D0224993

READERS' GUIDES TO ESSENTIAL CRITICISM

CONSULTANT EDITOR: NICOLAS TREDELL

Published

Nicholas Potter	Shakespeare: *Othello*
Berthold Schoene-Harwood	Mary Shelley: *Frankenstein*
Nick Selby	T. S. Eliot: *The Waste Land*
Nick Selby	Herman Melville: *Moby Dick*
Nick Selby	The Poetry of Walt Whitman
David Smale	Salman Rushdie: *Midnight's Children – The Satanic Verses*
Patsy Stoneman	Emily Brontë: *Wuthering Heights*
Susie Thomas	Hanif Kureishi
Nicolas Tredell	F. Scott Fitzgerald: *The Great Gatsby*
Nicolas Tredell	Joseph Conrad: *Heart of Darkness*
Nicolas Tredell	Charles Dickens: *Great Expectations*
Nicolas Tredell	William Faulkner: *The Sound and the Fury – As I Lay Dying*
Nicolas Tredell	Shakespeare: *Macbeth*
Nicolas Tredell	The Fiction of Martin Amis
Matthew Woodcock	Shakespeare: *Henry V*
Angela Wright	Gothic Fiction

Forthcoming

Pascale Aebischer	Jacobean Drama
Simon Avery	Thomas Hardy: *The Mayor of Casterbridge – Jude the Obscure*
Annika Bautz	Jane Austen: *Sense and Sensibility – Pride and Prejudice – Emma*
Matthew Beedham	The Novels of Kazuo Ishiguro
Jodi-Anne George	*Beowulf*
William Hughes	Bram Stoker: *Dracula*
Matthew Jordan	Milton: *Paradise Lost*
Sara Lodge	Charlotte Brontë: *Jane Eyre*
Matthew McGuire	Contemporary Scottish Literature
Timothy Milnes	Wordsworth: *The Prelude*
Steven Price	The Plays, Screenplays and Films of David Mamet
Stephen Regan	The Poetry of Philip Larkin
Michael Whitworth	Virginia Woolf: *Mrs Dalloway*
Gina Wisker	The Fiction of Margaret Atwood

Readers' Guides to Essential Criticism
Series Standing Order
ISBN 1-4039-0108-2
(*outside North America only*)

You can receive future titles in this series as they are published by placing a standing order. Please contact your bookseller or, in the case of difficulty, write to us at the address below with your name and address, the title of the series and the ISBN quoted above.

Customer Services Department, Macmillan Distribution Ltd
Houndmills, Basingstoke, Hampshire RG21 6XS, England

Postcolonial Literature

JUSTIN D. EDWARDS

Consultant editor: Nicolas Tredell

palgrave
macmillan

© Justin D. Edwards 2008

All rights reserved. No reproduction, copy or transmission of this publication may be made without written permission.

No paragraph of this publication may be reproduced, copied or transmitted save with written permission or in accordance with the provisions of the Copyright, Designs and Patents Act 1988, or under the terms of any licence permitting limited copying issued by the Copyright Licensing Agency, 90 Tottenham Court Road, London W1T 4LP.

Any person who does any unauthorised act in relation to this publication may be liable to criminal prosecution and civil claims for damages.

The author has asserted his right to be identified as the author of this work in accordance with the Copyright, Designs and Patents Act 1988.

First published 2008 by
PALGRAVE MACMILLAN
Houndmills, Basingstoke, Hampshire RG21 6XS and
175 Fifth Avenue, New York, N.Y. 10010
Companies and representatives throughout the world

PALGRAVE MACMILLAN is the global academic imprint of the Palgrave Macmillan division of St. Martin's Press, LLC and of Palgrave Macmillan Ltd. Macmillan® is a registered trademark in the United States, United Kingdom and other countries. Palgrave is a registered trademark in the European Union and other countries.

ISBN-13: 978-0-230-50673-2   hardback
ISBN-10: 0-230-50673-9   hardback
ISBN-13: 978-0-230-50674-9   paperback
ISBN-10: 0-230-50674-7   paperback

This book is printed on paper suitable for recycling and made from fully managed and sustained forest sources. Logging, pulping and manufacturing processes are expected to conform to the environmental regulations of the country of origin.

A catalogue record for this book is available from the British Library.

A catalog record for this book is available from the Library of Congress.

10   9   8   7   6   5   4   3   2   1
17 16 15 14 13 12 11 10 09 08

Printed and bound in China

For Churchill College, Cambridge University
Where much of this book was written

CONTENTS

CHAPTER FOUR   40

Orality

Focuses on the tradition of oral storytelling in postcolonial writing. With reference to the writings of Thomas King, Walter Ong, Mudrooroo and Patricia Grace, among others, this chapter explores the hierarchies and divisions associated with orality and textuality.

CHAPTER FIVE   51

Rewriting

This chapter addresses postcolonial rewritings of canonical texts and historical narratives. Criticism by Judie Newman, John Thieme, Gayatri Spivak, Benita Parry and Gauri Viswanathan, among others, is discussed alongside literary texts by Jean Rhys, E. M. Forster, Ruth Prawer Jhabvala and Salman Rushdie, and Patricia Rozema's film of Jane Austen's *Mansfield Park*.

CHAPTER SIX   62

Violence

This examines a range of key critical, theoretical and literary texts that analyse or represent the violence of colonization and resistance, as well as the fight for independence and internalized expressions of violence within a colonized community. Among writers considered are J. M. Coetzee, Patricia Grace, Frantz Fanon, Shimmer Chinodya and Toni Morrison. Gayatri Spivak's theory of 'epistemic violence' is also discussed.

CHAPTER SEVEN   74

Travel

Discusses the links between travel narratives, the rhetoric of empire and the expansion of European colonization. This chapter reflects upon how such narratives allowed Europeans to conceive of areas outside Europe as being under their control, as an extension of their nation's territory. Critics, travellers and writers explored include Jamaica Kincaid, Henry Morton Stanley, Mary Louise Pratt, Mary Kingsley, Amitav Ghosh, Tabish Khair and Caryl Phillips.

This chapter looks at representations of space, place and power in postcolonial literature and criticism. The establishment of a centre and periphery as well as the power dynamics of mapping territories and imposing borders are examined. Among the critics and writers considered are Brian Friel, Benedict Anderson, Michael Ondaatje, Graham Huggan, Margaret Atwood and Shani Mootoo.

Here, the masculinist assumptions found in some postcolonial criticism are highlighted with reference to the critiques by Reina Lewis and Jane Miller of Edward W. Said and Frantz Fanon. The feminist and postcolonial approaches of Gayatri Spivak, Chandra Talpade Mohanty and Trinh T. Minh-ha are presented as documenting issues confronting non-Western women. Fiction by H. Rider Haggard, Joseph Conrad and Tsitsi Dangarembga is also considered.

Traces how postcolonial issues of race, nationalism and gender intersect with queer theory on questions of power, oppression and hierarchical relations. This chapter scrutinizes debates about queer subjectivity, as well as the limits and strengths of queer theory, to inform an understanding of same-sexuality within a postcolonial context. Critics and writers discussed include John C. Hawley, Christopher Lane, Dionne Brand, Peter Dickinson, Jarrod Hayes, Tahar Djaout, Gayatri Gopinath and Hanif Kureishi.

Discusses the 'homely' and 'unhomely' in postcolonial writing, and focuses on criticism about the unsettling history of colonial settlement, oppression, displacement and migration. Considers texts that treat the postcolony as a place that is haunted by a history of trauma and suppression. Explores work by Toni Morrison, Homi Bhabha and Fred d'Aguiar, among others, and Margot Nash's film *Vacant Possession*.

CHAPTER TWELVE   129

Memory

Examines the importance of memory, remembering, trauma and historical narratives in postcolonial writing. The focus is on the significance of remembering the traditions of local (native) cultures and remembering the devastating effects of imperialism. Considers critics and writers such as Jamaica Kincaid, Benedict Anderson, Kali Tal, Joy Kogawa and Michael Ondaatje.

CHAPTER THIRTEEN   139

Hybridity

Here, influential theories of hybridity and the debates surrounding essentialism, authenticity and mimicry are discussed in relation to the work of, among others, Derek Walcott, Maria Campbell, Homi Bhabha, Robert J. C. Young, V. S. Naipaul, Benita Parry, Paul Gilroy and Tabish Khair.

CHAPTER FOURTEEN   150

Diaspora

Explores criticism and literature about the conflicting ties and demands, confusions and distances involved in diasporic conceptions of identity. Concepts such as home and belonging, displacement and migration are discussed. Critics and writers considered include Paul Gilroy, Caryl Phillips, Sunetra Gupta, Hanif Kureishi, Shyam Selvadurai, Stuart Hall and Arjun Appadurai.

CHAPTER FIFTEEN   160

Globalization

Elucidates literature and criticism about the contemporary international economic system that perpetuates many of the same power relations established between the sixteenth and twentieth centuries. Economic disparities and borderless form of 'Empire' are also discussed. Among critics and writers examined are Fidelis Odun Balogun, Jamaica Kincaid, Michael Hardt and Antonio Negri, Lisa Rofel, Arundhati Roy and David Punter.

ACKNOWLEDGEMENTS

The author and publishers wish to thank the following for permission to reproduce copyright material:

Tabish Khair for the extracts from the poem 'Unhybrid' from *Where Parallel Lines Meet* (Penguin, 2000). Reproduced courtesy of Tabish Khair.

Every effort has been made to trace the copyright holders, but if any have been inadvertently overlooked, the publisher will be pleased to make the necessary arrangement at the first opportunity.

Introduction

'Postcolonial literature' is an unstable and contested critical category. But it seems a necessary one to refer to that rich and diverse range of texts by writers who live in or have migrated from former colonies, even if some of them would reject the 'postcolonial' label. What is the appeal of postcolonial literature? After a tumultuous twentieth century marked by the politics and conflicts of decolonization, affecting nations across the globe, is it surprising that there are reading publics fascinated by such texts? In addition to this troubled history, we are also acutely aware, every day, of the continuing politics and violence of contemporary forms of imperialism, for example in Iraq and Afghanistan. What, then, is the purpose of writing literature about the aftermath of colonization and the independence of colonial nations? Does postcolonial literature simply represent the histories of violence and trauma that moved peoples, regions and countries from subjugation to liberation? Or does postcolonial writing tell us about what is happening in our own lives, mapping out where we come from and where we are going? These questions are addressed by postcolonial writers in the very acts of writing and theorizing literature from the (post)colonial world.

This Guide is unique. It presents new access routes into critical debates and literary works and offers new ways of thinking critically about postcolonial literature. Postcolonial criticism and theory are vital parts of studying contemporary literature but they can sometimes be overwhelming, confusing or intimidating. This Guide, organized in a thematic and conceptual way, provides 15 clear, accessible and succinct chapters, each of which focuses on a key word that has generated significant debate in postcolonial criticism: postcoloniality, difference, language, orality, rewriting, violence, travel, maps, gender, queer, haunting, memory, hybridity, diaspora and globalization. Since these terms often combine and clash with one another in critical debates, there are inevitably some fruitful overlaps between the chapters. By structuring the Guide like this, I seek to refrain from reducing the complex debates in the field to easy polemic, while also avoiding rigid taxonomies of the subjects at hand.

In this Guide, the concepts to which these key words refer are put into practice through an examination of particular literary texts from across the Anglophone (English-speaking) postcolonial world. This Anglophone focus responds to the bias towards English, which is inherent in the current structure of postcolonial studies, but it is not intended to deny the significance of postcolonial criticism and literature in African, Arabic, Asian or other European languages. Because postcolonial criticism and theory moves far beyond the political bounds of most forms of literary study and because its debates are global as well as local, I have chosen works that span the globe, moving from Australia and New Zealand to Kenya and Zimbabwe to India and Sri Lanka to North America and beyond. This is to show how texts from different regions reveal the asymmetrical power structures that lie behind imperialist discourses, and how such discourses have, at other times, been used as a political and ideological tool to advocate change and liberation.

This Guide constantly explores the relations between the postcolonial and the literary, considering not only academic critical texts but also literary works in a range of genres and, on occasion, films. Consequently, the critical texts necessarily work in dialogue with postcolonial writing (and cinema), and they often resonate with debates that return us to today's unresolved concerns about cultural imperialism, globalization and, more generally, inequities in economics and political influence. Such critical continuity, and the conflicting responses to postcoloniality, demonstrates the far-reaching and powerful allure of this dynamic area of literary studies.

No guide to the criticism of postcolonial literature can be exhaustive. As a result, this volume focuses on critical genealogies rather than rigid mappings, and it invites the reader to look beyond its content by further exploring the literary and theoretical matters addressed herein. The aim is not to wrap up or offer the final word on the many nuanced and unresolved debates within postcolonial criticism. Rather, the aim is to inform, stimulate and challenge, as well as offer signposts that the Guide reader can follow to undertake a series of sustained explorations. In this, the Guide focuses on the developing idea of what 'postcolonial literature' is, and what it signifies in a variety of key historical settings, while reminding the reader of the extent to which it has been challenged. The Bibliography at the end of the Guide is designed to help readers explore further the debates and controversies within a field that is striking for its irresolution and resistance to closure.

Contexts

It is important to mention at the outset that postcolonial writers often refer to specific historical events. These might include political movements or liberationist struggles or specific moments in the drive towards decolonization. Sometimes this Guide supplies historical contextualization in the chapters that follow. But as a starting point I have included some of the main historical references in this 'Introduction'. This material is highly selective, and thus it is not meant to be a homogenizing metanarrative or a positivist history. Rather, it is meant to introduce readers to some of the historical moments that are relevant to specific discussions that will be encountered as they make their way through this Guide.

The Middle Passage and slavery

The slavery of African peoples played a significant role in the development of European colonialism. In this, several of the postcolonial writers in this Guide refer to the 'Middle Passage', which was the journey of slave trading ships from the west coast of Africa, where the slaves were obtained, across the Atlantic, where they were sold or traded. The Middle Passage was the longest, hardest, most dangerous and most horrific part of the journey of the slave ships. The vessels were tightly packed with Africans, and the journey across the Atlantic would take anywhere from five weeks to three months. For many writers, the terrible Middle Passage has come to represent the ultimate in human misery and suffering. The abominable and inhuman conditions of the voyage clearly display the great evil of the slave trade.

During the early 1500s, the Portuguese and the Spanish dominated the African slave trade. At this time, Portugal claimed a monopoly on slave trading in the South Atlantic because of their colonies in South America. Spain also declared control of the trade in the North Atlantic because of their interests in the Caribbean Sea. But in 1562 the first Englishman, Sir John Hawkins (1532–95), carried a group of African slaves to the new world. This voyage was extremely profitable and, as a result, Queen Elizabeth I of England (1533–1603), who had previously denounced slave-trading voyages, secretly invested in several slaving expeditions. In fact, when Hawkins made his third voyage, Queen Elizabeth funded the two largest ships of the six vessels participating in the journey.

The 'scramble for Africa'

The slave trade was only one of the factors that led to the colonization of Africa. For European powers also had an interest in exploiting the rich natural resources of the continent. This led to what has been called the 'scramble for Africa', which was the proliferation of conflicting European claims to African territory between 1880 and World War I. At this time, there was a transition from the 'informal' imperialism of control through military influence and economic dominance to that of direct rule. Attempts to mediate imperial competition, such as the Berlin Conference (1884–5) between Britain, France and Germany, failed to establish definitively the competing powers' claims.

Britain was one of the main players in the colonization of Africa. In 1882, for instance, Egypt was occupied by British forces, and it was declared a British protectorate in 1914. In addition, large territories such as Sudan, Nigeria, Kenya and Uganda were subjugated by the British in the 1890s and early 1900s. Meanwhile, in the southern part of the continent, the Cape Colony – first occupied in 1795 – became the base from which the British could gain control of the neighbouring African territories, including Botswana and Zimbabwe. As early as 1877, the British annexed the South African Republic and consolidated their power over most of the colonies of South Africa in 1879 after the Anglo–Zulu War. Moreover, following the two Boer Wars (1880–1 and 1899–1902) the independent Boer republics of the Orange Free State and Transvaal were conquered and absorbed into the British Empire.

(Post)colonial Zimbabwe and Nigeria

The land of Zimbabwe was settled by the British in 1890 and named Rhodesia after the British-born South African businessman, mining magnate and politician, Cecil John Rhodes (1853–1902). The ideology of British superiority served as justification for taking control of the land and, as a result, the native Africans of Rhodesia were ruled by an all-white government, and only whites were granted the right to vote. Laws were passed which prohibited the presence of Africans in many public places, and ordinances allowed for an inequitable distribution of the land. During the colonial rule that extended from 1890 to 1979, the white minority dominated and oppressed the native population and divested them of their land.

Throughout the history of colonial rule, there was much civil unrest. But in 1962 the Zimbabwe African People's Union (ZAPU) was formed, and their radical ideas for liberation made it clear that violence was inevitable in order to achieve independence. As a result, ZAPU and other nationalist groups employed the tactics of guerrilla warfare, and their armed resistance to the colonial regime included attacking white farmers and destroying white-owned property. In the late 1960s armed resistance began to decline and members of the nationalist fighters began to call for political and military unity. The early 1970s were characterized by shifting alliances among the nationalists, and in 1979 the white Rhodesian government attempted to undermine the power of nationalist groups by offering 'Internal Settlement' which ended formal white rule, and installed the country's first black head of government, Abel Muzorewa (born 1925). Britain, however, refused to recognize this settlement and the nationalist forces continued to fight for liberation from colonial rule. The conflict ended when multi-ethnic elections were held in early 1980, and following these elections the newly independent and internationally recognized country was renamed Zimbabwe.

The history of Nigeria includes similar power struggles and conflicts. In 1900, the British government took control of the territory that had been chartered by the Royal Niger Company in 1885. Then, in 1901, Britain declared Nigeria a protectorate and part of the British Empire. Britain divided the nation into separate provinces: the north, the south and the Lagos colony. The imposition of western education and capitalist economics was more rapid in the south, and the consequences of this have continued to influence Nigerian politics. Nigerian nationalism began to flourish after World War II, and the British responded to calls for Nigerian independence by legislating successive constitutions. These changes moved Nigeria towards self-government on a representative and increasingly federal basis. In 1960 as nationalist movements were sweeping across Africa, Nigeria gained full independence under a constitution that provided for a parliamentary government and a substantial measure of self-government for the country's three regions. In October 1963 Nigeria proclaimed itself a Federal Republic, but Nigeria's ethnic and religious tensions were magnified by the disparities in economic and educational development between the south and north. The ensuing Nigerian Civil War resulted in over 30,000 deaths before ending in 1970.

Caribbean contexts

The history of the Caribbean reveals the significant role the region has played in the colonial struggles of the major European powers from the sixteenth to the twentieth century. In 1492, Christopher Columbus (1451–1506) was the first European to travel to the Caribbean, but soon afterwards Portuguese and Spanish ships began claiming territories in the region and throughout the Americas. Other European powers followed suit, and it was not long before Britain, the Netherlands and France sought to establish profitable colonies in the islands of the Caribbean Sea, thus making this region a contested territory and a hotbed of European wars for centuries.

In 1655, the British seized Jamaica, which remained under colonial rule for over 300 years. The British also expanded their influence in the region by controlling other islands, including Barbados, St. Kitts and Nevis, Antigua, Montserrat and Bermuda. During this expansionist project, the vast majority of the Caribbean natives were eradicated; in 1492, the native population of the islands was between 225,000 and 6 million. Today only a few thousand Caribs live in Dominica and on the mainland of South America.

The first Caribbean country to gain its independence was Haiti in 1804. This was followed by the Dominican Republic in 1844 and Cuba in 1902. After World War II, the islands were no longer considered to be of strategic or economic importance. Thus, the British islands formed an associated federation with the Britain in 1958, but Jamaica and Trinidad left the federation in 1962 to become independent nations. The federation was dissolved in 1966 when Barbados became independent and the other islands formed associated statehoods with Britain. Most of the smaller Caribbean islands gained independent status in the 1970s. Dominica, for instance, became independent in 1978.

British India and independence

British India is the expression that is sometimes given to the British rule of the majority of the Indian Subcontinent between 1858 and 1947 (which includes modern-day India, Bangladesh and Pakistan). Prior to Indian independence, these regions were under the colonial control of Britain and formed a substantial part of the British Empire.

The Indian independence movement liberated the region from British rule and formed the nation-state of India. This movement involved a wide spectrum of Indian political organizations, philosophies and rebellions that began as early as the 1850s and lasted until India became an independent country on 15 August 1947. But Indian independence also brought partition. For in 1947, the last Governor-General of India, Lord Mountbatten (1900–79), announced the partitioning of India into two independent nations: the Dominion of India (later the Republic of India) and the Dominion of Pakistan (later the Islamic Republic of Pakistan). Violent clashes between Hindus, Muslims and Sikhs followed, and the difficult job of unifying a diverse Indian nation began.

The Indian constitution was completed in 1949, and the following year the country became the Republic of India. Subsequently, the Constituent Assembly elected the first President of India, who took over from the Governor-General as the head of the country. In 1952, India held its first general elections, making it the largest democracy in the world. Soon thereafter India absorbed two other territories: Pondicherry (which the French ceded in 1954) and Goa (from Portuguese control in 1961).

First Nations and Métis cultures

First Nations is a Canadian term that refers to the Aboriginal peoples located in what is now Canada, and their descendants who are neither Inuit nor Métis. Collectively, First Nations, Inuit and Métis peoples are known as Aboriginal peoples, First peoples or Indigenous peoples, bands or nations.

Beginning in the late eighteenth century, First Nations were targeted for assimilation into what is often referred to as European-Canadian culture. These attempts reached a climax with the establishment of the Canadian residential school system, the prohibition of Indigenous cultural practices and the Indian Acts of the late nineteenth and early twentieth centuries. At present, many First Nations, along with the Métis and the Inuit, receive inadequate funding for education, and assert legitimate rights to lands that have been taken from them.

Aboriginal peoples in North America have often resisted Europeans who have attempted to disenfranchise them of land and cultural heritage. In 1869, for instance, the Métis leader Louis Riel (1844–85) orchestrated the Red River Rebellion in what is now Manitoba, and in 1885 he led the North-West Rebellion in Saskatchewan. In both cases, Riel attempted to establish a Métis homeland in a part of the country that was still considered 'open territory'. However, on both occasions, Riel failed and soon after the rebellions land speculators deprived the Métis of land by exploiting a government programme for its purchase. The Canadian province of Alberta distributed land to the Métis in 1938 to correct the injustice, but the provinces of Saskatchewan and Manitoba have not followed suit.

Indigenous Australia and New Zealand

Australia's Indigenous people, Aborigines, consist of approximately 2 per cent of Australia's total population. During the nineteenth century, Aborigines were subject to a combination of marginalization and assimilation. By the late 1880s, many had joined white rural and urban communities, where they often became economically disenfranchised and were exposed to devastating diseases. This led to massive depopulation and the extinction of several Aboriginal tribes.

The Aboriginal civil rights movement has developed a strong voice within Australia. As a result, Indigenous peoples gained the right to vote in Federal elections in 1965, but it was not until 1967 that they were counted in the distribution of electoral seats. In the 1970s, the fight for property rights fuelled important political debates and calls for restitution. Aboriginal groups spoke out for equal rights, and specifically for claims on property that had been forcibly taken from them by British settlers. The Aboriginal Land Rights Act, passed in 1976, became instrumental in territories with tribal associations. And the 1990s witnessed further milestones, including government legislation that returned a degree of autonomy to Indigenous groups, and increased wages and welfare benefits to Aboriginal people.

A similar civil rights movement has developed in New Zealand. Maori groups have legitimately demanded restitution for land that was taken from them when the British settlement was established in 1839. At this time, the New Zealand Company was ordered to establish British rule, and when more settlers arrived in 1840 the Maori were forced to sign the Treaty of Waitangi.

The treaty has been a great source of disharmony between Maori and Pakeha (New Zealanders of European descent). It was drawn up by a European settler who was not fluent in the Maori language, and it was read to chiefs who were unfamiliar with instruments of European politics or diplomacy. The greatest ambiguities of the treaty turned on ideas of sovereignty and ownership that were not necessarily part of Maori culture. In 1975, the Waitangi Tribunal was established to hear claims of abuse of the treaty. Many claims have resulted in return of land, financial compensation, restoration of rights to natural resources and the transfer of businesses to Maori groups.

In the 1980s and 1990s urban Maori organizations continued to advocate for political, social and economic rights, as well as working towards the regeneration of the Maori language. In 1998, the New Zealand Parliament attempted to settle a long-standing legal complaint by the Ngai Tahu tribe of the South Island. The government offered several million dollars in compensation and apologized for injustices dating from the 1840 Treaty of Waitangi. Such conflicts over the ownership of territory in New Zealand continue today.

The aim of this Guide will be to equip readers with an understanding of key approaches, so that they can read further into the topic with a critical awareness of the area. Thus, the next chapter offers an overview of postcolonial theory and criticism and a discussion of definitions in the field.

CHAPTER ONE

Postcoloniality

In his now infamous 'Hong Kong Diary', Prince Charles (born 1948), the heir to the throne of England, describes the chartered British Airways 747 flight that took a large party of official representatives from Heathrow to Hong Kong for the 30 June 1997 handover celebrations:

■ 'It took me some time to realize that this was not First Class, although it puzzled me as to why the seats were so uncomfortable. I then discovered that others [...] were comfortably ensconced in First Class immediately below us: "such is the end of empire", I said to myself'.[1] □

The end of Empire indeed. After all, the celebrations marked an end to Hong Kong's status as a British colony, thus concluding the final chapter in the history of the once expansive and powerful British Empire. But the Prince's comments betray a sense of personal loss at the end of this Empire: the British heir to the throne is no longer treated as he once was. He is no longer pampered as the influential leader of an Empire that once stretched from London to Sydney, from Auckland to Cape Town, from Kingston to Delhi and from Montreal to Hong Kong. Nor is he perceived to be the symbolic leader of a thriving Commonwealth. Instead, he is forced to cram himself into the British Airways 'cheap seats' on his way to a ceremony to celebrate the decolonization of Hong Kong.

But Charles's comments do not only reflect a personal loss of privilege; they also highlight an historical shift in the fight for political control over former British territories. For the end of Empire marks the beginning of postcolonialism and, as such, the political independence of Britain's colonies. Thus, I invoke Charles's comments at the beginning of this Guide because his de-throning, his displacement from the lofty seats of First Class, signals a symbolic shift in power: 'the centre cannot hold', Chinua Achebe (born 1930) writes, 'things fall apart'.[2] And, indeed, the once commanding centre of the British Empire – the crown – has not held; it no longer holds the political currency or authority that it once did. In the wake of political decolonization (of which Hong Kong is just one example), the monarchy has been replaced by other structures of power and new forms of imperialism – the independent governments of former colonies, media moguls, multinational corporations, the International Monetary Fund and the World Bank. This change, this de-centring, is an example of what many contemporary theorists and critics refer to as postcoloniality.

However, defining 'the postcolonial' is not an easy task. As a result, we must begin by reflecting on a significant question – what is postcolonialism? According to the *Shorter OED*, 'postcolonialism' is concerned with what 'occur[s] or exist[s]' after the end of colonial rule. It is a condition that arises out of political independence'. This is confirmed by *Longman's Dictionary*, which defines the postcolonial as the 'period following a colony's achieving independence'. Based on these definitions, the Hong Kong celebrations on 30 June 1997 marked an important postcolonial moment. For the first time in decades, Hong Kong was no longer to submit to British authority. Therefore, according to the *OED* and *Longman's*, Hong Kong was entering an era of postcolonialism. However, some politicians and historians have suggested that the Hong Kong handover was not a moment of political independence for the region. Instead, they have argued, 30 June 1997 was the day when Hong Kong became subject to the political, social and economic domination of China, effectively transforming the region into a Chinese colony. In effect, Hong Kong was not, according to this school of thought, achieving independence or self-determination.

This debate is just one example of the countless disputes over how to define the postcolonial condition. In fact, postcolonial critics have long been divided on the meaning of the term 'postcolonial'. For instance, the authors of *The Empire Writes Back* (1989) have argued that the word 'postcolonial' should be applied to 'all the culture affected by the imperial process from the moment of colonization to the present day'.[3] Moreover, Ania Loomba writes that the term postcolonial 'cannot be used in any single sense'. This is because decolonization has 'spanned three centuries, ranging from the eighteenth and nineteenth centuries in the Americas, Australia, New Zealand and South Africa, to the 1970s in the case of Angola and Mozambique'.[4] Loomba's multifaceted definition of postcolonialism has been scrutinized by the critic Bart Moore-Gilbert, who worries about expansive definitions of the term. He writes,

■ Such has been the elasticity of the concept 'postcolonial' that in recent years some commentators have begun to express anxiety that there may be a danger of it imploding as an analytic construct with any real edge [...]. [T]he problem derives from the fact that the term has been so variously applied to such different kinds of historical moments, geographical regions, cultural identities, political predicaments and affiliations, and reading practices. As a consequence, there has been increasingly heated, even bitter, contestation of the legitimacy of seeing certain regions, periods, socio-political formations and cultural practices as 'genuinely' postcolonial.[5] □

This book is about these debates. Thus, the ideas explored in this Guide illustrate how the term postcolonial has been applied to writing – to literature, criticism and theory – in contemporary literary studies. Above all, postcolonial literature, criticism and theory are about scrutinizing power relations and resisting imperialist prerogatives. Postcolonial writing, then, offers a 'symbolic overhaul' to reshape meanings in light of dominant hegemonies and powerful ideologies. According to Elleke Boehmer,

■ postcolonial writers [have] sought to undercut thematically and formally the discourses which supported colonization – the myths of power, the race of classifications, the imagery of subordination. Postcolonial literature, therefore, is deeply marked by experiences of cultural exclusion and division under empire.[6] □

The earliest works of postcolonial writing discussed in this Guide are Frantz Fanon's *Black Skin, White Masks* (1952) and *The Wretched of the Earth* (1961). Born on the French colony of Martinique in 1925, Fanon actively supported and organized resistance to French colonialism and disseminated ideas about decolonization in his writings. His critical trajectory moves across the political and academic disciplines of philosophy, psychiatry, social science and literature. But his contributions must be contextualized historically; unlike many of today's postcolonial critics, Fanon's contribution to current understandings of nationalism and decolonization emerged during the exigencies of colonial rule. It is therefore important to contextualize his writing in light of the colonial struggle for self-determination – a moment of social transformation that preceded the emergence of the poststructuralist approaches that underwrite the projects of so many postcolonial critics today.

Another key figure in the early development of postcolonial criticism and theory is Edward W. Said (1935–2003), who, like Frantz Fanon, was an academic activist, although it must be noted that Said's moderation contrasts sharply with Fanon's ideas of revolutionary violence. Said was born in Jerusalem and was for many years America's foremost spokesman for the Palestinian cause. His two most influential books are *Orientalism* (1978) and *Culture and Imperialism* (1993), both of which displace monolithic and oppressive assumptions about racial and ethnic difference by highlighting the power of discourse and offering alternative ways of reading – what Said calls contrapuntal reading.[7] Such an approach suggests ways of reading that are informed by multiplicity, a questioning of binary oppositions and an affirmation of racial otherness. Often engaging in analyses of nineteenth-century literary discourse strongly influenced by the writings of Noam Chomsky (born 1928) and Michel Foucault (1926–84), Said's work also examines contemporary realities and has clear political implications. His texts are often associated with postmodernism and postcolonialism, both of which share various degrees of scepticism about representation itself.

Fanon's writing has also had a profound influence on the work of Homi K. Bhabha, the postcolonial theorist and literary critic who was born in Mumbai, India in 1949. Bhabha's early work on Fanon was informed by poststructuralist thought, most notably the writings of Jacques Derrida (1930–2004), Jacques Lacan (1901–81) and Michel Foucault. In his book *Nation and Narration* (1990), Bhabha argues that our sense of nationhood is discursively constructed: it is narrativized. He thus challenges the tendency to treat postcolonial countries as a homogeneous block, refuting the assumption that there is a shared identity among excolonial states. In *The Location of Culture* (1994), Bhabha deploys concepts – mimicry, interstice and hybridity – influenced by semiotics and psychoanalysis to argue that cultural production is most productive when it is also most ambivalent. Both of these works attack the Western production of binary oppositions, traditionally defined in terms of centre and margin, civilized and savage, enlightened and ignorant. Bhabha thus questions the easy recourse to consolidated dualisms by repudiating fixed and authentic centres of truth, suggesting that cultures interact, transgress and transform each other in a much more complex manner than typical binary oppositions allow.

Derridean deconstruction and other forms of poststructuralism have also influenced the postcolonial theory espoused by Gayatri Chakravorty Spivak. Born in Calcutta, India in 1942, Spivak first achieved recognition as the English translator of Derrida's *Of Grammatology* (1976), after which she carried out a series of historical studies (as a member of the 'Subaltern Studies Collective') and literary critiques of imperialism and international feminism. Spivak's essay 'Can the Subaltern Speak?' (1988) demonstrates her concern for the processes whereby postcolonial studies reinscribe, co-opt, and rehearse the imperialist imperatives of political domination, economic exploitation and cultural erasure. According to Spivak, the Western postcolonial critic often unknowingly reasserts the asymmetrical power relations that he or she is attempting to critique. This is because the privileged male academic has institutionalized discourses of postcolonial studies that classify and survey 'the East' in the same measure as the actual modes of colonial dominance have done in the past. Similarly, in her essay, 'Three Women's Texts and a Critique of Imperialism' (1988), Spivak examines the complicated interface of competing critical practices. She argues that *Jane Eyre* (1847) by Charlotte Brontë (1816–55) may well uphold its protagonist as a new feminist ideal, but it does so at the expense of Bertha (Rochester's Creole bride) who legitimates Jane's ascent to domestic authority. Thus, a feminist approach to this text perhaps precludes an understanding of the novel's depiction of the 'epistemic violence' (and physical restrictions) imposed upon the Other. These restrictions, Spivak concludes, silence the subaltern. In her more recent work, *A Critique of Postcolonial Reason: Towards a History of the Vanishing Present* (1999), Spivak continues to write about the subaltern and epistemic violence: she explores how major studies of European metaphysics by, among others, the German philosophers Immanuel Kant (1724–1804) and Georg Wilhelm Friedrich Hegel (1770–1831) not only exclude the subaltern, but also actively prevent non-Europeans from occupying positions as fully human subjects.

The early work of Spivak and Bhabha has undoubtedly inspired the authors of *The Empire Writes Back: Theory and Practice in Post-Colonial Literatures* (1989), which clearly established the relationship between the postcolonial and the literary. Drawing on the work of Fanon, Said and others, the authors of this volume – Bill Ashcroft, Gareth Griffiths and Helen Tiffin – employ a comparative approach that brings the experiences of colonization and the challenges of postcolonialism to bear on new writing in English. This book, simply put, explores postcolonial criticism and theory about literature from the Indian Subcontinent, Australasia, North America, the Caribbean and African nations. It thus maps out the debates surrounding the interrelationships of literary traditions and investigates the powerful forces acting on language in the postcolonial text, showing how these texts constitute a radical critique of the assumptions underlying Eurocentric notions of literature and language. In so doing, Ashcroft, Griffiths and Tiffin challenge traditional canon formation and dominant ideas about literature and culture, offering insights into the politics of storytelling and the power of representation.

The political dimension of postcolonial literary criticism has been influenced by Marxist approaches to reading texts. In 1983, for instance, Benedict Anderson published *Imagined Communities: Reflections on the Origin and Spread of Nationalism*, in which he systematically describes, using an historical materialist and Marxist approach, the major factors contributing to the emergence of nationalism in the world during the past three centuries. He argues that the main causes of nationalism and the creation of 'imagined communities' are the reduction of privileged access to particular script languages, the movement to abolish the ideas of divine rule and monarchy, as well as the emergence of the printing press under a system of capitalism (or, as Anderson calls it, 'print-capitalism').[8] Anderson's book has had a profound impact on postcolonial literary studies, but it has also elicited criticism from some scholars and activists.

Another postcolonial critic influenced by Marxist approaches is Aijaz Ahmad, who published the influential book *In Theory: Classes, Nations, Literatures* in 1992. Ahmad, an Indian political commentator, activist and intellectual, has critiqued the growing tendency to homogenize 'Third World' literature and culture. He thus provides rigorous criticisms of major theoretical statements on 'colonial discourse' and postcolonialism, challenging many of the commonplaces and conceits that dominate contemporary cultural criticism. With lengthy considerations of the essentialist assumptions of, among others, Fredric Jameson (born 1934), Edward Said and the Subaltern Studies group, Ahmad's work contains important analyses of the concept of Indian literature, of the genealogy of the term 'Third World', and of the conditions under which so-called colonial discourse theory emerged in metropolitan intellectual circles.[9]

A further strand of postcolonial literary studies is scholarship that investigates travel writing. David Spurr's *Rhetoric of Empire: Colonial Discourse in Journalism, Travel Writing, and Imperial Administration* (1993) and Mary Louise Pratt's *Imperial Eyes: Travel Writing and Transculturation* (1992) are two such studies, both of which interrogate how travel writing often supports the discourses of imperialism. In her seminal work, for instance, Pratt attempts to 'decolonize knowledge' by examining how travel books by Europeans about non-European parts of the world create the 'domestic subject' of Euroimperialism.[10] She thus foregrounds how such books have engaged metropolitan reading publics with expansionist enterprises whose material benefits accrued mainly to the elite. Travel writing has been used, she argues, as a tool for explaining and justifying colonization, for naturalizing it, and for promoting its underlying assumptions. Pratt thus identifies a number of important concepts such as contact zones, transculturation and autoethnography to explain the political ramifications of travel texts. Taken together, these three concepts explain and describe the social spaces where different cultures meet, clash and grapple with each other, often in highly asymmetrical relations of domination and subordination. What makes Pratt's work so influential for postcolonial studies is its insistence on new visions in culture and citizenship and the 'traffic in meaning', and how travel and exploration writing have 'produced Europe's differentiated conceptions of itself in relation to something it became possible to call the rest of the world'.[11]

Pratt's look at cultural movements and the exchange of ideas in the wake of colonial contact has also been addressed by Ann McClintock, whose postcolonial criticism draws upon gender studies, feminism and queer theory. In *Imperial Leather: Race, Gender, and Sexuality in the Colonial*

Context (1995), for instance, McClintock argues that to understand colonialism and postcolonialism, one must first recognize that race, gender, sexuality and class are not distinct realms of experience. She writes that these aspects of identity do not 'exist in splendid isolation from each other; nor can they be simply yoked together retrospectively like armatures of Lego. Rather, they come into existence in and through relation to each other – if in contradictory and conflictual ways'.[12] McClintock thus makes an important contribution to postcolonial studies, convincingly arguing that the discourses of colonialism are connected to race, class and gender in ways that promoted expansionism abroad and classicism at home. These connections, she adds, have proved crucial to the development of Western modernity. For imperialism, she explains, 'is not something that happened elsewhere – a disagreeable fact of history external to Western identity. Rather, imperialism and the invention of race were fundamental aspects of Western, industrial modernity'.[13] Hence, the social construction of race in the imperial centres became fundamental to the self-definition of the middle class, while simultaneously demonizing a 'dangerous class' of 'Others' that spanned everything from blacks and Jews to feminists and radicals to prostitutes and homosexuals. Such modes of classification, then, sanctioned discourses that justified colonization.

Some critics assert that the theories and practices pertaining to postcolonialism pose a necessary antidote to late twentieth- and early twenty-first century globalization and contemporary forms of imperialism. David Punter's *Postcolonial Imaginings: Fictions of a New World Order* (2000) picks up on these issues by drawing upon Edward Said's argument in *Culture and Imperialism* that colonialism was not – and is not – limited to a specific historical moment. Punter continually queries the definition and scope of the 'postcolonial', which is seen throughout his book as a phenomenon that is not restricted to ex-colonies but that impacts all of our lives at the beginning of the twenty-first century. Postcoloniality is, he argues, an indissoluble part of the development of national imaginings and, at the same time, an alibi for the emergence of a violently assertive 'new world order' committed to the management and obliteration of difference. Drawing on deconstruction and psychoanalysis, his examination of postcolonial writing raises significant questions about the relation between the literary, the meaning of the notion of 'theory' and the wider global political and economic climate. For Punter, we are globally living in 'the postcolonial' and, as a result, the 'process of mutual postcolonial abjection is', he maintains, 'one that confronts us every day in the ambiguous form of a series of uncanny returns'.[14]

Following Punter, some literary critics and theorists have begun to see postcolonial studies as in a state of crisis, where the overlap with globalization theories and methodologies is potentially diffusing the field of study. Michael Hardt and Antonio Negri's *Empire* (2000) has, for some, fuelled this sense of crisis and, for others, calmed an anxiety about the potential death of postcolonial studies. Hardt and Negri theorize an ongoing transition from a 'modern' phenomenon of colonization, centred around individual nation-states, to an emergent postmodern construct created among ruling powers. They argue that the globalization and informatization of world markets since the late 1960s have led to a progressive decline in the sovereignty of nation-states and the emergence of a new form of sovereignty, composed of a series of national and supranational organisms united under a single logic of rule. This new global form of sovereignty is what they call Empire, a consolidation of power that represents 'the real subsumption of social existence by capital' and a 'post-modernized global economy'.[15]

These ideas are further explored in *Multitude: War and Democracy in the Age of Empire* (2004), in which Hardt and Negri adopt the term 'multitude' from the Dutch philosopher and theologian Benedict Spinoza (1632–77) to refer to the population of the world that they believe is increasingly networked and has the potential to resist 'Empire' and establish genuine democratic principles. Indeed, 'the multitude' focuses on the masses within the Empire, a body of people who are defined by diversity rather than commonalities. The challenge for the multitude in this new era is 'for the social multiplicity to manage to communicate and act in common while remaining internally different'.[16] In this, 'the multitude' is envisioned as the political subject of a counter-Empire, an alternative political organization of global flows and exchanges. Thus, Hardt and Negri imagine a new, more global version of the proletariat (the multitude) who are united by a common desire for liberation. The authors, then, bring back a dialectic of human struggle to the development of global capitalism, in contrast to other scholarly work that describes capitalism as developing globally from within its own internal financial or accumulation logic.

As we have seen in this chapter, postcolonial criticism and theory moves far beyond the political bounds of most literary studies. It has, at times, been used to reveal the asymmetrical power structures that lie behind colonial discourse, and it has, at other times, been used as a political and ideological tool, advocating change through decolonization. In the next chapter we will consider how postcolonial writers have engaged with the concept of 'difference', and examine the political implications of ontologies based on binary oppositions and dichotomies.

CHAPTER TWO

Difference

On the opening pages of the Australian novel *Remembering Babylon* (1993) by David Malouf (born 1934), the protagonist, Gemmy Fairley, an English citizen who has lived most of his life with the Aborigines of Australia, emerges from the bush and, upon meeting some white settlers, raises his arms and, in almost forgotten English, declares: 'Do not shoot … I am a B-b-british object!'[1] This declaration suggests a number of ways of thinking about 'difference' in postcolonial literature and criticism. Gemmy, of course, means to identify himself as a British *subject*, not object, and thus indicates to the settlers that he is no different from them. He seeks to save his life by presenting himself as British, white, non-threatening, Christian and 'civilized'; in short, to maintain his status as a British citizen, not Aborigine.

This scene in *Remembering Babylon* highlights the ways in which postcolonial literature exposes categories of difference. By categories of difference we mean, quite simply, the discourses that constructed the colonizing distinctions between, among others, 'us' and 'them', 'civilized' and 'savage', 'Christian' and 'heathen', 'self' and 'other', 'British' and 'Aborigine', 'subject' and 'object', 'colonizer' and 'colonized'. Gemmy's utterance, then, calls attention to the ways in which the project of imperialism structures the colony around a series of hierarchical differences based on nationality, religion, race and ethnicity. And yet it is significant that Gemmy mistakenly substitutes the word 'object' for 'subject', for the absurdity of Gemmy's adoption of British objecthood foregrounds the hierarchical divisions that differentiate between subject and object. In this context, one cannot be both 'British' and 'object' because colonial discourse reserves subjecthood for the colonizer and objecthood for the colonized.

It is also significant that Lachlan, the white youth who first meets Gemmy, cannot *see* that the newcomer is British. This likewise calls attention to the social construction of difference, for, in looking at Gemmy, Lachlan cannot tell the difference between a British subject and a native of Australia: Gemmy must *tell* Lachlan that he is British, not Aborigine. Language, then, becomes necessary for identifying differences and hierarchies, and, as a result, any assumption that these differences have an essential basis beyond language is exposed to be false. This is significant because it highlights the fact that difference constitutes the linguistic and cultural demarcations that set the native 'other' apart from the Eurocentric 'I'. This way of seeing the world, from the perspective of the colonizing gaze of the imperialist, engenders a colonist discourse that aims to normalize and position the 'other' according to the terms of reference constructed by the group at the centre of power. This sets up a seemingly clear-cut distinction between colonizer and colonized through the imposition of a dichotomized hierarchy that distances the 'other' and generates stereotypes to suggest that he or she is entirely knowable and therefore subjectable.

Exposing discourses of difference is one of the projects of postcolonial literature and criticism, a project that is, in this respect, connected to poststructuralism. Difference is, for instance, central to Jacques Derrida's considerations of the distinctions between signs within text. In fact, in *Speech and Phenomena* (1973), Derrida uses the term 'différance', punning upon both spatial and temporal meanings of the verb 'différer' – to 'differ' and to 'defer'. The ambiguities between these two meanings become meaningful only on the written page; as Derrida notes, in spoken French *'différance'* (with an 'a') and 'différence' (with an 'e') are indistinguishable. In other words, since the difference between 'différance' and 'différence' inheres only in writing and not in speech, Derrida reverses the assumption that speech (an indicator of presence or being) precedes the written word that approximates it. In his essay 'Signature, Event, Context' (1977), Derrida furthers this argument by deconstructing binary oppositions (particularly between speech and writing). Here, Derrida examines a hierarchical binary opposition (in this example, speech/writing) in which one term is privileged over the other. Derrida reverses the binaries by re-privileging writing, but with the important caveat that this inversion is itself unstable and susceptible to continual displacement. In terms of logocentrism, to privilege writing over speech is to characterize writing as a new 'centre' of meaning.[2]

These ideas have had a profound impact on postcolonial literature and criticism. This is because deconstruction has exposed the cultural assumptions and dynamics of power that lie behind our everyday encounters with language. As Derrida suggests in *Writing and Difference* (1978), writing does not passively record social 'realities' but in fact precedes them and gives them meaning through a recognition of the differences between signs within textual systems. Cultural differences, then, are disseminated through representation, speech and writing.[3] Postcolonialism thus draws on the lessons of poststructuralism and deconstruction to challenge the writing and speech which supports hierarchical divisions, disseminates cultural assumptions, furthers the power of empire and contributes to the subjugation of the colonized.

It is perhaps not surprising, then, that the English translator of Derrida's major work, *Of Grammatology* (1976), is the postcolonial critic Gayatri Spivak. In 'Bonding in Difference' (1993), an interview with the Chicano poet and scholar Alfred Arteaga (born 1950), Spivak describes her indebtedness to deconstruction. Here, she explains that the postcolonial critic's responsibility is to question the assumptions of social formations through an examination of difference and power. She states,

■ Deconstruction does not say there is no subject, there is no truth, there is no history. It simply questions the privileging of identity so that someone is believed to have the truth. It is not the exposure of error. It is constantly and persistently looking into how truths are produced. That's why deconstruction doesn't say logocentrism is a pathology, or metaphysical enclosures are something you can escape. Deconstruction, if one wants a formula, is among other things, a persistent critique of what one cannot not want.[4] □

Deconstruction, in other words, draws on 'difference' to question assumptions about 'truth' and the ideologies or hierarchies that lie behind various versions of the truth. It does this by interrogating the margins, borderlines and zones of contestation in language. This, in turn, carries implications of social and political conflict which have had a significant impact on postcolonial literature and criticism. For what postcolonialism takes from deconstruction is a suspicion of the structuralist project's desire to produce a neutral science of language and discourse that negates difference. As a corrective, postcolonial writers seek to analyse language in its relation to political history and political power by being sensitive to difference. One area in which postcolonial criticism has drawn on Derrida's ideas has been in analyses of binary oppositions, which are no longer seen as innocent structural relations but rather as hierarchies. In Derrida's work, and in the work of many postcolonial critics who develop his ideas, there is always a sense that an opposition is not an innocent structural relation. Rather, it is a power relation, in which one of the oppositions dominates the other. In the case of binaries such as white/black or civilized/savage, there are clear relations of power that ascribe privilege, priority and positive value to one term at the expense of the other.

But, you might ask, what is the difference between deconstruction and postcolonialism? Well, some postcolonial critics see deconstruction as apolitical because of its desire to destabilize truth. In this, it has been said that deconstruction actually maintains the status quo because it leaves little, if any, terrain upon which a critic or writer can take a political stand. Within deconstruction, then, one can argue that there is no room for the political engagement that lies at the heart of the postcolonial project. Spivak, for instance, points towards deconstruction's limitations in conceptualizing and sustaining an engagement with the politics of domination. Since deconstruction involves the infinite displacement of hierarchical binary oppositions (rather than their tacit reversal), the postcolonial critic aiming at substantive social transformation or revolution finds herself in an inadequate position to revise dominant power structures.[5]

The figure of Gemmy in *Remembering Babylon* illustrates the political limitations of deconstruction. Gemmy's very existence deconstructs the binaries of subject/object, white/black, British/Aborigine: his very presence, and the way he is marginalized by both the British and Aboriginal communities, exposes the hierarchies of these oppositions. And yet where does this leave him? Where does he belong? He is a stranger among the Aborigines and an outsider within the white Australian settlement. How can he take a stand? And how can he resist the inequity of the dominant power structures that are so oppressive to him and the natives of the area? Yes, he deconstructs the social construction of power relations, but where does this get him? Under these circumstances there is no possibility for political action or resistance. Instead of inspiring the white community to rethink their colonizing relation to the Aborigines, the settlers marginalize, abuse, silence and eventually displace Gemmy. As a result, Gemmy is robbed of voice and influence, for there is no ground upon which he can speak. He is therefore perpetually in between the British and Aboriginal cultures, displaced from both the centre and the margin. This lack of belonging forces Gemmy to disappear into the outback, after which Lachlan hears vague rumours of Gemmy's death at the hands of white settlers.

Yet Edward Said, one of the most politically engaged postcolonial critics, has also been influenced by the lessons of deconstruction and poststructuralism. One of his major works, *Orientalism* (1978), interrogates the binary oppositions and hierarchies of East/West and Oriental/Occidental. Such categories of difference, Said argues, are entrenched in the very structure of Western discourse, and they disseminate generalizations about the part of the world known as the 'East'. Said did not invent the term 'Orientalist'; it was used by 'Middle East' specialists, Arabists and those who studied both East Asia and the Indian subcontinent. But Said did point out that the vastness alone of the part of the world that European and American scholars think of as the 'East' is, in itself, highly problematic. Stretching from Morocco to Japan and from Sri Lanka to Northern China, Said observed, the 'East' and the 'Orient' in the Western imagination comprises an absurdly vast geography and includes many different languages, cultures and religions. The labelling of this massive terrain and the images imposed upon it have been, Said maintains, ideologically driven and contribute to a conception of the 'East' as 'the Other' – as different. As Said puts it, 'Orientalism was ultimately a political vision of reality whose structure promoted the difference between the familiar (Europe, West, "us") and the strange (the Orient, the East, "them")'.[6]

Said, then, links the colonizing discourses of Orientalism to stereotypes. The Oriental is, in the Western imagination, characterized as clannish and potentially despotic. He cannot be trusted or relied upon. The men are sexually incontinent and the women are treated as slaves. The Oriental is, in short, different and strange. In *Orientalism*, though, Said asks a significant question: Where is this untrustworthy, clannish, desiring and abusive (or abused) Oriental?[7] Has anyone met a person who matches this description in all of its particulars? No, the imagined characteristics often attributed to the Oriental are, Said argues, generated out of myths that have been disseminated through European thought and writing since the eighteenth century. *Orientalism*, then, is an attempt to deconstruct these myths and identify the discourses of Orientalism as supporting imperialism.

Referring to a practice more than a profession, Said employs the term 'Orientalism' to shift attention away from methods and even subjects of inquiry to the modes by which cultures control and manipulate one another through representation and discourse. For Said, Orientalism refers explicitly to the West's discourses and representations about the Middle and Far East – discursive practices that have denigrated, stereotyped, exoticized, eroticized, mythologized and sought to control 'the Orient'. One of the by-products of this phenomenon is, according to Said, Western self-validation through clear-cut demarcations of difference: East is East and West is West, as Rudyard Kipling famously put it.

The term 'Orientalism' has now entered the critical lexicon, though not without contestation, as a term to describe instances when the 'West' constructs critical generalizations about the 'East' for the sake of reinforcing a superior self-image. Said's work has thus made scholars sensitive to the cultural politics of knowledge by highlighting how a collective identity is frequently constructed in opposition to, and at the expense of, a different culture. To put it simply, Said argues that societies often create superior images of themselves by representing another place or culture as inferior, savage, demonic, exotic and, in general, culturally different. Said sums up his project in the following statement:

> ■ My contention is that Orientalism is fundamentally a political doctrine willed over the Orient because the Orient was weaker than the West, which elided the Orient's difference with its weakness. [...] As a cultural apparatus Orientalism is all aggression, activity, judgment, will-to-truth, and knowledge [...]. My whole point about this system is not that it is a misrepresentation of some Oriental essence – in which I do not for a moment believe – but that

it operates as representations usually do, for a purpose, according to a tendency, in a specific historical, intellectual, and even economic setting.[8] □

Postcolonial literary critics have taken up Said's ideas and applied them to a range of texts, from the Romantic poem 'Ozymandias' (1818) by Percy Bysshe Shelley (1792–1822) to the American science fiction novel *Do Androids Dream of Electric Sheep?* (1968) by Philip K. Dick (1928–82). In postcolonial literature, Tayeb Salih (born 1929), the Sudanese novelist, examines the discursive practices of Orientalism in his 1969 novel, *Season of Migration to the North*. Critics often read Salih's text as a dramatic analysis of colonial politics, wherein a narrator realizes the danger of becoming a Europeanized Arab who wishes to wreak vengeance on the West for his 'Orientalization'. The processes of Orientalization experienced by the anonymous narrator and one of the characters, Mustafa Sa'eed, arise out of the Europeans' historical manufacturing of symbols, tropes and stereotypical representations when writing about, or otherwise 'knowing' the 'Oriental' (usually Arab) in order to prop up and further perpetuate racially essentialist views of the East. Most critics of Salih's text focus on its colonial politics, from Mustafa Sa'eed's adoption of an Oriental persona to his conquests of Englishwomen in order to avenge the ways in which the East has been penetrated and possessed by the West. Such readings of the novel usually focus on Mustafa Sa'eed and develop arguments that link the novel's postcolonial politics to its sexual politics.[9]

The story is told by a narrator who, after living in England for many years, returns to the small Sudanese village of his youth. Soon after his return, he uncovers the story of Mustafa Sa'eed, who has also lived in England and has recently returned to this village. The narrative reveals Mastafa's life in the West. While in England, he adopts a 'mask' in which he becomes 'unaffected by outside forces' and a 'heartless machine'.[10] Extremely well educated and with a very bright future ahead of him, Mustafa chooses to be a conqueror, a man who shall 'liberate Africa with [his] penis', and who regards English women as 'cities to be sieged' or 'mountain peaks' on which to climb.[11] In this, he reverses the European imperialist penetration of Africa (as exemplified in works such as Joseph Conrad's *Heart of Darkness*) and he willingly adopts the Orientalist stereotypes disseminated in the Western discourse. He cannot be trusted; he has a thirst for power; and he is abusive to women. Moreover, by acting out a phallocentric form of hyper-masculinity, his mask fits with what Edward Said calls the Western image of the 'lustful, phallic Oriental subject'.[12] Mustafa thus appropriates 'different units of Orientalist discourse' through 'a set of representative figures, or tropes', 'figures which are to the actual Orient [...] as stylized costumes are to characters in a play'.[13]

Yet the objects of his possession reveal Mustafa to be a hollow symbol constructed out of Orientalism: he is reduced to an Oriental phallic symbol of 'cruelty and sensuality'.[14] This appropriation and internalization of Western discourse exposes the power dynamics inherent to categories of difference. Orientalization thus plays an indispensable role in the fulfilment of Mustafa Sa'eed's dark destiny, the violent dénouement of this novel in which sexual violence is the gruesome and excessive metaphor for the clash between colonizers and the cultures they dominate, shape and ultimately destroy. In the end, though, Mustafa mysteriously disappears and the narrator recognizes his companion's desire to conquer as a meaningless and bare pursuit that is destructive for the conqueror and the conquered.

Edward Said's theory of Orientalism has had a profound impact on other literary critics who are interested in examining representations of racial difference. In fact, the concept of 'difference' is central to the book *'Race', Writing, and Difference* (1987) edited by Henry Louis Gates (born 1950). Here, the authors interrogate the idea of 'race' as a category of difference in the study of literature and the shaping of critical theory. In so doing, they explore the dynamics of racial 'otherness' in various modes of discourse to get at the complex interplay between representations of race and social constructions of difference. In his introduction to the volume, 'Writing "Race" and the Difference It Makes', Henry Louis Gates illustrates how race has been 'written' into existence as a way of keeping racially marked populations in subordinate positions. Throughout the nineteenth and twentieth centuries, representations of race in literature have, Gates argues, sought to 'naturalize' and therefore legitimate the racially marked body as essentially inferior. 'Race, in these usages', he writes, 'pretends to be an objective term of classification, when in fact it is a dangerous trope'.[15] Following from this, a role of the postcolonial critic is to analyse the ways in which writing relates to race, and how attitudes towards racial differences generate and structure literary texts. This can, in turn, lead to a combination of critical methods that can effectively disclose the traces of racial and ethnic differences in literature. But the literary critic, Gates suggests, must also recognize that certain forms of difference and the language used to define these supposed distinctions not only reinforce each other but also create and maintain each other.

Hence, Gates adopts a materialist position to argue for the economic basis of racial oppression. 'Literacy', he suggests, 'is the emblem that links racial alienation with economic alienation'.[16] To illustrate this point, Gates reminds us that Western imperialism institutionalized a system of chattel slavery under which slaves were denied literacy. His central argument here is that slaves, denied the 'right to write', met exclusion from the opportunities available to literate whites: 'Black people and other people of color', Gates continues, 'could not write'.[17] He thus describes how the majority of salient Enlightenment thinkers – such as Kant and Hegel – denied Third World subjects the access to the notion of 'reason' that underwrites their philosophical inquiries. What Gates seeks is not so much an equivalence of 'black' and 'white' writing, but rather a nuanced confrontation of the discursive modes by which 'blackness' and 'whiteness' have come to be understood and defined as different.

Henry Louis Gates is often identified as a ground-breaking scholar in the field of African American literary studies. It is therefore worth pausing a moment and asking an important question: What is the difference between African American literary criticism and postcolonial literary criticism? Well, in the past, scholars have tended to see them as two different areas, but recent trends in criticism have illustrated that they share a central goal: destabilizing racial hierarchies and exposing the linguistic and discursive modes that contribute to the perpetuation of unequal power relations. After all, discussions of the relationship between the colonizer and colonized are sometimes similar to analyses of the master-slave relation in the context of American slavery. Another connection arises out of the lingering forms of discrimination and racism towards minority populations in both the United States and many postcolonial nations. In this, African American studies and postcolonial criticism examine how a hegemonic white or Western culture has come to dominate non-white cultures, and how the subordinated culture has reacted to and resisted domination.[18] In the United States and former European colonies, slavery and racism produced a hegemonic white culture that enforced its systems and values on the non-white population, and the non-white population both obeyed and resisted those systems and values.

From this perspective, Henry Louis Gates and other critics point to the possibility for postcolonial approaches to writing in the United States. American systems of racial imbalance, segregation and disenfranchisement are, they suggest, every bit as 'postcolonial' (perhaps even as 'colonial') as the legacies of imperial rule in developing countries. What's more, because of its racial, religious and cultural heterogeneity, the United States becomes a particularly volatile site of colonial contestation for political visibility and dominance.

This issue is taken up in *The Empire Writes Back*. The authors – Ashcroft, Griffiths and Tiffin – argue that the United States, despite its current 'neo-colonial' position in the world, produces literature that is as postcolonial as the cultural traditions originating in the Third World. They write,

■ So the literatures of African countries, Australia, Bangladesh, Canada, Caribbean countries, India, Malaysia, Malta, New Zealand, Pakistan, Singapore,

South Pacific Island countries, and Sri Lanka are all post-colonial literatures. The literature of the USA should also be placed in this category. Perhaps because of its current position of power, and the neo-colonizing role it has played, its post-colonial nature has not been generally recognized. But its relationship with the metropolitan centre as it evolved over the last two centuries has been paradigmatic for post-colonial literatures everywhere.[19] ☐

The use of postcolonial approaches in analyses of US writing has been particularly productive in understanding how racial difference contributes to the construction of the American categories of nation, class and gender. Such approaches lead to possible deconstructions and reconstructions of 'race' as a meaningful political category.

June Jordan (1936–2002), the African American poet and scholar, insists on examining racial difference by connecting her experience as a black American woman to other non-white populations of the postcolonial world. In this, she connects her struggle for independence not only to the American civil rights movement, but also to the independence movements in countries such as Zimbabwe and South Africa. In her essay, 'Declaration of an Independence I Would Just as Soon Not Have' (1981), Jordan calls for minority groups to unite on a global scale in order to effect change and work towards justice. Here, she writes of the 'hunger and famine afflicting some 800 million lives on earth' as 'a fact that leaves [one] nauseous, jumpy, and chronically enraged'.[20] Exploitation and abuse, she continues, can only be eradicated through the unity of 'the multimillion-fold majority of the peoples on earth [who] are neither white, nor powerful, nor exempt from terrifying syndromes of disease, hunger, poverty that defies description, and prospects for worse privation or demeaning subsistence'.[21]

Discourses of difference and their devastating effects are represented in Jordan's most famous poem, 'Poem about My Rights' (1980). In this highly personal piece, she identifies the power of discourse to identify her difference (her race and gender) as 'wrongness'. The poem begins by describing a society that identifies her gender, race, age and sex as 'wrong', as marginalized by the dominant culture. Thus, Jordan sets up the binaries of white/black, man/woman in order to link them to the dichotomy of right/wrong. By laying out these differences, Jordan exposes the injustice of the hierarchies that are constructed out of these oppositions: being white is right and being black is wrong; being a man is right and being a woman is wrong. Critics have observed that Jordan opens the poem *in medias res* (in the middle of things), which gives form to Jordan's repeated thesis that self-determination is precluded by all oppressions that arise from being outside the white, male, heterosexual centre of power.

'Poem about My Rights' represents racism, sexism, classicism and ageism through situational analogies and projections that meld personal experience with the struggles of other non-white women. In the following passage, Jordan connects the violation of her body – her experience of being violently raped – to violence that is enacted on a national, geographical and political level:

■ they fucked me over because I was wrong I was / wrong again to be me being me where I was wrong to be who I am.[22] □

Like many African American and postcolonial poets, Jordan uses language boldly and fully, not shying away from expressing the anger and rage that results from oppression and injustice. Thus, she often adopts a liberationist discourse by writing about the asymmetrical power structures that rob individuals of liberty and freedom.

More importantly, though, is the fact that 'Poem about My Rights' captures most completely the unbounded range of Jordan's subjects, moving from autobiographical sections to global political issues. She powerfully uses the personalized image of rape to capture political issues in South Africa, Namibia and Zimbabwe. In this sense, Jordan tries to overcome difference by uniting people over common struggles. For instance, she clearly links the violence inflicted upon her to the South African struggle against apartheid. In a 1981 interview, Jordan said the following about 'Poem about My Rights': 'I wrote it in response to having been raped, but I tried to show as clearly as I could that the difference between South Africa and rape and my mother trying to change my face and my father wanting me to be a boy was not an important difference to me. It all violates self-determination'.[23]

Clearly, Jordan is calling for a global resistance movement. This is significant in that global movements are often blamed for ignoring, negating and even eradicating difference. In fact, postcolonial critiques of globalization sometimes equate the global flows of capital and a subsequent rise in consumerism with a process of homogenization and Americanization. Cultural difference is, these critics argue, under threat because of the homogenization of political discourses and socio-economic policies across the globe. After all, globalization is, for the elite, resulting in the increasing breakdown of borders and trade barriers through the increasing integration of world markets, communication systems and media outlets. However, Jordan's writing asserts the need for a transnational resistance to oppression that connects people of African descent, from America to Angola and beyond. As such, Jordan recognizes the necessity of negating differences between oppressed peoples of the world in order to combat the potent forces of globalization and the neocolonial economic movements that exert influence throughout the world.

Discourses of difference have attracted much attention in postcolonial literature and criticism over the last 30 years. As we have seen in this chapter, 'difference' has been attacked as a tool of colonial administration, responsible for disseminating hierarchical distinctions between the colonizer and colonized. By extension, it has also been condemned for maintaining divisions between the Orient and Occident – East and West – through colonizing discourses and problematic modes of representation. Other writers and critics stress the need for colonized peoples of the world to come together – to overcome their differences – and unite under a common aim of economic, social and political equality. In the next chapter, we will examine different approaches to language and the various ways in which postcolonial writers have resisted the homogenizing process of losing a native language and writing in the language of the colonizer.

CHAPTER THREE

Language

> Although, everybody in Dukana was happy at first.
>   All the nine villages were dancing and we were eating plenty maize with pear and knacking tory under the moon. Because the work on the farm have finished and the yams were growing well well. And because the old, bad government have dead, and the new government of soza and police have come.[1]

Thus begins *Sozaboy: A Novel in Rotten English* (1985) by the Nigerian writer Ken Saro-Wiwa (1941–95). The disarming grammar of these first lines continues throughout the entire book and, by the novel's end, the playful simplicity and the lyrical voice of the protagonist take on a sinister and dark quality. For the optimism and hope of narrator at the beginning becomes lost in the violence, conflict and aftermath of the Nigerian civil war of 1967–70. The melancholy ending is, in fact, foreshadowed by the ungrammatical wording of the opening line: the odd displacement of 'Although' and the contingency of the expression 'at first'.

Saro-Wiwa's vivid and idiosyncratic language is a unique literary construct. The author explains that the 'Rotten English' used in the novel is a blend of pidgin English (the lingua franca of the West-African ex-colonies), corrupted English and occasional flashes of standard, idiomatic English.[2] The language, then, is a composite; it is not a mere written version of the language spoken in Nigeria. Nor do Nigerians speak or write in this way. Instead, the small and yet vibrant vocabulary captures the voice of Sozaboy ('soza' means 'soldier') who narrates the terror and horror of the war from his perspective. The 'Rotten English' therefore captures the immediacy of the subjective point of view, and the replication of the Nigerian accent along with the use of local words and phrases (which are explained in a glossary) locates the voice in a specific place. Concerning the novel's language, the novelist and critic William Boyd (born 1952) remarks that

■ Saro-Wiwa has both invented and captured a voice here, one not only bracingly authentic but also capable to many fluent and telling registers.

I cannot think of another example where the English language has been so engagingly and skillfully hijacked – or perhaps 'colonized' would be a better word. Indeed, throughout the novel, Saro-Wiwa exploits Rotten English with delicate and consummate skill. We see everything through Sozaboy's naive eyes, and his hampered vision – even in the face of the most shocking sights – is reproduced through inevitable understatement. Sozaboy's vocabulary simply cannot encompass the strange concepts he encounters or the fearful enormity of what he is undergoing. Yet these silences, these occlusions and fumblings for expression exert a marvelous power.[3] □

If we can leave aside Boyd's own problematic language ('authentic', 'hijacked', etc.), then it is worth noting that he makes an important point. For he correctly argues that Saro-Wiwa engages in an active appropriation of the English language for his own purposes. That is, Saro-Wiwa creates a written vernacular code to 'Nigerianize' the text, departing from a standardized form of English by using oral techniques, culturally specific vocabulary and word morphologies found only in Nigeria. Rather than rejecting the language of the colonizer, Saro-Wiwa appropriates, shifts and changes English (the medium of the centre) as a tool that allows for a renewed sense of local expression. In this, Saro-Wiwa celebrates the survival of a local, Nigerian culture in the language and literary form of the colonizer.

This is a paradoxical issue that has, of course, invited analytical and theoretical response in postcolonial writing. After all, if language is power, then language must be a site of contestation in the struggle for decolonization – a struggle that continues to this day. For the extent to which cultures all over the world have been devalued in the movement of social history is reflected through the dual processes of language repression and the worldwide dominance of English. Postcolonial writing *in English*, then, poses a challenge, for the native writer as well as for the non-native reader, because both enter into domains that are foreign to their own backgrounds.

As early as 1952, Frantz Fanon situated language at the centre of the predicament of colonization, marginalization and servitude. In *Black Skins, White Masks* (1952), he declares that a man who has a language consequently possesses the world expressed and implied by that language.[4] Fanon argues that language becomes an index of both cultural difference and power imbalance: 'What we are getting at becomes plain: Mastery of language affords remarkable power.'[5] Here, he laments the fact that the French language assumed a certain privilege over the 'jabber' of native dialects. The native bourgeoisie, he states, undermined the workings of revolution by coveting the agency or subjectivity ensured by the ability to speak the language of the colonial bourgeoisie. For Fanon, the assimilation and valorization of a European language in

Africa (or elsewhere) underscores the native intellectual's complicity with the 'mother' country that uses the language as a discursive instrument to subordinate colonized subjects and legitimate its comparative privilege: 'the colonized is raised above jungle status [in the eyes of the colonizer] in proportion to his adoption of the mother country's cultural standards.'[6] The person who has taken up the colonizer's language runs the risk of internalizing the perspectives, points of view and cultural assumptions of the dominant group.

What Fanon is getting at here is the fact that language has the 'power to name' and therefore to construct the lens through which understanding takes place. As the most potent instrument of cultural control, the language of the colonial power therefore played an essential role in the process of colonization. Today, the literature of the ex-colonies often decentralizes the power of language and, to a certain extent, it decolonizes by its very nature. Language choice, though, has raised some heated debates in postcolonial writing. This is, in part, because the bilingual postcolonial writer must choose a language of communication and then negotiate the power dynamics regarding such tensions as colonized-colonizer and indigenous-alien. Postcolonial literature itself is a battleground in which the active pursuit of decolonization continues to be played out. Armed with their pen, the postcolonial writer addresses the dominance of imperial language as it relates to educational systems, to economic structures and perhaps more importantly to the medium through which anti-imperial ideas are cast. The postcolonial voice can decide to resist imperial linguistic domination in two ways – by rejecting the language of the colonizer or by subverting the Empire by writing back in a European language.

One of the major voices in this debate has been Ngugi wa Thiong'o (born 1938), a Kenyan writer of Gikuyu descent. Following Fanon, Ngugi argues that decolonization in Kenya can only take place through a rejection of the English language. Although he began a very successful career writing novels in English, he has in recent years worked almost entirely in his native Gikuyu.[7] In his 1986 book *Decolonising the Mind: The Politics of Language in African Literature*, Ngugi includes a chapter, 'Farewell to English', in which he describes language as a means by which the individual makes sense of the world and gains an understanding of himself. For Ngugi, English in Africa is a 'cultural bomb' that continues to wound the individual by erasing his memories of pre-colonial cultures and installing the dominance of new, more insidious, forms of colonialism.[8] By choosing to write in Gikuyu, then, Ngugi reinvigorates Gikuyu history and traditions, while also developing Gikuyu culture in the present. From this perspective, Ngugi is not concerned primarily with universality (though local models of resistance sometimes influence other cultures): his aim is to preserve the specificity of his own community. In a general statement, he points out that language and culture are inseparable, and that therefore the loss of the former results in the loss of the latter:

> ■ [A] specific culture is not transmitted through language in its universality, but in its particularity as the language of a specific community with a specific history. Written literature and orature are the main means by which a particular language transmits the images of the world contained in the culture it carries. Language as communication and as culture are then products of each other [...]. Language carries culture, and culture carries, particularly through orature and literature, the entire body of values by which we perceive ourselves and our place in the world [...]. Language is thus inseparable from ourselves as a community of human beings with a specific form and character, a specific history, a specific relationship to the world.[9] □

Here, Ngugi points out the specific ways that the language of African literature manifests the dominance of the Empire. He presents a compelling argument for African writers to write in traditional languages of Africa rather than in the European languages. Writing in the language of the colonizer, he claims, means that many of one's own people are not able to read one's original work. For him, texts written in a European language cannot claim to be African literature and, as a result, the work of Ken Saro-Wiwa, Wole Soyinka (born 1934) and Chinua Achebe is, from his perspective, Afro-European literature.[10] Ngugi's main unease with African writers' reliance on colonial languages has to do with the limits that choice puts on possible postcolonial readerships, particularly in a country like Kenya where English is the language of the elite. Consequently, Ngugi's concern has to do with privilege and class.

Ngugi reminds us that the teaching of English language and literature was a prominent part of the administration of the British Empire in Kenya. In 1954, in response to the Mau Mau uprising against colonial rule, the British government took control of Ngugi's school and made instruction in English mandatory. Prior to this event, Ngugi had been taught by native Kenyans as part of an independent education system. However, after the uprisings, the British imposed a curriculum on students that emphasized English history, literature and a Eurocentric vision of the world. Ngugi has written extensively about transformation and the devastating effects of the colonial education system in Kenya. In 1968, for instance, Ngugi wrote a collaborative essay, 'On the Abolition of the English Department', which stages a revolt against the vestiges of British colonial rule. This piece depicts English not as a neutral or natural subject but as an instrument of imperialism. And, as a result, Ngugi promotes the study of indigenous national literatures and languages. It was originally

meant to be a university memorandum, but today it is seen as an inau-
gural expression of postcolonial literary criticism. What lies behind an
English department in Kenya, Ngugi suggests,

> ■ is a basic assumption that the English tradition and the emergence of the
> modern west is the central root of our [African] consciousness and cultural
> heritage. Africa becomes an extension of the west, an attitude which, until a
> radical reassessment, used to dictate the teaching of History in our University.
> Hence, in fact, the assumed centrality of the English Department, into which
> other cultures can be admitted from time to time, as fit subjects for study, or
> from which other satellite departments can spring as time and money allow.
> A small example is the current, rather apologetic attempt to smuggle African
> writing into an English syllabus [...]. Here then, is our main question: If there is
> need for a 'study of the historic continuity of a single culture', why can't this be
> Africa? Why can't African literature be at the centre so that we can view other
> cultures in relationship to it?[11] □

This passage spells out a direct connection between language, culture and politics, viewing the influence of a dominant language and
culture as the central vehicles for colonial control. The English Department at an African university is, for Ngugi, an agent of cultural imperialism which, during colonial rule, supplemented direct military and
political occupation, but which continues to be a major player in the
institutionalization of neocolonialism.[12]

'On the Abolition of the English Department' argues that literature
is not neutral nor does it merely impart truth and beauty; instead, the
ways in which literature is taught includes an ideological dimension
through the choice of texts and their interpretation. Ngugi and his
co-authors suggest specific ways to fix this problem. First, African universities must dismantle departments centred on English language and literature. Second, new departments must be created in order to focus on
the study of African languages and literatures, as well as relevant foreign
ones. Third, studies should be geared towards neglected topics such as
the African oral tradition. And, finally, there should be a focus on modern
African literature, which includes Caribbean and African American
literature. Throughout these proposals, the authors do not dismiss English
or European literature, but argue for the benefits of opening literary
study to wider currents. Within the debate over the literary canon, they
take an expansionist position, arguing that the canon must encompass
more texts from different cultures rather than be artificially limited, and
that students should study representative rather than 'classic' texts.

Since the 1990s postcolonial critics have sometimes questioned
the nationalistic character that can dominate the debates over language choice. This is because the struggle for political and cultural

independence can, at times, lead to the same logic of imperialism. This is because postcolonial assertions of nationalism can rest on the fictive construct of an 'imagined community' that is neither natural nor essential to a particular place. Decolonization and Afrocentrism can, in other words, generate essentialist discourses that echo the colonizing Eurocentric ideologies that privilege particular nations, races, ethnicities, cultures and traditions.[13]

For some postcolonial writers in the contexts of slavery, the Caribbean and in regions where indigenous languages have been obliterated through genocide or long-term cultural deracination, language choice is not an issue. English, in these areas, is a site of demolition that leaves behind no linguistic alternative or possible choice. This removal of the 'native tongue' is a direct consequence of the spread of English, and the Antiguan writer Jamaica Kincaid (born 1949) captures the effect of this situation. In her essay, *A Small Place* (1988), for instance, Kincaid writes,

> ■ What I see is the millions of people, of whom I am just one, made orphans: no motherland, no fatherland, no god [...] and worst and most painful of all, no tongue [...]. For isn't it odd that the only language I have in which to speak of this crime is the language of the criminal who committed the crime?[14] □

Here, Kincaid points out that the original languages of Antigua are no longer spoken because the original inhabitants have been genocidally exterminated. But Kincaid is also pointing out that her ancestors were slaves from Africa who would have spoken an African language. But this too has been lost, and she is left only with the 'Queen's English'. Antiguans, as a result, have no 'mother' tongue to call their own. Instead, they are forced to speak in the very language of the people who have ruled over them. This imposed language is, Kincaid maintains, inadequate for expressing the criminal deeds perpetuated by the colonial power. For this language is built to express an Englishman's point of view, and thus it cannot adequately articulate the horror, injustice and agony of colonization from an Antiguan perspective.

Kincaid links the spread of English to the administration of a colonial education and cultural imperialism. She continues her discussion of language by stating that, once the native language of Antigua was eradicated, the ground was laid for the British to 'educate' the natives. Such an education seduced Antiguans with a story told to them by the colonial powers, who taught them to love this story before they became aware that it was erasing Caribbean culture. When the story was seen to be false, Kincaid writes, Antiguans were left with an immense sense of loss, so overwhelming that they tried to cling to the old beliefs, though on some level they realized how destructive it was to do so.

These feelings of betrayal and loss profoundly affect Jamaica Kincaid, and these emotions resurface when she describes the destruction of Antigua's library in the earthquake of 1974. Although the building is still standing, it has been seriously damaged and, as such, it cannot be used. Kincaid, then, uses the image of the broken-down library as a complex metaphor to capture the connections between language, cultural imperialism and the legacy of British rule.[15] She clearly loved the old library, and she is saddened by the temporary library, the 'dung heap', that has replaced it.[16] At the same time, she is fully aware that the library's primary function was to 'educate' Antiguans about the 'greatness', 'wonder' and 'beauty' of British culture, society and history. In lamenting the loss of the library, Kincaid also laments the loss of Caribbean culture in the wake of linguistic and cultural domination. But she is most upset by the loss of the beautiful, yet treacherously seductive, stories that she was told by her British teachers. Kincaid writes,

■ But if you saw the old library [...] its rows and rows of shelves filled with books, its beautiful wooden tables and chairs for sitting and reading [...] the beauty of us sitting there like communicants at an altar, taking in, again and again, the fairy tale of how we met you, your right to do the things you did, how beautiful you were, are, and always will be; if you could see all of that in just one glimpse, you would see how my heart would break at the dung heap that now passes for a library in Antigua.[17] □

The dissemination of English language and culture is, Kincaid recognizes, a function of the material housed in the library (a building constructed by the British). For the holdings were meant to acquaint Antiguans with narratives and stories that promoted an idealized view of English history and society. The library's collection, Kincaid writes, disseminated the tale of England as a benevolent nation that was nurturing the island. From this perspective, she states, the books are a source of lies that the English used in order to justify colonization.

Kincaid's essay, though, falls short of offering any solutions to the problems of Antigua's lost languages or the 'lies' of her teachers. By contrast, Edward Kamau Brathwaite (born 1930), the poet and literary critic from Barbados, argues that it is important to develop a regional form of English to articulate a specific identity that resists Standard English. In 1984, Brathwaite published a critical work, *History of the Voice: The Development of Nation Language in Anglophone Caribbean Poetry*, which put forward his ideas about what he called a 'nation language'. In this, Brathwaite points out that although English is the official language of many Caribbean nations, the citizens do not stick to the prevailing norms of the English language. While some linguists refer to this 'other' language as a simple dialect, Brathwaite views Caribbean English as something much more unique. Writing about language in Anglophone Caribbean poetry, for instance, Brathwaite states,

■ We in the Caribbean have a [...] kind of plurality: we have English, which is the imposed language on much of the archipelago. It is an imperial language, as are French, Dutch and Spanish. We also have what we call creole English, which is a mixture of English and an adaptation that English took in the new environment of the Caribbean when it became mixed with the other imported languages. We have also what is called nation language, which is the kind of English spoken by the people who were brought to the Caribbean, not the official English now, but the language of slaves and labourers, the servants who were brought in.[18] □

Following this description, Brathwaite proposes 'nation language' as a way for the people of the Caribbean to reclaim (or to form) a sense of cultural identity. Such an identity, he explains, has been influenced by colonial, European powers, by native Amerindian culture and by the imported culture of the African slaves. Still, he insists that there is a unique Caribbean culture and identity that is separate from all of these individual influences; it is something unique to the islands themselves. For Brathwaite, then, Caribbean citizens must not be encumbered by the weight of imperial history; they must assert their own independent identity in their own nation language.

A nation language, he argues, decentralizes the control of the imposed European language systems in the postcolonial era. The term, then, is used in contrast to dialect, since dialect carries pejorative connotations, suggesting that it is an inferior version of the European language. Nation language, by contrast, describes a creative system that infuses the imposed language with the attributes of the suppressed system. This assumes that certain 'underground language codes' continue to live on in the dominant code.[19] According to Brathwaite, the rich plurality of the Caribbean has contributed to a variety of underground linguistic patterns that continue to survive:

■ Ashanti, Congo, Yoruba, all that mighty coast of western Africa was imported into the Caribbean. And we had the arrival in our area of a new language structure. It consisted of many languages but basically they had a common semantic and stylistic form. What these languages had to do, however, was to submerge themselves, because officially the conquering peoples – the Spaniards, the English, the French, and the Dutch – insisted that the language of public discourse and conversation, of obedience, command and conception should be English, French, Spanish, or Dutch. They did not wish to hear people speaking Ashanti or any of these Congolese languages. Its status became one of inferiority. Similarly, its speakers were slaves. They were conceived of as inferiors – non-human, in fact. But this very submergence served an interesting interculturative purpose, because although people continued to speak English as it was spoken in Elizabethan times and on through the Romantic and Victorian ages, that English was, nonetheless, still being influenced by the underground language, the submerged language that the slaves had brought.[20] ☐

Here, Brathwaite defines nation language as the language that is influenced by the African model, the African aspect of the Caribbean heritage which was suppressed by European colonizers. The resulting language, then, includes English lexical features, but its contours, rhythms and explosions are not Anglophonic, even though the vocabulary might be, to a greater or lesser degree, English. This form of expression is, Brathwaite suggests, revolutionary, for it can combat the hegemony of conventional English and provide a medium to develop non-European narratives. Brathwaite goes on to write,

■ The underground language was constantly transforming itself into new forms. It was moving from a purely African form to a form which was African but which was adapted to the new environment and adapted to the cultural imperative of the European languages. And it was influencing the way in which the English, French, Dutch, and Spaniards spoke their own languages. So there was a very complex process taking place, which is now beginning to surface in our literature.[21] ☐

In this passage, Brathwaite begins to connect the nation language to a national literature, suggesting that a specific language can generate a specific literature that expresses a unique identity through the rhythm, storytelling styles and orality of the subversive language system. Such a linguistic form can, he suggests, foreground the complex Caribbean heritage and its African roots, and thus resist a potential erasure of that history through the imposition of Eurocentric narratives.

The pluralistic cultural background of the Caribbean is also linguistically expressed in the poetry and drama of Derek Walcott (born 1930). Although he does not necessarily subscribe to Braithwaite's call for a 'nation language', Walcott mixes Standard English with Caribbean expressions to explore the folk and Creole traditions of the region. As such, Walcott's style combines oral storytelling, singing and calypso with richly metaphorical voices and speech patterns. In his essay on Caribbean aesthetics, 'What the Twilight Says: An Overture' (1970), Walcott reflects on the complexity of artistic expression in his native island of St. Lucia. Here, he bemoans the lasting effects of over 400 years of colonial rule, highlighting the political and aesthetic problems presented by a region with little in the way of indigenous forms, and with little national or nationalist identity. 'We are', he writes, 'all strangers here [...]. Our bodies think in one language and move in another'.[22] In this manner, Walcott shifts his poetic language between formal English and 'patois' to highlight the linguistic dexterity of Caribbean citizens. While recognizing the profound psychological and material wrongs of the colonial project, Walcott simultaneously celebrates the hybridization of Antillean cultures: his epic poem *Omeros* (1990), for instance, exposes the complex cultural strains and languages that converge in St. Lucia, and he celebrates the European, Amerindian and African heritage shared by the islanders.

Thus, Walcott has chosen a position that places him in direct opposition to those postcolonial writers who find the English-language literary tradition problematic. Walcott affirms,

■ I am primarily, absolutely a Caribbean writer. The English language is nobody's special property. It is the property of the imagination: it is the property of the language itself. I have never felt inhibited in trying to write as well as the greatest English poets. Now that has led to a lot of provincial criticism: the Caribbean critic may say, 'You're trying to be English', and the English critic may say, 'Welcome to the club'. These are two provincial statements at either end of the spectrum.[23] □

Here, Walcott points out that English may have originated in England, but it has now spread to many countries across the globe. In consequence, it no longer belongs to one place. He thus maintains that there's 'no distinction between someone in Ceylon who's a young poet, and someone in England who's on the same level of talent or whatever, enjoying the language'.[24] This statement, then, challenges Brathwaite's 'nation language', for Walcott seeks to connect poets writing in English (from Sri Lanka to England to St. Lucia) and therefore negate differences between nations. Yet Walcott does not wish to erase difference entirely. On the contrary, in his writing and in interviews, he has acknowledged the divisions of power that can arise out of the dynamics of language choice, suppression and resistance. 'Language is not a place of retreat', he states, 'it's not a place of escape, it's not even a place of resolution. It's a place of struggle.'[25]

This struggle over language can become particularly fierce in nations where full political independence has not been realized. Recently, a heated battle was played out when the Scottish novelist, James Kelman (born 1946), was awarded the Booker Prize for *How Late It Was, How Late* (1994). Written in Glaswegian English, the protagonist and virtual narrator, Sammy, repeatedly uses the word 'fuck' as an adjective, verb and noun. For instance, at the beginning of the novel, Sammy wakes up, after a drunken night out, on a 'wee bed of grassy weeds' with a group of plain-clothes policemen staring at him. The narrator states,

■ How come they were all fucking looking at him? This yin with his big beery face and these cunning wee eyes, then his auld belted raincoat, shabby as fuck; he was watching; no watching but fucking staring, staring right into Sammy christ maybe it was him stole the leathers. Fuck ye! Sammy gave him a look back then checked his pockets; he needed dough, a smoke, anything, anything at all man he needed some fucking thing instead of this, this staggering about, like some fucking down-and-out winey bastard.[26] □

This use of language continues throughout the text and, when it was awarded the Booker Prize, two of the judges furiously dissented, arguing that 'the whole novel constituted an impoverishment of the language'.[27] Moreover, the review in the conservative broadsheet the *Daily Telegraph* called the book 'ugly' and claimed that the novel was a 'pollution of the language which forms an essential part of our culture'.[28]

These reactions to Kelman's use of language betray a defensiveness that attempts to 'protect' the 'Queen's English' and assert a standardized authoritative version of the language that is tied to England. But Kelman responded to his critics in his Booker Prize acceptance speech, in which he spoke of the necessity of using the language that is actually spoken on the streets, whatever the implications may be.[29] For Kelman, the English nationalist discourse that asserts authority over its language and culture is yet another tool of imperialism. 'I write in *my* language and *my* culture', Kelman asserts, 'They say I'm subverting their tradition, but I say this is my tradition. And my tradition has nothing to do with them.'[30]

Kelman uses local vernacular language as a way of expressing the issues of political and economic marginalization faced by the working community of Glasgow. In this, he seeks to capture the voice of the people. By extension, he argues that the 'Eng Lit' taught in schools and universities of the United Kingdom is a means of control by England and the upper classes. As a corrective, his writing continually challenges the very idea of a 'Great Literary Tradition' and concentrates on issues that are immediate and relevant, moving from issues of class speech to a general concern with political freedom of speech.[31]

In recent interviews, Kelman has expressed the value of a literary culture that is pluralistic, inclusive of the voice and use of the vernacular. But, more importantly, he celebrates his affinity with writers from the former colonies of Britain in Africa and the Caribbean whose work he considers to be equally 'subversive' of English:

■ Writers from Africa and the Caribbean proved that what was sneered at as 'dialect', 'patois' or 'pidgin' could be a poetic, lyrical language expressive not only of vulgar realism or comedy but of inner truths and emotions – often with an ear to the rhythm, pace and pulse of the spoken word.[32] □

This connection is fruitful. For the defensive critiques of Kelman's writing echo those critics who have denigrated the authors writing in Caribbean or African Englishes. At issue is acceptance of the hybridity of English and the recognition that English is subject to transformation and change.

David Punter's analysis of *How Late It Was, How Late* correctly suggests that the negative response to Kelman's novel raises precisely the same debates that have arisen among postcolonial writers from other parts of the world. At the centre of this debate is, as we have seen, an important question: What language should the postcolonial writer use? For the outraged Booker Prize judges, Kelman's language does not respect what they see as the sacred nature of the English language and, by extension, the so-called Great Literary Tradition which is, for them, also sacred and desirable to be included. On their side of the struggle, they exert a discourse of linguistic and literary standardization and control that attempts to police the borders and limits of language. Like Customs Officers, they see themselves as protecting the customs and culture of the land.

In this chapter, we have seen how several postcolonial writers and critics treat the issue of language. Some writers develop new forms of English, while others choose to reject entirely the language of imperialism, while still other writers lament the loss of an ancestral language. In the next chapter, we will consider the critical responses to another form of linguistic expression in postcolonial literature – orality – and examine how the oral can relate to the textual in order to develop new forms of writing.

CHAPTER FOUR

Orality

In the previous chapter, we explored how postcolonial writers use the vernacular – the common speech of a region or place. Vernacular literature is, as we saw, a term often applied to works not written in the standard or dominant language of their time and place. The Australian poet Les Murray (born 1938) writes that when poets use the vernacular, they resist the 'colonial hangover' that would otherwise compel them to identify with a British literary tradition. By writing in the language of a self-respecting 'ordinary' Australia, Murray states, the poet uses the spoken language of the nation – what he calls the 'vernacular republic' – as a mode of poetic validation.[1]

Vernacular literature, then, creates a written language out of an oral language and, in this sense, the vernacular is linked to orality. A vernacular text, then, captures an oral language in writing. However, when literary critics speak of the oral tradition, they are referring to something much more specific and complex. For they are identifying a way of transmitting stories, history and culture from one generation to another in a society that does not rely upon writing as a means of communication. An oral tradition is therefore defined by the transmission of cultural material by word of mouth rather than through written documents. The academic study of oral traditions has had a profound impact on the areas of literature, linguistics, communication, folklore, theology, anthropology and history. Moreover, recent developments in the examination of orality have contributed to a reconsideration of the construction of systematic hermeneutics and aesthetics. As a result, the study of oral cultures has influenced criticism in the areas of film studies, popular culture and, of course, postcolonial literature.

Some analyses of oral culture have focused on periodization, treating it as a closed cultural system. Such studies have conventionally identified oral culture as beginning between 60,000 and 100,000 years ago and ending with the arrival of writing around 4000 BC or moveable print in Europe (between 1451 and 1453). But the anthropologist Eric Michaels has demonstrated that periodization overlooks the continuities of oral culture, and the ways in which new cultural forms may simply be overlaid onto pre-existing processes and experiences. In his article 'Constraints on Knowledge in the Economy of Oral Information' (1985), Michaels argues that oral culture ought to be characterized by the pre-eminence of orality, though the fundamental language technology may have been supplemented by graphic and visual artistic forms, dance, music, rituals and other meaning codes like smoke signals.[2] What Michaels points to is the problem of framing oral culture within a specific period. After all, the beginnings of an oral culture remain elusive since spoken language leaves no residue, no artefacts for possible investigation. However, cultural critics agree that a complex system of oral communication is associated with the migrations of peoples across the globe and the imperatives of new living conditions and social organization. Oral language seems necessary for such social and transitory activities, including the movement and settlement of people in the Americas and through South East Asia to Australia. Recent evidence suggests that these migrations took place as long as 100,000 years ago. It is unthinkable that these long, complex journeys could have occurred without a complex system of oral culture that would facilitate the communication necessary for organizing such movements.[3]

Postcolonial critics have identified certain traits of oral cultures. Oral language is, of course, fixed in time and space. It cannot be recorded, so it only exists while the vocal sounds are occurring. This means that oral information is ephemeral and relies on memory for its durability. Oral communication is also constrained by the range of a person's voice. In this, the human voice becomes the range limit, so the presence of the person's body is essential to the communication. In oral cultures, information is connected with immediacy and relies on ritualized practices of memory. As a result, information is closely linked to narrative and storytelling. This means that social laws are repeated, communicated and performed in practices like dance and ceremonies. But memory is not always perfect; it can distort or change information. Moreover, because knowledge is difficult to accumulate, it follows that a limited corpus of knowledge can be transmitted. Thus, the limitations of knowledge and memory are supplemented with rituals, totems, symbols and art. Examples of these include cave paintings, totem poles, wood carvings and stone monuments. Within many oral cultures, past and present are not separated from each other. This is because history lives on (it is restored) in every utterance. Since memory does not work like lineal time or a chronology, the past seems forever preserved in the present utterance. The language use of oral cultures appears to compress time into an ever-unfolding now. Therefore, lived experience embodies all history, reinterpreted and refashioned to make sense of present events, social practices, relationships and other conditions of daily life. Finally, mythology structures the present time, and it thus becomes the conduit to human perpetuity.

Generally speaking, the ideological force of writing and print culture has relegated orality to the margins. But it is important to remember that oral culture has remained an important part of human communication, interaction and cohesion for the past millennium. Moreover, Marshall McLuhan (1911–80) points to the arrival of electronic communication not just as a 'secondary orality', but as a continuity between orality in the present and oral cultures of the past.[4] Jeff Lewis also notes that 'postmodernism, with its emphasis on de-centralization, imagery and the compression of time, has in many respects reinvigorated this underlying orality'. He goes on to note that 'the communalism in decorative art, the intensification of time and immediacy as "all-time", the experience of ephemera and the pleasures of the communicable bodily presence – all are shared by orality and postmodernism'.[5]

Until relatively recently, however, the predominant belief among anthropologists, mission societies, media theorists and government policy makers was that oral and literate cultures were successive, mutually exclusive stages in a single, unavoidable path of cultural evolution. This way of thinking had a profound impact on colonial administration and imperialist ideologies. For in settler nations like Canada, Australia and New Zealand, it justified assimilation policies, which were considered merely a means of hastening the inevitable 'progress' of 'primitive' Aboriginal peoples into the 'modern' world. Today, such ideas are discredited as relics of a colonist ideology that justified European cultural domination by picturing Aboriginal peoples as Europe's primitive ancestors. Nevertheless, the postcolonial literary critic Penny Van Toorn asserts that Aboriginal peoples are, 'living with the legacies of such ideas, having seen their cultures threatened or destroyed by missionaries who prohibited traditional languages and ceremonies, and [...] obstructed cultural transmission by separating children from their families. Erroneous though it was, the idea that cultures evolved from orality to literacy became a self-fulfilling prophecy because it was enforced through government policies.'[6]

Many of today's postcolonial writers emphasize the importance of an oral cultural heritage both as a source of meaning in their lives and as a resource for their writing. This can be found in English language literature from all parts of the postcolonial world: from Africa and the Indian Subcontinent to North America and Australasia. While direct interaction with family and community life remains the primary means of oral cultural transmission, oral cultures are now also passed down through a variety of additional means such as books, magazines, films, television, radio and the Internet. This has led to a significant question: How can orality be translated into writing? In fact, the expression 'oral literature' is an oxymoron (a contradiction in terms) and, as a result, some critics use the word 'orature' to refer to forms of oral discourse such as stories, songs and various kinds of ritual utterance.

The 'translation' of orality into writing is a problem faced by many Aboriginal writers. The Métis (Canadian) writer Maria Campbell (born 1940) stresses the difficulty of fusing together the oral and the written. In her Preface to a collection of short stories titled *Achimoona* (1985), she writes, 'Now came the big job, to take those oral stories and put them on paper. It was hard, we had to change from telling a story to a group of people to being alone and telling the story to the paper.'[7] For Campbell, the difficulty of this 'translation' lies in the fact that the communal experience of telling a story needs to be adapted to the solitary acts of reading and writing. But this also means that the isolation and lack of immediacy associated with textuality changes the narrative patterns of the oral story. For the circular communication of the oral process that occurs between teller and listener(s) is, when written down, transformed into a linear narrative structure. Similarly, another Métis writer, Emma LaRocque (born 1949), sees the juxtaposition between orality and textuality as a source of conflict in Aboriginal writing. Commenting on the 'translation' of oral stories into text by First Nations' writers in Canada, she claims: 'What is at work is the power struggle between the oral and the written, between the Native in us and the English.'[8] Echoing Campbell's frustration with translating the oral into the textual, LaRocque views 'the oral' as intrinsically 'Native' and in conflict with 'the written', which is identified as the colonizer's medium – 'the English'.[9] Here, LaRocque articulates the problem of being an Aboriginal writer who writes in the dominant language of the nation and publishes for a mainstream audience. This situation forces her to reflect upon the power struggle in which her writing is situated, and she expresses these difficulties in the introductions to her work.

The power struggle involved in the relationship between orality and textuality is also highlighted in *The Post-Colonial Studies Reader*. Here, Bill Ashcroft, Gareth Griffiths and Helen Tiffin suggest the possibility that 'orality' empowers the colonial subject with a mode of resistance. As they argue in the passage below, despite the subordination of 'oral traditions' in Western modernity, spoken performances often reject the discursive subordination as a result not only of colonization but academic conceptualizations of colonization:

■ In 'modern' societies the oral and the performative continues to exist alongside the written but is largely ignored or relegated to the condition of pretext in many accounts, represented as only the beginning or origin of the written. Yet in many postcolonial societies oral, performative events may be the principal present and modern means of continuity for the pre-colonial culture and may also be the tools by which the dominant social institutions and discourses can be subverted or repositioned, shown that is to be constructions naturalized within a hierarchized politics of difference.[10] □

In this passage, the authors suggest that orality can be used as a method of resistance to the epistemic and material violence of imperialism and neocolonialism. Oral traditions can, in other words, function as an alternative to the dominant discursive modes and ideologies disseminated by the colonizer. Orality can, in short, offer a way of structuring stories and conceiving of the world that is outside of a Eurocentric textual framework.

Yet for the Canadian First Nations novelist Thomas King (born 1943), this mode of resistance runs the risk of repeating simple binaristic oppositions between orality and textuality, Native and non-Native. As a result, King's novels and short stories strive to develop what he has termed a Native 'interfusional literature', a hybrid of heretofore oppositional traditions. In so doing, his writing combines aspects of oral Native culture and Western narrative traditions both to expose the intrinsic imperialist biases of Eurocentric thought and the possibilities for resistance through hybridity. This technique is illustrated in the opening lines of King's novel *Green Grass, Running Water* (1993):

> ■ So.
> In the beginning, there was nothing. Just water.
> Coyote was there, but Coyote was asleep. That Coyote was asleep and that Coyote was dreaming. When that Coyote dreams, anything can happen.
> I can tell you that.
> So, that Coyote is dreaming and pretty soon, one of those dreams gets loose and runs around. Make a lot of noise.
> Hooray, says that silly Dream, Coyote dream. I'm in charge of the world.[11] □

Here, the first word of the novel 'So' gestures towards an oral story through its colloquialism, but also through its resistance to the teleology of linear textual narratives. After all, King's use of the word 'so' suggests that something has come before it and, as such, the beginning of the story is not really the beginning at all. However, the influence of an oral tradition in this passage is fused with Western discourse through the Biblical reference, 'In the beginning …', which repeats the first words of Genesis (the first book of the Old Testament). This Judeo-Christian story of the origin of the world is, then, mixed with a Native oral creation cycle that renders an origin of the world in the figure of Coyote (the trickster) and the dream. The result is that King is able to combine the conventions of an Aboriginal oral tradition with Western stories and discourses in order fluidly to cross the borders that have traditionally separated Native and non-Native cultures.

King's literary project is partly explained in his critical writing. In his 1990 essay 'Godzilla vs. Post-Colonial', King challenges the view that all Native literature is a reaction to colonialism, rather than an extension of a much longer Native tradition. The problem with postcolonial literary criticism, he argues, is that it often reduces Native literature to a political reaction to imperialism. This positions the writing of Natives as a mere by-product of Western politics and textual production. In this, postcolonialism can reinscribe the colonizing discourses of Eurocentrism by, once again, placing the colonizer at the centre and the Native on the margin. From this perspective, King interrogates the origin and the precise definition of the term postcolonial, asserting that in terms of Native literature, 'we can say that pre-colonial literature was that literature, oral in nature, that was in existence prior to European contact, a literature that existed exclusively within specific cultural communities'.[12] By extension, King refutes the idea that Native literature is an exclusively postcolonial form of writing, for it is not simply literature that has emerged out of (or after) the period of colonization. Instead, contemporary First Nations writing in Canada is, from King's perspective, part of a much longer tradition that connects back to an oral culture that existed before colonization. Having said this, King concedes that contemporary Native writing has been influenced by colonization and the impact of European settlement in North America. However, he maintains that the unique voices of Native writers resist attempts to categorize their texts within the limiting confines of a postcolonial paradigm.

One of King's problems with the term postcolonialism is that it assumes too much, for it conveys the idea 'that the struggle between guardian and ward is the catalyst for contemporary Native literature, providing those of us who write with method and topic'.[13] By extension, postcolonialism supposes that contemporary Native writing is merely a construct and consequence of oppression, and that it removes Natives from traditions which existed long before the advent of imperialism.

King also argues that the term 'postcolonial' implies a sense of progress and improvement, moving from 'savagery' to 'civilization'. As a corrective, King proposes other terms that emphasize the fact that Native literature is not dependent on a European imperialist project. For instance, he uses the expression 'tribal literature' to refer to writing that exists primarily within a tribe or a community, literature that is 'shared almost exclusively by members of that community and literature that is presented and retained in a Native language'.[14] This form of cultural production is important for the Native community, but has no interest in being accessible to other audiences. 'Associational literature' is, on the other hand, accessible to a wider audience; it is work that, according to King, details the daily lives of Natives through plots that are linear, while not necessarily foregrounding the climaxes and resolutions of much non-Native fiction. Here, non-Native readers can associate with the native world without actually being encouraged to feel part of it. King also uses the expression 'polemical literature' to define writing which is written in either English or a Native language, and which describes Native–European conflict and/or advocates Native values. King describes how 'polemical literature chronicles the imposition of non-Native expectations and insistences (political, social, scientific) on Native communities and the methods of resistance employed by Native people in order to maintain both their communities and cultures'.[15] Finally, as far as orality and textuality are concerned, King uses the term 'interfusional literature' to describe literature which is a mix of both oral and written narratives. Although these texts are written in English, their grammatical structures, themes and characters are drawn from the oral tradition. King explains that the reader of this literature must be encouraged to read the text aloud to avoid the problem of losing the voice of the storyteller, which is the biggest problem in the transfer of oral literature to the written word.

King's voice is an important intervention in the recent debates over orality. As Terry Goldie points out in *Fear and Temptation* (1989), orality came to be one of the important ways in which the Aboriginal 'Other' was defined as different from the white 'self'. Within this dichotomy, orality was associated with the primitive and set in opposition to civilization. It was thus characterized as inferior and, as such, it was associated with irrationality, fantasy and impermanence. Moreover, the world-views and belief systems of orality were defined as pre-modern in relation to the so-called advanced knowledges of 'civilized' Europe. Here, Goldie's discussion of orality is influenced by Walter Ong's *Orality and Literacy* (1982), an extensive study of the two concepts, which must, as Goldie points out, be deconstructed before its insights can be of any value in the postcolonial context: 'Orality as defined by [...] Ong is a major part of the primitivist attraction of the Indigene for the white text. A part of this is simply primitivism, a desire for an earlier time, before the technology represented by writing.'[16]

Ong's ideas rest on the assumption that writing is totally artificial and yet necessary for the development of complex, analytical, sequential and linear thought. Oral cultures, he continues, do not order thoughts in this way because their narratives and cultural belief systems rely on 'rhapsodizing' and the 'stitching together' of stories that are not necessarily linear or teleological. Ong, then, praises orality as 'natural', a form of communication that is in direct opposition to the artificiality of literacy.[17] Orality is, for Ong, superior to writing because it is immediate and communal, as well as offering a lyricism and mysticism that is lacking in the written word. Such a binaristic model romanticizes orality and expresses a nostalgia for its loss. This, then, assumes a 'progressive' notion of history in which literacy is associated with progress, while the death of orality is associated with the illiteracy of the past. Moreover, by associating orality with nature, Ong displaces it from culture, effectively reinscribing the nature-culture binary that feeds into the colonizing opposition between uncivilized (nature) and civilized (culture). All of these ideas illustrate how Ong's praise of orality is supportive of Euro-centric hegemonic discourses that link oral traditions to the Rousseau's figure of the 'Noble savage'.[18]

It is not surprising, then, that Aboriginal writers such as King in Canada and Mudrooroo (born 1938) in Australia highlight the ways in which European scholarship and criticism tend to reinscribe colonizing discourses and ideologies. In his article 'White Forms, Aboriginal Content' (1985), for instance, Mudrooroo sees the wave of postcolonial studies as threatening to deny the fact that Australian Aborigines are still colonized, always invaded and never free from the history of white occupation. 'The indigenous minorities', he writes, 'are submerged in a surrounding majority and governed by them' and, in this sense, the effects of colonization cannot be relegated to the past, as the prefix 'post' in postcolonial seems to suggest.[19] This continuing interfusion of cultures has meant that 'Aboriginality in Australia is often defined as an assimilative state, as an admission of conflicting and hybrid cultural allegiances.'[20]

Throughout his fiction, Mudrooroo focuses his energies on revising the language, narrative styles and historical representations of the colonist invader. His aim is not to replace white with black. Instead, he seeks to accentuate hybridity: to write Indigenous stories and oral narratives using what he calls 'white forms' like the novel. He thus adapts the mnemonic codes of orality, totemic symbols, cyclical patterns, myths, as well as Aboriginal demotic speech into his texts, in this way creating a composite literature – literature that mixes oral and written forms of communication. For instance, in the conclusion of Mudrooroo's novel *Doctor Wooreddy's Prescription for Enduring the Ending of the World* (1983), one of the Aboriginal characters, Waau, tells Wooreddy, a native Tasmanian, an oral creation story. Speaking of *Puliliyan*, the controller of the waters, Waau says,

■ Once *Puliliyan* thumped the water until it became very thick, as thick as mud and he could no longer see far down into the depths. Something appeared to move in the murk and he took a branch and divided the waters [...]. He broke a twig off the branch and fashioned a hook which he let down into the water, and he drew up those creatures. They were similar to the ones Our Father had created on land. So he took these two strange creatures to him. Our father took them and gave one each to the men he had created. They were women and were to be their wives. He gave each man a spear and each woman a digging stick, then told them to live together and divide the work between them.[21] □

By including this passage towards the end of his novel, Mudrooroo resists the linearity of textuality, ending the text with a beginning – a creation story. This ending/beginning is rendered through an oral transmission – one person tells the story to another – and it is in this way that the history and culture of the place and people are kept alive. Moreover, the inclusion of Indigenous words and phrases (in Bruny) alongside oral forms enables Mudrooroo to re-enter Aboriginal history and cultures. Writing of *Doctor Wooreddy*, the literary critic Elleke Boehmer states that Mudrooroo is able to infuse the white, textual genre of the novel with the orality of,

■ Aboriginal [...] myth and historical legend, re-telling the contact story from an Aboriginal perspective, muddling chronology to create a sense of 'the unity of three times', and ... incorporating the 'text' of a traditional corroboree, in which Bruny words and song symbols are not translated for the benefit of non-Aboriginal readers.[22] □

In this, Mudrooroo is able to assert his own resistant metaphysic, and come to terms with the uneasy concerns surrounding his complex cultural background (Aboriginal and Australian), as well as writing in the language and form of the colonizer. As Mudrooroo argues in his critical work, *Writing from the Fringe* (1990), Indigenous Australian writers often include aspects of traditional oral culture in their texts, inscribing a camouflaged or hidden metatext which does not open itself up to the understanding of the un-initiated reader. The initiated or aware reader can, however, uncover the hidden metatext of Indienality or maban reality.[23]

The relationship between orality and writing, Indigenous traditions and appropriations, identity and representation is central to Eva Rask Knudsen's book, *The Circle and the Spiral: A Study of Australian Aboriginal and New Zealand Maori Literature* (2004). This analysis of an illustrative corpus of Indigenous Australian and Maori novels outlines the field of Indigenous writing in Australian and New Zealand in the period between the mid-1980s and the early 1990s.[24] In Aboriginal and Maori literature, Knudsen argues, the circle and the spiral are structurally important because of the influence of the traditions of orature. But this formal quality is also echoed in the metaphoric cadence of the circle and the spiral as a never-ending journey of discovery and rediscovery. For Knudsen, the journey itself, with its Indigenous perspectives and sense of orientation, is the most significant act of cultural recuperation. Orature, then, resists Eurocentrism and theories of postcolonialism that try to fix positions and even 'centre the margins'. Indigenous writers, Knudsen suggests, are often keen to escape the particular centring offered by contemporary theory by searching for other positions more in tune with their creative sensibilities, traditional Indigenous cultures and orality. Thus, throughout the 1980s and early 1990s, Indigenous writing turned away from social realism in favour of what Mudrooroo calls a camouflaged or hidden metatext that represents the secret/sacred prescriptions of their ancestry.

Following in Mudrooroo's footsteps, Knudsen searches for 'the black words on the white page […] in the Indigenous subtexts of contemporary Aboriginal and Maori literature'.[25] This reading strategy is pursued by means of searching for enquiries into the historical, anthropological, political and cultural determinants of the present state of Aboriginal and Maori writing. Her readings thus often reveal underlying oral patterns that are part of what she calls 'New Traditionalism'. Thus, her combination of Indigenous and European theorizations of orality and Indigenous spirituality responds to her desire to leave an ear open to what the texts are telling. This hybrid combination points out that postmodern, poststructuralist and postcolonial theorizations were influenced by Indigenous Australian and Maori culture. By extension, Knudsen attempts to adopt some oral tools in her own writing such as a circular structure and what she terms 'indigenized' reading. In her application of the latter, Knudsen explores the possibilities offered by Mudrooroo's theory of the hidden metatext or matrix.

Patricia Grace (born 1937), a New Zealand writer of Maori descent, further examines the relationship between orality and textuality in her 1975 short story 'A Way of Talking'. Here, Grace looks at not only the ways in which people speak, but also the political, generational and communal implications of how speech is uttered. Although the story is written in English, the first-person narrator, Hera, uses non-English words such as 'Kamakama', 'Pakeha' and 'hoha'. And yet these words are not the only ways of talking that signal their Maori background: Hera, for instance, highlights a linguistic uniqueness in her family when she tells us of her grandmother's 'lovely way of talking', quoting her Nanny as saying things like 'Time for sleeping. The mouths steal the time of the eyes.'[26] This highly lyrical and metaphoric utterance implies that too much talking can rob one of sight and obscure a person's perspective. As such, she vocalizes the tenet of an oral culture in which there is an understanding that words are not to be uttered lightly.[27] Later in the story, Hera is 'wild' with her sister Rose because she has embarrassed her in front of Jane Frazer, but she 'couldn't think what to say' and threatens to withdraw into a childish sulking.[28] Hera recognizes, however, that as a woman coming of age and 'about to be married', she must speak out and tell her younger sister of her disapproval.[29] Finally she blurts out: 'Rose, you're a stink thing, […] you made me embarrassed.'[30] Here, Grace contemporizes the Maori oral tradition, which places a prescription on speaking out about knowledge and understanding of genealogical status.

Grace is, of course, highlighting the importance of speaking through her writing. Thus, the way of speaking (or speaking out) for and within the Maori community opens up the space of writing as a potential site of responsible communication. What Grace's story explores, then, is a combination of orality and textuality as a site of enunciation that forces a clear establishment of speaking positions. Indeed, one of the most important requirements of the oral tradition is the recurrent questioning and acknowledgement of the 'positionality', accountability and responsibility in a community of speakers. As a result, for Grace and other Indigenous writers, it is important to reconceptualize discourse as an event which includes speakers, words, hearers, locations, language and so on. This is important because all of these aspects of discourse are, in one way or another, related to power. This simply follows from the fact that an utterance (oral or textual) will be based on the specific elements of historical discursive context, as well as the location of speakers and hearers and so forth.

This chapter has traced the reasons why postcolonial writers turn to orality in their writing. For some, it is a form of resistance to the forceful hegemony of European technological narrative practice. For others, it is a link to the past, a way of continuing Indigenous cultural expression in the present. And still, for others, the act of 'writing orality' is a way of capturing a contemporary hybrid native culture that mixes native modes of expression with the cultural practices of the colonizing group. As we will see in the next chapter, some critics link orality to the postcolonial practice of 'rewriting' the canonical narratives of the imperialist.

CHAPTER FIVE

Rewriting

> Achille moved Philoctete's hand, then he saw Helen
> Standing alone and veiled in the widowing light.[1]

At a glance, it might seem as if these lines come from one of Homer's epic poems, *The Iliad* or *Odyssey*.[2] But they don't. The passage is, in fact, from Derek Walcott's poem *Omeros*, published in 1990. In this epic, Walcott presents us with a rewriting of Homer's work: he offers the reader a contemporary postcolonial setting that corresponds to Homer's world through a sequence of story lines, flashbacks, conversations, monologues, episodes and descriptions. Above all, Walcott depicts, in minute detail, life on the Caribbean island of St. Lucia.

But the poem does not only evoke a Western epic tradition through a repetition of character's names and Homeric parallels. For it is important to note that Walcott's poem replicates the very epic form that was established by Homer, Dante (1265–1321, Italian poet), Milton (1608–74, English poet) and others. The metre is a loose hexameter (with six metrical feet per line), approximating the Homeric style (though it contracts occasionally to five or even four-beat lines). In this, Walcott also acknowledges the influence of Milton's blank verse, the accentual tetrameter (four iambic feet per line) of *Beowulf*[3] and the English poem 'Piers Plowman' (ca. 1360–99), as well as the folk music of the Caribbean. Moreover, the *Omeros* stanza, with the exception of one section in tetrameter rhymed couplets, is composed in the tercet (in which three lines of poetry form a stanza) of Dante's *Divine Comedy* (1308–21). But Walcott adapts the stanza freely, departing from Dante's strictly linked rhyme to accommodate ad hoc variations on terza rima (a three-line stanza using chain rhyme in a specific pattern).

Furthermore, Walcott even has Homer appear as a character in several sections. He appears as the blind Greek poet himself and the blind popular poet Seven Seas. He pops up again as the African rhapsodist, as well as the famous American painter Winslow Homer (1836–1910), with his paintings from the Atlantic Ocean such as *A Fair Wind* (1876) and *The Gulf Stream* (1899). And, finally, he returns as the blind barge-man who stands on the steps of the London church St. Martin-in-the-Fields with a manuscript refused by his editors. The influence of Homer on *Omeros* is also present in the fact that Walcott writes Helen-of-Troy into the heart of his poem, presenting his Caribbean Helen as the symbolic and actual centre of a complex imperialist struggle in the competition for power and control over the island. Walcott thus draws upon the thematics of anger, division, competition, lust, battle, domination, oppression, suffering, and eventually love, homecoming and redemption that are prominent in Homer's verse as well as in other European epics.

This begs a series of important questions that are addressed throughout this chapter. Why would Walcott, a prominent postcolonial writer, draw on a Classical as well as European literary tradition? Does he, as a Caribbean poet, find it necessary to rely on the mainstays of Western literature, 'the World's Great Classics', when writing his narratives? Or is such rewriting part of the process of challenging and subverting the literary canon? Perhaps, by alluding to this tradition, the postcolonial writer is claiming membership into the club of 'Great writers'. Or maybe he is exploring the diversity and hybridity of a postcolonial culture in which 'Classics' are just one aspect of the literary tradition. At the heart of these questions are debates about writing and rewriting, as well as canon formation and canon revision – questions that are highlighted throughout postcolonial literature and criticism.

Walcott's desire to rewrite Classical and European texts is shared by many other postcolonial writers. Rewriting is, in fact, a common postcolonial practice, and works such as *The Tempest* (1611) by William Shakespeare (1564–1616), *Robinson Crusoe* (1719) by Daniel Defoe (1659–1731) and *Great Expectations* (1860) by Charles Dickens (1812–70) have been revised, restructured and scrutinized from non-European perspectives. After all, the telling of a story from another point of view can be an extension of the deconstructive project to explore the gaps and silences in the canonical text. And since writing has long been recognized as one of the strongest forms of cultural control, the rewriting of central narratives of an imperialist culture can be a liberating act for authors subjugated by imperialism.

In his book *Postcolonial Con-texts: Writing Back to the Canon* (2001), John Thieme argues that rewriting canonical Western texts offers the postcolonial writer a way of 'writing back' to the imperial centre and developing 'counter-discursive' works of resistance – what he calls 'con-texts'.[4] With reference to the English-language literary tradition, he writes that 'con-texts are [...] a body of postcolonial works that take a classic English text as a departure point, supposedly as a strategy for contesting the authority of the canon of English literature'.[5] Rewriting the 'classics', then, becomes a way of challenging and dismantling English literary hegemonies that tend to represent the world through a white, imperialist lens. But the act of rewriting is not simply a dismissal of the earlier text, for the relationship between the two works must be seen as existing in dialogue with each other, however strained that conversation might be. Thieme states,

■ Whether or not they set out to be combative, the postcolonial con-texts [rewritings] invariably seemed to induce a reconsideration of the supposedly hegemonic status of their canonical departure points, opening up fissures in their supposedly solid foundations that undermined the simplism involved in seeing the relationship between 'source' and con-text in terms of an oppositional model of influence. Attractive though binary paradigms have been to some post-colonial theorists, the evidence invariably suggested a discursive dialectic operating along a continuum, in which the influence of the 'original' could seldom be seen as simply adversarial — or, at the opposite extreme, complicit.[6] □

Thieme notes that the process of rewriting sets up a complex and ambivalent relationship between the new text and the old. The rewriting might be oppositional and counter-discursive or it might simply engage in direct dialogue with the canon by virtue of responding to a 'classic' English or European text. To put this another way, the combative nature of rewriting is always potentially limited by the fact that it invokes an original work and, in so doing, the new work positions itself in relation to the English 'original'. In short, the postcolonial rewriting meets the colonial text on its own ground. This has inspired some post-colonial writers and critics to be dismissive of rewritings. They argue that any rewriting, no matter how combative, is always implicated in the process of reinscribing the Western canon. As a corrective, these writers and critics suggest that the postcolonial project must dismiss Western canonical texts and seek out other non-Western influences with which to engage in a dialogue.

By contrast, other postcolonial writers and critics embrace the process of rewriting as a way of challenging the Western literary canon and, by extension, Western perspectives, ideologies and discourses. They argue that whatever the relationship is between the postcolonial work and the canonical text, the newer piece helps us to read the older work in new ways. This is because the postcolonial rewriting often foregrounds voices that are silenced in the original and reveals areas of the 'Classic' text that have been veiled in darkness. Rewriting, then, provides alternative ways of reading. The authors of *The Empire Writes Back* put this quite clearly:

■ The subversion of a canon is not simply a matter of replacing one set of texts with another. This would be radically to simplify what is implicit in the idea of canonicity itself. A canon is not a body of texts per se, but rather a set of reading practices [... that] are resident in institutional structures, such as education curricula and publishing networks. So the subversion of a canon involves the bringing-to-consciousness and articulation of these practices and institutions, and will result not only in the replacement of some texts by others, or the redeployment of some hierarchy of value within them, but equally crucially in the reconstruction of the so-called canonical texts through alternative reading practices.[7] □

These authors describe how postcolonial rewritings can offer new insights into the 'Classic' work. A rewriting can shed new light on how the previous text may be read and analysed by offering new perspectives and by exposing the ways in which conventional reading practices contribute to the consolidation of a variety of individual and community assumptions. These assumptions work to construct a canon by privileging certain points of view and aesthetic preconceptions about genre, literature, language and writing.

Arguably, one of the most famous postcolonial rewritings in English is the novel *Wide Sargasso Sea* (1966) by Jean Rhys (1890–1979), which confronts the possibility of another side to the novel *Jane Eyre* (1847) by Charlotte Brontë (1816–55). Rhys reframes the narrative *Jane Eyre* as the story of Antoinette/Bertha, the Creole heiress and Rochester's first wife. By retelling the story from this perspective, Rhys is able to deconstruct Brontë's legacy and offer a damning critique of the history of colonialism in the Caribbean. Set in the wake of the British abolition of slavery, the narrative explores the strained relations of race and gender in Jamaica, and it is in this context that Rhys depicts Rochester's unethical treatment of Antoinette, whom he abuses and renames Bertha. Because she is of mixed racial background, Antoinette/Bertha finds herself in between races and cultures, dismissed by both the black and white communities. One might argue, then that, as a Creole, she is utterly marginalized, for, within the contemporary discourses of racism, she displays the so-called blemish of racial impurity.

The narrative voice of *Wide Sargasso Sea* is divided between Rochester and Antoinette and, as such, Rhys attempts to avoid the same suppression of an alternative voice she critiques in Brontë's novel. The 'Rochester character' in Rhys's narrative holds a position of race and class privilege that engenders and justifies his irrational bigotry, hypocrisy and pride. He perpetuates a master-slave dynamic that is potentially destructive for Antoinette/Bertha. Such a rewriting enables Rhys to renegotiate and reposition perspectives and points of view in order to foreground that which is silenced in Brontë's text. Because *Jane Eyre* is a highly canonical work, the conflation of Antoinette's fate into that of Bertha's death is a distinct possibility. But Rhys allows for unique interpretations and possibilities by resisting closure and leaving the ending open. Antoinette dreams of the fire and the leap to her death, but the novel ends with her resolution to act; we are not left with a mere description of her death or an exact repetition of Brontë's words. In the end, the possibility of a different fate for Rhys's character is left intact, and *Wide Sargasso Sea* offers an agency for 'the mad woman in the attic' that is denied in *Jane Eyre*. This unique ending is analyzed by the postcolonial literary critic Judie Newman, who writes,

> ■ The ending of *Wide Sargasso Sea*, the burning of Thornfield Hall, has aroused considerable critical debate. For some readers, the idea that Antoinette is tied to a destiny created by Charlotte Brontë makes the whole novel an exercise in cultural determinism. Antoinette may have been revised from the malevolent vampire, but she is a passive victim just the same. It is worth noting, however, that Rhys ends her novel before Antoinette's death. As readers, we may choose to 'finish her off' in Brontë's terms – or not. We know that her death lies just beyond the ending, but we are at liberty to ignore that knowledge; our imaginations are not the slaves of Charlotte Brontë. After all, Rhys was perfectly free to rewrite *Jane Eyre* in any way she pleased.[8] □

The process of rewriting can sometimes represent the political empowerment of the postcolonial subject – an empowerment denied in the canonical text. However, as Newman suggests, the question of agency in *Wide Sargasso Sea* has fuelled much critical debate in feminist postcolonial studies. In her essay 'Three Women's Texts and a Critique of Imperialism', Gayatri Spivak reads *Wide Sargasso Sea* alongside *Jane Eyre* and *Frankenstein* (1818) by Mary Shelley (1791–1815) to criticize feminist theorists for reading 'Bertha Mason only in psychological terms, as Jane's dark double'.[9] Spivak insists that nineteenth-century feminist individualism was necessarily influenced by the culture of imperialism, and that it marginalized and dehumanized the native woman even as it sought to assert the white woman as speaking and acting subject. For Spivak, Rhys's rewriting of *Jane Eyre* falls short of offering agency to Antoinette.

Spivak argues that Rhys chooses to focus on the character of Antoinette, who is a Creole and thus caught between the English imperialist and the black native.[10] Rhys, then, posits Antoinette as both native and Other, even though the Creole did not suffer the same oppression, abuse or voicelessness as those who were enslaved. This is problematic because, according to Spivak, Rhys chooses to give a voice to a 'white creole' rather than to a former black slave such as Christophine. Such a move effectively reinforces the silence of the most oppressed people of the Caribbean – the black women and former slaves – in favour of a Creole character. For Spivak, then, the unmediated access to the subaltern's voice is impossible because Christophine is 'tangential to a narrative written in the interest of the white Creole protagonist'.[11] Such a reading emphasizes that our very effort at resuscitating the subaltern's voice/self by invoking historical contexts reproduces the 'epistemic violence' of imperialism. Such violence imposes on the subaltern Western assumptions of embodied subjectivity and fails to acknowledge that the Other has always already been constructed according to the colonizer's self-image and can therefore not simply be given her voice back.

Spivak's argument has been challenged by Benita Parry. Parry contends that the role of the feminist postcolonial critic is to recover historically repressed voices and to construct 'the speaking position of the subaltern'.[12] This would, she argues, offer readers a 'conception of the native as historical subject and agent of an oppositional discourse'.[13] In Parry's reading of *Wide Sargasso Sea*, then, Christophine *is* given a voice, thus rendering Rhys's text far less problematic than Spivak suggests. Christophine's voice, Parry argues, arises out of the fact that she is a black nurse and obeah (voodoo) woman whose knowledge of these non-Enlightenment practices is the source of a counter-discourse that is rooted in the historically potent function of black magic in African and West Indian cultures. By focusing on Christophine (who does not appear in *Jane Eyre*), Parry asserts that Bertha Mason, tormented Caribbean woman as she is, is not the real 'woman from the colonies in Rhys's novel'.[14] Rather, Christophine, an exploited black plantation slave, is the authentic Caribbean subject who refuses to be silenced or reduced to the margins. For Parry, Chistophine articulates a critique of Rochester and race relations on the island. Such a reading thus runs counter to the analysis offered by Spivak, who asserts that any interaction between ruler and ruled is doomed to voicelessness. Parry concludes by saying that 'The story of colonialism which she [Spivak] reconstructs is of an interactive process where the European agent, in consolidating the imperialist Sovereign Self, induces the native to collude in its own subject(ed) formation as other and voiceless'.[15] By contrast, Parry asserts that the colonized subject can have a voice with which she can express counter-discources and resistance.

The literary critic Peter Hulme's article on *Wide Sargasso Sea* suggests that the Spivak–Parry debate is useful for rereading the English canon, but he also maintains that critics of Rhys's novel must remain sensitive to the historical and political contexts of the work. *Wide Sargasso Sea*, he writes, is

■ a novel published in 1966, at a time when the general decolonization of the British empire was well under way but before Dominica, the island of Jean Rhys's birth, had gained independence; a novel written by, in West Indian terms, a member of the white colonial elite, yet somebody who always defined herself in opposition to the norms of metropolitan 'Englishness'; a novel which deals with issues of race and slavery.[16] □

Hulme implies that any reading of Rhys's rewriting ought to be contextual: readers must acknowledge that *Wide Sargasso Sea* was written after *Jane Eyre*, but that Rhys's work is set before the events of Brontë's novel take place. This latter point is particularly significant, for various critics have pointed out that Rhys's novel reconstitutes itself as the 'mother text' or point of origin of the English novel.[17] Indeed, because the events and setting of *Wide Sargasso Sea* occur prior to those of *Jane Eyre*, Rhys constructs her novel as a 'postdated prequel' to Brontë's novel. In this, Rhys is able to reconstitute *Jane Eyre* as the sequel to her own work and, by extension, she represents Victorian Britain as dependent on her colonies, just as 'Brontë's heroine depends upon a colonial inheritance to gain her own independence'.[18] Finally, Rhys's repositioning of her text in relation to *Jane Eyre* is also dependent on the reader, for the critic must take into account which text he or she has read first. If the reader is familiar with *Jane Eyre* before reading *Wide Sargasso Sea*, then Rhys's novel will be haunted by Brontë's text. But if the reader has read *Wide Sargasso Sea* first, then it will influence any subsequent reading of *Jane Eyre*.

This last point arises out of the fact that Rhys's novel can stand on its own: the reader does not need to be familiar with *Jane Eyre* in order to understand *Wide Sargasso Sea*. This is not always the case with postcolonial rewritings.[19] Sometimes postcolonial rewritings simply gesture towards a canonical text or author. For instance, in the Indian novel *Heat and Dust* (1975) by Ruth Prawer Jhabvala (born 1927) one of the two storylines is set more or less contemporaneously with *A Passage to India* (1924) by E. M. Forster (1879–1970). This part of the narrative depicts an Englishman, Harry, who visits India and criticizes the British presence in the country. Harry is a thinly disguised E. M. Forster – an English homosexual who idealizes the Indian princely state as the antithesis of imperialism. In fact, Harry dreams of a future in which humanism triumphs and India becomes a place where interpersonal relations transcend politics. The literary critic Richard Cronin demonstrates how Jhabvala uses the figure of Harry to rewrite Forster's liberal humanist narratives about India. Cronin correctly points out that Forster's *A Passage to India* and *The Hill of Devi* (1953) assert the primacy of friendship over divisive political ideologies, thus sweeping the politics of imperialism under the rug. By contrast, Jhabvala's portrait of Harry rewrites Forster's liberal humanist plots in order to repoliticize the English writer's stay in India.

Richard Cronin notes that Forster visited India in 1921, spending six months as a private secretary to the Maharajah of Dewas. As part of his research for *A Passage to India*, Forster wanted to experience the 'heat and dust' of the hot season, for he conceived of the novel as having three sections (Mosque, Caves, Temples) to reflect the three seasons of India (cold, hot, rain). The middle section, with its emotional and sexual confusion, was thus meant to correspond with the heat of India's hot season. Cronin points out that in the 1983 edition of *The Hill of Devi* it was revealed that Forster had edited the letters that form the basis of his account. Forster thus deleted any reference to his sexual relationship with an Indian boy, whose services were procured and paid for by the Maharajah, and who then boasted publicly of going to bed with Forster. Cronin suggests that the Maharajah orchestrated this public display of homosexuality to gain power over Forster and humiliate the English.

This strategic display of power is foregrounded by Jhabvala in *Heat and Dust*. For instance, in her depiction of Harry's relationship with the Nawab, Harry is enthralled and overpowered by the attractive Indian ruler. 'He looks devastatingly handsome', Harry says of the Nawab, a fact that he communicates to Olivia with 'exhaustion' rather than 'pleasure'.[20] This 'devastation' of the Englishman – the conquering of Harry – is furthered by the Nawab's characterization of Harry as a 'very improper Englishman'.[21] For Cronin, Harry is 'a living exemplar of all the possibilities of Englishness that the British in India would rather deny existed. His [the Nawab's] patronage of Harry is a delicate affront. Racial hatred is the motive of much of his behaviour.'[22] From this perspective, Jhabvala replaces Forster's narratives of transcendent friendship with power struggles and political ideologies that are played out in the relationship between the Indian Nawab and the English Harry. This, then, suggests that the power structures of the past and the ideologies of imperialism cannot be simply ignored or dismissed. As a result, Jhabvala emphasizes the need not to be complicit with those forces that would erase historical truth, reducing events to myth, fantasy or silence. The problem with Forster's text, Jhabvala's rewriting seems to suggest, is its insistence on a 'higher law' over a recognition of particular crimes committed against particular people. In counter-distinction to an erasure of power, Jhabvala's revision of Forster's work asserts the specificity of a history that is linked to the power structures of colonization. This maintains the necessity of keeping political ideologies in full view, rather than placing the imperialist past in a generalized history of Indian suppression for which nobody in particular, or anyone in general, may be held accountable.

Heat and Dust serves as one example of how rewritings of the English canon can be acts of resistance to the cultural hegemony of the British. In her book *Masks of Conquest: Literary Study and British Rule in India* (1989), Gauri Viswanathan examines how the study of 'English Lit' can be traced back to colonial India in the early nineteenth century. She demonstrates that the discipline was established in India long before it became a subject in British schools and universities. The literature of England was, she argues, used to convey an ideal Englishman to Indians, particularly after the implementation of the 1835 English Education Act, which required natives of India to study English language, literature and culture. Thus, 'English Lit' was not only used to help disseminate the English language; it also functioned as a tool for promoting Christianity, Western values and British culture. Canonical English writers (like Shakespeare) were thus taught as the purveyors of common sense and universal truths; the words of the Bard and others were therefore promulgated as words to live by. This was significant in that 'English Lit' presented the Indian student with models for disciplining the mind and thinking objectively. As a result, these cultural products – the products of mental labour – could be used to distract the Indian student from the British imperialist project in India. Commenting on the colonial education system in India, Judie Newman states,

■ Production of thought came to define the true essence of the Englishman. His material reality as subjugator and alien ruler was dissolved in his mental output. Viswanathan thus fully substantiates the [...] idea that cultural hegemony can be best established and maintained through the consent of the dominated.[23] □

In this passage, Newman, following Viswanathan, points to the power dynamics of literature, the canon and the role of 'English Lit' in imperial control and legitimization. Newman, moreover, extends this insight to argue that postcolonial rewritings of the English canon include an awareness of these power dynamics, as well as the ways in which stories influence events, perceptions and political agendas. Thus, postcolonial rewritings can highlight the politics of storytelling by engaging with colonial narratives of the past and refusing to be confined to the ivory tower or limited by purely literary bounds.

Postcolonial rewritings, though, do not always question dominant ideologies, political legitimacy or the English literary canon. In some cases, rewritings simply engage in a form of intertextuality that highlights the overlapping cultures of the colonizer and colonized. In *Culture and Imperialism*, for instance, Said explores the existence of 'overlapping territories' and 'intertwined histories' that are found in many colonial and postcolonial texts. Here, Said examines literary works that may, on the surface, seem to offer a clear-cut separation of colonizer and colonized but that, upon closer inspection, show that the experiences of ruler and ruled are not so easily separated, divided or disentangled. On both sides of the imperial divide, Said argues, people have shared experiences (though differently inflected experiences) through education, civic life, memory and war. Postcolonial rewritings, then, sometimes illustrate the ways in which the cultures of the colonizer and the colonized are inseparable, thus reflecting the intertwined histories that have developed out of colonial enterprises.[24]

The novel *Midnight's Children* (1981) by Salman Rushdie (born 1947) is a good example of this. Rushdie's text is, among other things, an enquiry into the appropriate subject matter and form for an Indian novel that is written in English. Should an Indian English novelist draw on a British/European literary tradition? Or should he stick to Indian sources and influences? Rushdie answers these questions by rejecting separations and divisions between literary histories. As a result, *Midnight's Children* includes a range of literary references and diverse sources that include everything from the Koran, ancient Sanskrit writings, classical Arabic literature, as well as contemporary German, American and Latin American fiction.[25] This is, as John Thieme points out, only a partial list of the novel's many references, but they all contribute to Rushdie's portrait of the diversity of Indian culture and the range of cultural traditions with which many Indians are familiar (Muslim and Hindu texts are referenced alongside European and American works). Moreover, Rushdie takes the eccentric, self-referential and metafictional novel *Tristram Shandy* (1759) by Laurence Sterne (1713–68) as his main 'English' reference point. As such, Rushdie's choice is strategic in its 'overlapping' with the English literary canon, for *Tristram Shandy* deconstructs the conventions of the realist novel and, in so doing, ruptures the colonial narrative traditions of works like *Robinson Crusoe*.

The expansive literary genealogies found in *Midnight's Children* are also reflected by the main character, Saleem Sinai, who is born at the exact moment of Indian Independence. Although Saleem mentions that Methwold is his biological father, he looks elsewhere for different versions of his background. In fact, the absence of his biological parents enables him to adopt an 'endless series of parents' and continually rewrite the history of his origins.[26] Thus, Saleem moves between a series of different mothers and fathers of different cultural backgrounds (an Englishman, a Hindu woman, a Goan Catholic nurse, a Muslim family), all of whom represent India's diverse society. Such diversity resists attempts to fix Saleem into a specific cultural identity that would define him through a single set of cultural markers. In this, the formal aspects of Rushdie's intertextuality are reflected in the main character and narrator: Saleem embodies the cultural diversity that is found in the novel's many different literary affiliations.

By way of conclusion, it is worth noting that another form of rewriting can arise in the 'translation' of canonical novels into films. In the 1999 film version of *Mansfield Park* (1814) by Jane Austen (1775–1817), for instance, the Canadian director Patricia Rozema (born 1958) rewrites sections of Austen's narrative to insert scenes that are not in the book. At the beginning of the film, as Fanny Price departs from her family in Portsmouth to live in the grand household of her aunt and uncle, she hears someone wailing on a ship off the coast. 'Black cargo, Miss', explains the coachman. The ship is a slave transport and it is meant to remind the audience that around 1800, when this scene takes place, England was still a slave-trading nation that profited from its colonies in the Caribbean. It is also a portent of what the heroine will eventually discover is the dark side of her new home: the wealth of Mansfield Park is made from the West Indian sugar plantations that are worked by slaves transported from the west coast of Africa to the Caribbean. This scene does not exist in Austen's novel and, as such, Patricia Rozema's rewriting injects important social and political issues into the quintessentially domestic concerns of the original narrative. In short, Rozema refuses to negate, ignore, overlook or silence the source of the income that fuels the lavish lifestyle of the Mansfield estate.

Rozema's rewriting of *Mansfield Park* is, in fact, inspired by Edward Said's rereading of the novel. In *Culture and Imperialism*, Said argues persuasively that *Mansfield Park* and its author were deeply implicated in the question of both slavery and imperialism in the Caribbean, the location of the sugar plantations that funded some of England's grand estates, including that of the novel's title.[27] By focusing on the privilege of an English elite and by negating the source of their privilege, Austen's silence worked to celebrate Englishness at the expense of those slaves who were kidnapped and forced into a life of deprivation and hard labour. Said argues that Austen's text contributes to support the system of bondage by what it chooses to say and not say. Published in 1814, *Mansfield Park* was, Said notes, one in a long line of literary products that supported English imperial interests. In this, he does not identify Austen's novel as an isolated text. Rather, he states that 'a quick inventory' reveals 'poets, philosophers, historians, dramatists, statesmen, novelists, travel writers, chroniclers, soldiers, and fabulists' whose writing ignored the sources of wealth and, in so doing, furthered the interests of imperialism.[28] From this perspective, it is important to analyze what is silenced in the work of Jane Austen and what is, by extension, left out of the canon of Western literature. Breaking the silence through rereading and rewriting is thus important, for recognizing the crimes of the past can inform those who might seek to perpetuate the culture of exploitation.

In this chapter, we have seen how several postcolonial writers address the European literary canon through acts of rewriting. Such rewritings might invoke the canonical text directly (*Omeros*) or they might refer to the European work indirectly (*Heat and Dust*). Rewritings can be, as we have seen, oppositional (*Wide Sargasso Sea*) or they can be intertextual (*Midnight's Children*). But regardless of the approach taken by the author, postcolonial writings have fuelled debates within literary criticism – debates that are not easily resolved and which will undoubtedly continue into the future. In the next chapter, though, the emphasis shifts slightly, as we will consider representations of violence in postcolonial writing. As we will see, postcolonial texts depict several forms of violence, from the violent oppressions of colonization to the violence of resistance and revolution.

CHAPTER SIX

Violence

The project of colonialism was, more often than not, carried out through the force of violence. The conquest of a region, as well as the subsequent 'clearing' of the terrain and the imposition of a new law of the land, engendered a violence that was often brutal and uncompromising. White settlers would frequently kill natives with impunity, for such murders were supported by a colonial administration and a legal system that justified certain forms of violence in the name of 'spreading civilization' and colonial rule. 'The colonists', writes Aimé Césaire (born 1913) in *Discourse on Colonialism* (1955), 'reserve the right to kill in Indochina, torture in Madagascar, imprison in Black Africa, crack down in the West Indies'.[1] Violence is, as Césaire indicates, a tool that is used by the colonizer to repress and control the colonized. To put this simply, the colonists' power over a colony is gained and maintained through violence.

Colonial violence, then, sought to impose borders and boundaries. These included the new borders imposed on the native's land after the European power declared its ownership of the colony. But such borders were conceptual as well as physical. For they included an identificatory boundaries that divided the colonizer from the colonized. Aimé Césaire goes on to ask, 'has colonialism really placed civilizations in contact? [...] I answer no [...] No human contact, but relations of dominance and submission'.[2] Such relations of power, we must recognize, included several forms of violence. In this chapter, we will begin by examining the violence of conquest. We will then turn to what critics call 'epistemic violence', before moving on to discuss the violence of resistance and liberation that was often part of decolonization. Finally, the chapter will conclude by considering the violence that occurs within a previously colonized community.

An example of the violence of conquest arises in the novella *The Narrative of Jacobus Coetzee* by J. M. Coetzee (born 1940), which was published as the second part of *Dusklands* in 1974. The novella is based on the travel writing of the seventeenth- and eighteenth-century 'explorers' of the South African Cape (the original Jacobus Coetsé was a distant ancestor of the author). Throughout the text, the author foregrounds graphic scenes of violence between the white settlers and the native inhabitants of South Africa. As a result, *The Narrative of Jacobus Coetzee* invites us to draw parallels between the violence of South African apartheid (in the 1970s) and the violent origins of Afrikaner domination of the region. Moreover, Coetzee encourages the reader to examine the question of authorial complicity in violence, both as a general issue, and through recognition of the specific self-analysis of Coetzee's historical associations.

The fictional *Narrative* identifies itself as a 1760 'deposition', and it begins with Jacobus's first-person description of the best way to hunt the native Bushmen. He states,

■ The only sure way to kill a Bushman is to catch him in the open where your horse can run him down [...]. It is only when you hunt them as you hunt jackals that you can clear a stretch of country. You need plenty of men. The last time we swept this district we had twenty farmers and their Hottentots, nearly a hundred hunters all told [...]. We waited till they were out in the open running from the Hottentots at a nice steady trot, the sort they can keep up all day. Then we broke cover and rode on them. We picked out our targets beforehand, for we knew they would scatter as soon as they saw us [...]. That day, we got all of them, the whole band.[3] □

In this passage, the white settler offers instructions about the best methods and techniques for murdering members of the native community. He attempts to justify his violence by envisioning the Bushmen as non-human, conflating them with the wild dogs of southern Africa (jackals). This vision of the native – as an animal to be hunted down and killed – engenders the colonizing rhetoric that Jacobus invokes: he states that he is engaged in the project of 'clearing the land' and 'sweeping the district'.[4] Control over the land, then, is gained through violence, and Jacobus believes that he must hunt the Bushmen in order to implement a system of private property and establish borders that are foreign to the natives' way of life. In this, Jacobus contributes to the European colonization of southern Africa by reshaping physical territories, social terrains as well as human identities through violence.

In his book *J. M. Coetzee* (1997) the literary critic Dominic Head writes that Jacobus presents 'imperial violence as a quest for ontological reassurance'.[5] The imperialist of Coetzee's text, in other words, attempts to define himself through the brutal violence that he inflicts upon others. But, as Head points out, Jacobus's desire to define himself as a subject through the brutalization of the other is self-defeating, for his desire for self-confirmation and contact leads to increasing levels of brutality that produce inevitably dehumanized victims. As a result, Jacobus's enthusiasm for murder and violence as a path towards self-actualization is undermined through the very discourses of difference that he sets up. This is because his acts of violence threaten his claim to civilized subjectivity. As Head writes, 'Jacobus, in short, is barbaric. His solipsism, philistinism and phallocentric aggression are all impulses inimical to civilization. The obvious master–savage inversion that we witness in his narrative is quite clearly stated when he is reduced to leading a Bushman's life (as he imagines it), though by this stage his savagery is already self-evident'.[6]

Jacobus's attitudes about the spread of 'civilization' and the subsequent violence that he perpetuates are, in many respects, representative of colonial domination. He articulates a set of cultural assumptions that both engender violence and justify conquest. The use of weapons' technology was also central to this process, for cannons and guns were important tools in the development of European imperialism. In fact, in Coetzee's text, the colonizer's technology of violence – the gun, in particular – becomes a way for the white settler to define himself. Jacobus, then, identifies his gun as the thing that differentiates him from the other and establishes his relationship to the world. He states,

> ■ The gun is our last defence against isolation within the travelling sphere. The gun is our mediator with the outside world and therefore our saviour. The tidings of the gun: such and such is outside, have no fear. The gun saves us from the fear that all life is within us. It does so by laying at our feet all the evidence we need of dying and therefore a living world [...].
>
> The instrument of survival in the wild is the gun, but the need for it is metaphysical rather than physical.[7] □

In this passage, Jacobus describes his gun as an object of worship. It is not only the form of technology that enables him to gain power over the natives, but it is the very source of his identity. It reinforces his belief in his own superiority, and it enables him to overcome his fear of the other. But, as the critic Rosemary Jolly points out, Jacobus's 'gun-worship' both creates his sense of self and also destroys it. 'The desire for absolute mastery that the gun represents', she writes, enables Jacobus to receive 'self-gratification from destruction'.[8] But the evidence of violence associated with the gun also causes him to see that this technology is a potential source of his own destruction and that, in turn, he must face his own mortality. The gun is, then, simultaneously creative and destructive.

Having said this, colonial violence must be situated in the broader frame of regulating and controlling the other. Thus, violence (and the threat of violence) plays a complex social role in the institutionalization of political, economic, legal, educational, social and cultural systems within colonies. In this, violence can be seen as a political tactic for exercising power and displaying the means of subjection. Indeed, subjection through violence and terror is one way of instituting a regime of power over colonized subjects. Within this paradigm, the conquered group is the object over which an imperial authority is exercised: they are stripped of their subjectivity, restrained from running their own affairs and, more generally, possessed and ruled over by a foreign power.

It is therefore important to note that the mastery of the gun is combined with the mastery of discourse. That is, the manipulation of language and thought becomes a form of control that empowers the colonizer and subjugates the native. Ania Loomba puts this quite clearly when she states that 'Colonial violence is understood as including an "epistemic" aspect, i.e. an attack on the culture, ideas and value systems of the colonized peoples.'[9] Here, Loomba is following on the work of Gayatri Spivak, who argues that the violence of the colonizer is not reducible to physical domination, but also includes a discursive aspect. Spivak raises this idea towards the end of her essay, 'Can the Subaltern Speak?' (1988), when she asks: 'On the other side of the international division of labor from socialized capital, inside and outside the circuit of the epistemic violence of imperialist law and education supplementing an earlier economic text, can the subaltern speak?'[10] Here, Spivak uses the expression 'epistemic violence' to mean the powerful projection of a white European epistemology on the rest of the world. Epistemology is often defined as the theory of the origin, nature, methods and limits of knowledge. As a result, the question of epistemic violence is related to issues such as who produces knowledge, or how power appropriates and conditions the production of knowledge. In Spivak's formulation, epistemic violence results when the subaltern is silenced by the colonial power.[11]

For Spivak, the violence of the episteme of the dominant power arises in the very fact of articulation and through the imposition of a certain form of knowledge on a marginalized group. She writes that the epistemic violence of imperialism has meant the transformation of the 'Third World' into a sign whose production has been obfuscated to the point that Western superiority and dominance are naturalized.[12] In short, Spivak argues that epistemic violence is the forcible replacement of one structure of beliefs with another. At first, the term might indicate how the British Empire forcibly imposed its ideology on the colonies, but Spivak extends the meaning to the 'complicity in the persistent constitution of the Other as the Self's shadow'.[13] That is, she criticizes the first world scholars who claim that they can represent the subaltern people and speak for them, or who think of themselves as having an objective point of view to analyse the subaltern issue. For within this frame of reference, the subaltern loses her voice because she is represented by the scholar's conception of her.

Epistemic violence arises when those people who hold power begin to silence a less powerful group. It thus points to the interplay between the pre-colonial and colonial structures of dominant discourses that erase the space from which the subaltern can speak. This is because, for Spivak, a speech act is a transaction between the speaker and the listener. Often, the subaltern makes an attempt at self-representation, yet this act of representation is not heard. The hegemonic listener does not recognize it, because it does not fit into the official institutional structures of representation. The failure of the fulfilment of the speech act is what Spivak calls 'not speaking'.[14] And she clarifies further that within the very definition of subalternity there is an implicit not-being-able-to-make-speech-acts, for if the subaltern could speak she would no longer be a subaltern.[15]

Examples of epistemic violence can be found throughout postcolonial writing, from the representations of residential schools in *Kiss of the Fur Queen* (1998) by Tomson Highway (born 1951) to the exploration of mental illness in *A Question of Power* (1973) by Bessie Head (1937–86). Perhaps one of the most disturbing examples is depicted in Patricia Grace's novel *Baby No-Eyes* (1998), when the young Maori child, Riripeti, is 'Killed by school'.[16] Here, Riripeti is sent to school with her older sister, Kura, where the Principle demands that all of the pupils speak English. Riripeti's mother tongue is Maori, and she cannot understand the commands of the Principle or her teachers. However, instead of recognizing Riripeti's lack of understanding, her instructors perceive her as stubbornly dismissing the authorities of the school; and, as punishments, she is smacked and humiliated, separated from her sister and restrained while she is caned in front of her peers. The misunderstandings and punishments continue until the school closes for summer. Kura narrates that

■ during the holiday [...] Riripeti was happy and we played together, then when it was near time to go to school again she became sick and couldn't eat. Her throat closed and wouldn't let any food go down. Her skin was moist all the time and she couldn't get out of bed.

Not long after that she died.
Killed by school [...].

After that I became sick too. I couldn't eat and couldn't go to school. I went to bed and couldn't get up, just like Riripeti. I think I nearly died too. There were people coming and going, talking to me, talking amongst themselves, putting their hands on me, speaking that language over me — that evil language which killed mỹ teina and which I never spoke again.[17] □

Riripeti's death arises out of a form of epistemic violence that robs the Maori child of her language and replaces it with a new linguistic system that is not understood. In this process, the teachers indicate that the Maori language is 'wrong', and that a Maori utterance will engender physical punishment. This, then, silences the monolingual Maori speaker, taking away her voice and leaving her with no means of communication. The sequence of events engendered by this situation has dire consequences for Riripeti, but Kura is also deeply wounded by this violence. From her perspective as a young girl, Kura sees the Maori language as responsible for her sister's death. 'What an evil thing', she thinks, 'our language was to do that to my teina'.[18] This also silences Kura, who feels that she must protect herself against her own language. Thus, her fear of speaking Maori causes her to dismiss her mother tongue and subsequently to lose touch with important aspects of her native culture and heritage.

In her analysis of *Baby No-Eyes*, the postcolonial critic Michelle Keown argues that Grace's novel challenges white cultural hegemony and epistemic violence. The text's political commitment is, for Keown, located in its narrative and linguistic strategies as well as its socio-political context. This resistance develops out of Grace's polyphonic narrative structure, a structure that draws upon the patterns of Maori speech-making and oral traditions:

■ *Baby No-Eyes* [...] is a testament to resistance. If silence is complicity, Grace seeks to end the silence and to challenge the grammatical and social structures that have enforced that silence. The semiotic, manifested in Grace's corporeal lingualism, becomes a fundamental and powerful weapon, a site of resistance, an expression of political awareness and anger; Grace's semiotized language reaches beyond the text, engaging in the symbolic structures whose function is to repress its representative and constitutive power.[19] □

Keown's reading documents the ways in which Grace's text draws on Maori language – particularly grammatical structures – to 'invade' English with 'syntactical errors'.[20] Such an invasion is, for Keown, a challenge to epistemic violence through a transgression of mood and tense in the modification of verbal particles and inflections. In addition to infusing English with Maori language, Grace also uses these new linguistic forms to mimic the rhythms of Maori oratory.

More generally, epistemic violence as well as the violence of conquest (the loss of land and the decline of Maori ontology) is a central concern in Maori English writing. Thus, in *The Bone People* (1983) by Keri Hulme (born 1947), for instance, we find an appalling case of child abuse – a form of violence that calls for spiritual renewal on the basis of a Maori ethos. Patricia Grace's *Potiki* (1986) also explores violence through the confrontation between a Maori family and a private land development company that wants to buy the land to build a resort.

The failure of communication leads to violence: the company burns the Maori meetinghouse and the Maori retaliate by destroying the company's building site. Similarly, in *The Matriarch* (1986), Witi Ihimaera (born 1944) focuses on the New Zealand land wars of the 1860s, especially the campaigns led by the founder and leader of the Ringatu movement, Te Kooti. Yet while violence is sometimes shockingly prominent in these texts, they all also explore the prospects of cultural revival and demonstrate the possibility of renewing traditions by incorporating Pakeha (non-Maori) resources into Maori cultural expression. Thus, Maori texts from the 1980s give rise to the impression that the culture is expanding and developing. Central to this expansion is the confidence that Pakeha forms and tools can be adapted to Maori purposes, made to serve key Maori values such as guardianship over economic, cultural and spiritual resources. The incorporation of Pakeha elements notably shows itself in the use of these texts made of literary and non-fictional traditions of Pakeha and European writing. Both *The Bone People* and *Potiki*, for instance, weave broad intertextual networks, drawing on both Maori culture and Western literary traditions, while they also resist epistemic violence.

The revival of native languages and cultures since the 1960s and 1970s (of which Maori is just one example) has been part of a much larger liberationist movement towards freedom and self-determination throughout the former European colonies. Many of these liberation movements have included armed uprisings whereby the colonized group has attempted to gain political and economic control of the nation. In many cases, as Frantz Fanon points out, violence was the only means by which the project of decolonization could succeed. Writing about the French colonization of Algeria in *The Wretched of the Earth* (1961), for instance, Fanon argues that the colonized person can only find freedom through violence:

■ Decolonization is always a violent phenomenon [...]. Decolonization, which sets out to change the order of the world, is, obviously, a programme of complete disorder [...]. For the native, life can only spring up again out of the rotting corpse of the settler.[21] □

The decisive role that Fanon attributes to violence in the colonial context has had an inexorable afterlife in many postcolonial societies. For he writes that violence functions like a language in the colonial system: the militant who seeks to overthrow the colonizer through violence is only writing back in the colonizer's own language. After all, he claims, the colonized people have suffered from the brutality of European colonial policies and the oppressive forces of a foreign power. In this context, Fanon argues, political repression *must* breed armed resistance.

The first chapter of *The Wretched of the Earth*, 'Concerning Violence', contains an open advocacy of armed struggles. Fanon goes into great detail explaining that revolutionary groups should look to the most oppressed members of society for the force needed to expel colonialists. 'Violence', Fanon writes, 'is a cleansing force. It frees the native from his inferiority complex and from his despair and inaction; it makes him fearless and restores his self-respect.'[22] To grasp Fanon's insistence on the absolute necessity of violence, one has to understand that violence is more than a political method or tool to force the removal of the European oppressor. For Fanon, it is a vital means of psychic and social liberation. And he states that 'violence is man recreating himself: the native cures himself through force of arms.'[23] Thus, Fanon implies that if the colonialists peacefully withdraw, the decolonization process is somehow aborted, that liberation is incomplete, for the native will remain an enslaved person in a neo-colonial frame of mind.

What Fanon means is that if violent resistance to colonization does not occur, then the native's inner violence (his anger and resentment towards the colonizer) will remain pent up. This will, in turn, lead to a potentially negative situation in which unexpressed violence explodes in renewed inter-tribal war, civil war, coups or other forms of post-independence civil violence. The way of avoiding this, Fanon argues, is to project that violence at the appropriate group – the colonizer. Thus, the function of violence is only incidentally political; its main function is psycho-social. Or, as Fanon puts it, 'The native's weapon is proof of his humanity. For in the first days of the revolt you must kill – to shoot down a white man is to kill two birds with one stone, to destroy an oppressor and the man he oppresses at the same time.'[24]

The Zimbabwean writer Shimmer Chinodya (born 1957) explores these issues in *Harvest of Thorns* (1989), a novel that represents the transition from the white-dominated Southern Rhodesia, through the Bush War, to postcolonial black self-determination. In this text, the main character, Benjamin Tichafa, is a teenager who joins the black liberation movement and takes up arms against the colonial government. As part of his initiation into the liberationist army, he attends lectures and discussions about the colonial history of violence and oppression. Recounting one of these meetings, he states,

■ You sat there and listened, your fist raised over your head, stabbing the air, chanting slogans and you heard about capitalism and socialism and democracy and equitable distribution of wealth and racism and discrimination and equal rights and justice and the Land Appropriation Act and segregation and exploitation and neo-colonialism [...] and you gasped to be told five per cent of the population owned the better half of Rhodesia and earned more than the other ninety-five per cent together, that they had the best jobs, homes, schools, hospitals – everything – because their skin was lighter than yours.[25] ☐

What lies behind this message is clear: the violent uprising of the black revolutionaries is necessary and justified. In this, the leaders of the insurgency recount the injustices suffered by the black majority at the hands of the white minority. The history of colonization, they assert, has enslaved the black population, and the only way to overcome this repression is through violence. But, at the same time, the speakers make it very clear that violence must be directed at the right group: the white colonizer.

This is highlighted in Baas Die's commanding lecture to his fellow insurgents. Here, he recounts the story of first contact, in which he describes the initial arrival of white settlers in Rhodesia. These white strangers, he states, first claimed to be friends with the black villagers, but the whites continued to take more and more of the fertile land. When the natives protested, the white settlers shot and killed many of the villagers, who were unable to defend themselves against the European guns. The spiritual leader of the village – the *svikiro* – advised the natives to respond with violence: '"*Cut the throats of the strangers' children*", the *svikiro* said, "*cut the throats of their children and they will go away.*"' But before the villagers can act, the *svikiro* is hanged by the strangers and the villagers 'became slaves' to the whites.[26] Baas Die's story is not only meant to educate the soldiers; it is also meant to motivate his army to kill. He wants his soldiers to identify with the black villagers and follow through on the svikiro's command: they must cut the throats of white children. In this, they will be directing their violence at the correct group, and fighting for control of their homeland.

Having said this, Shimmer Chinodya's novel does not glorify violence. As the critic Ranka Primorac points out, 'Chinodya's novel was among the first [of the post-independence Zimbabwean novels] to desist from glorifying nationalist guerrillas as flawless, invincible heroes.'[27] Indeed, Chinodya depicts violence as a necessary part of the struggle for independence, but he also shows the destructive consequences of that necessity. In this, *Harvest of Thorns* has been identified as including a nuanced representation of violence. For the main character does not even join the war for ideological reasons. Instead, a series of contingencies draws him into the armed conflict: he rebels against his Christian extremist parents, he is expelled from high school after taking part in a protest march, and he blunders his way across the Rhodesia–Mozambique border and into a guerrilla base. The novel follows him through training and life as a guerrilla in operational areas inside Rhodesia: its central episodes point accusing fingers at the Rhodesian army's atrocities committed against civilians in Mozambican camps, but also at guerrilla cruelty against peasant civilians suspected of collaborating with the authorities. However, Chinyoda's novel also supports Fanon's assertion that the anger of the colonized group must be directed outwards, not inwards. By the end of the novel, the violence of the revolution has led to political independence, and Zimbabweans are depicted as united in the common cause of rebuilding their nation. The expression of violence, then, has engendered political and psychic liberation.

By contrast, the novel *The Bluest Eye* (1970) by Toni Morrison (born 1931) depicts what happens when the violence of imperialism is internalized by the oppressed group and directed inwards. To put it simply, the novel is about Pecola, a girl who is raped by her father, Cholly Breedlove. The context in which this rape occurs is one of violence, destruction and self-destruction: Cholly is an alcoholic who frequently beats his wife, he burns down their home and he is symbolically raped by two white men. In Morrison's text, the African American characters are wounded by the history of slavery and repression, and, as such, they are haunted by the violence of the past. Here, the suffering of violence becomes internalized, for it cannot be directed towards the white community. The characters thus direct the violence inwards, inflicting it upon themselves and other members of the black community. Domestic violence is, for instance, commonplace in the novel, and Cholly and Pauline Breedlove see the 'violent breaks' in their marriage as ruptures in the 'tiresomeness of poverty' and breaks in the routine of their 'ugly' lives.[28] The narrator states,

■ They [Cholly and Pauline] tacitly agreed not to kill each other. [...] He fought her the way a coward fights a man – with feet, the palms of his hands, and teeth. She, in turn, fought back in a purely feminine way – with frying pans and pokers, and occasionally a flat iron would sail toward his head. They did not talk, groan, or curse during these beatings. There was only the muted sound of falling things, and flesh on unsurprised flesh.[29] □

The cycle of violence begins as white-on-black violence and then moves into the black community and continues as black-on-black violence. This is in part because Cholly is unable to fight back against the white men who have abused him. As a consequence, he attacks his wife and daughter instead. The context for Cholly's rage against his family is explained by the narrator, who describes Cholly's first sexual experience and his humiliation at the hands of two white men:

■ When he was still very young, Cholly had been surprised in some bushes by two white men while he was newly but earnestly engaged in eliciting sexual pleasure from a little country girl. The men had shone a flashlight right on his behind. He had stopped, terrified. They chuckled. The beam of flashlight did not move. 'Go on', they said. 'Go on and finish. And, nigger, make it good.' The flashlight did not move. For some reason Cholly had not hated the white men; he hated, despised, the girl.[30] □

The last sentence of this quotation is particularly significant. Cholly, who Morrison states is 'symbolically raped' by the two white men, does not direct his hatred at the source of his humiliation.[31] Instead, he directs it towards the black girl, who is powerless to fight back. Cholly thus compensates for his own powerlessness at the hands of white men by inflicting pain and suffering on black women – women who he can physically overpower and brutalize.

It is in this context that Cholly rapes his daughter Pecola. Once again, Cholly violently attacks someone who cannot resist. Pecola is physically overpowered by him; she loses consciousness and falls to the floor; she cannot fight back or even struggle to remove his grip. In this, Morrison depicts the devastating effects of violence on women, for Pecola becomes a receptacle for abuse and brutality. In the end, she is destroyed because a brutal violence has been inflicted upon her and she cannot express her trauma in any external way. She is thus destroyed by violence – a violence that is passed from one community to another, from one race to another and, finally, from one gender to another.

In *Postcolonial Imaginings: Fictions of a New World Order* (2000), David Punter comments on the devastating repetition of violence in *The Bluest Eye*. Writing about Cholly's rape of Pecola, Punter calls attention to the relationship between violence, freedom and slavery and, in this light, he asks what it means when the author tells us that Cholly is 'free':

■ What might this [freedom] mean in the context of his [Cholly's] immediate and subsequent actions? What might it mean in the immediate context of the postcolonial? I suggest that one way of interpreting it is like this. When loss in the past has been painful, then indeed it might be as though, to use those oft-repeated words, 'the dreadful has already happened'. All that can happen now falls under the sign of a repetition compulsion; there is nothing new under the sun, and therefore no possibility of acting badly; all that can happen has already occurred – under the guise of transportation and slavery. Pecola's loss, the loss of everything good that Pecola might want, the loss of Pecola herself, these multiple and intertwined losses are doomed to come anyway given her home circumstances and the 'colonized' history of her race'.[32] □

Punter points to the repetition of violence in the postcolonial context. Violence, to put it simply, begets violence. Thus, the violence inflicted upon African Americans from the time of the Middle Passage and slavery through to segregation and discrimination, as well as in more contemporary forms of marginalization and racism, is repeated in the black community itself. Violence haunts Cholly and the other characters and, as a result, that violence returns like a spectre to destroy the weakest members of the society – those who cannot fight back.

This chapter has traced several of the main depictions of violence in postcolonial writing, moving from representations of the physical acts of domination to the imposition of modes of thought to the struggle of resistance and liberation to the violence that sometimes erupts within a postcolonial community. All of these forms of violence have arisen out of the movement, migration and displacement of people through imperialism. In the next chapter, we will consider the critical work on travel and travel writing to examine how the traveller and his discourses have contributed to the debates within postcolonial studies.

CHAPTER SEVEN

Travel

In her critique of tourism and the history of travel that facilitated the development of colonization, the Antiguan writer Jamaica Kincaid asserts the following about those imperialists who travelled from Europe to the Caribbean:

> ■ You came. You took things that were not yours [...]. You murdered people. You imprisoned people. You robbed people. You opened your own banks and you put our money in them. The accounts were in your name. The banks were in your name. There must have been some good people among you, but they stayed home.[1] □

The 'good people', in other words, did not travel. And because they did not travel, they did not exploit, rob or brutalize the natives of foreign lands. Kincaid's distinction between the European traveller and the non-traveller is an important one. This is not only because she seeks to avoid the same discourses of racism that she critiques in others, but is also because she wants to highlight the destructive history of travel. If Europeans had stayed at home, she points out, then the brutal histories of the slave trade, the Middle Passage and the global spread of European colonialism would not have taken place. However, because many Europeans did not stay at home, Kincaid continues, they must be held responsible for a history of 'domination', 'destruction', 'corruption' and 'cruelty'.[2]

Kincaid's *A Small Place* has been described by Patrick Holland and Graham Huggan as a piece of 'countertravel writing'.[3] This is because Kincaid exposes the compulsion of those traditional travellers, tourists and writers who have tried to fit what they see into familiar narratives. Kincaid reminds us that the traveller is not a passive subject who sits back and enjoys the view. Rather, he is often an important player in a culture of consumption and exploitation that established and continues the European colonial project. In this, Kincaid's text is, among other things, a critique of more conventional works of travel writing that invoke discourses designed to describe and interpret a 'foreign' location for a familiar audience, thus focusing on the unique nature, people, culture and society of the foreign place. More often than not, this kind of conventional travel writing tells us more about the assumptions and cultural values of the traveller than it does about the land in which the author is travelling.

One of the most infamous examples of this is *In Deepest Africa* (1890) by Henry Morton Stanley (1841–1904), which sold 150,000 copies within a few weeks of publication. Stanley's text mixes descriptions of African geography with scenes of adventure, suspense and violence. Here, Stanley repeatedly depicts the 'savagery' of the Africans – particularly their appetite for blood and human flesh – in order to demonize them and justify the Western expansion of 'civilization' and missionary interventions. His message is clear: the European imperialist who murders natives and massacres villages does so with justice on his side. For he is the product and agent of 'progress', law and order. By contrast, the African is depicted as a primitive, irrational, uneducated, non-Christian savage.

At the beginning of volume two, for instance, Stanley describes an African Pigmy in the following manner:

> ■ The little body of his represented the oldest types of primeval man, descended from the outcasts of the earliest ages, the Ishmaels of the primitive race, for ever shunning the haunts of the workers, deprived of the joy and delight of the home hearth, eternally exiled by their vice, to live the life of human beasts in morass and fen and jungle wild.[4] □

This passage is typical of Stanley's writing. He repeatedly identifies Africans as pre-modern and animalistic, referring to them as members of 'wild tribes' who are 'incorrigibly fierce in temper, detestable in their disposition, and bestial in their habits'.[5] In this way, he reduces the Indigenous people to beings of an inferior status by removing them from the realm of modernity. The literary critic David Spurr has called this rhetorical device 'debasement' and he gives two reasons for the perseverance of this trope. First, Spurr contends, travel writers like Stanley had the 'need for positive self-definition', which led to the establishment of opposites like savage versus civilized. Second, the demonization and 'accursedness of the other [...] has its origin in anxiety over the preservation of cultural order and in the need to designate the unknown by a set of signs which affirm, by contrast, the value of culturally established norms'.[6] The rhetoric of debasement, in other words, has been used to create a clear-cut division between colonizer and colonized.

In Deepest Africa illustrates how travel writers and their readers were intimately tied to the formation, justification and maintenance of European imperialism. David Spurr writes that 'the rhetoric of empire' was disseminated in travel narratives, and that these texts offered colonial administrators information about what was happening throughout the Empire, facilitating imperial expansion and administration, while constituting the colonies for their readers. Such narratives allowed Europeans to conceive of areas outside of Europe as being under their control, as an extension of their nation's territory. Subsequently, travel writing contributed to the construction of modern identities that were based on, among other things, race, sexuality, gender and nationality. This is explored in Douglas Ivison's cogent article on travel writing and Empire. He argues that

■ travel and travel writing are determined by and determine gender, racial identity, economic status and a host of other interrelated markers of status and privilege. Travel is inextricably implicated in a history of European, literary, male, bourgeois, scientific, heroic, recreational meanings and practices, and simultaneously invokes and disavows those connotations in producing the travelling subject [...]. Furthermore, the genre of travel writing [...] was the cultural by-product of imperialism, often written by those actively involved in the expansion or maintenance of empire (explorers, soldiers, administrators, missionaries, journalists), and dependent upon the support of the institutions of imperialism in order to facilitate the writers' travels.[7] □

For many recent critics, then, travel writing is read as an instrument of colonial discourse to reinforce colonial rule.

One of the most influential studies of imperialism and travel writing is Mary Louise Pratt's *Imperial Eyes: Travel Writing and Transculturation* (1992). Here, Pratt examines how travel and exploration writing has 'produced Europe's differentiated conceptions of itself in relation to something it became possible to call the rest of the world'.[8] In order to 'interrupt the totalizing momentum of both the study of genre and the critique of ideology', Pratt goes beyond the production of the 'domestic subject of Euroimperialism' to examine the dynamics of what she calls 'transculturation'.[9] Transculturation is an ethnographic term that she uses to emphasize the varied responses of a subordinated culture to domination. In taking transculturation as a conceptual frame for her work, Pratt engages current efforts in the field of colonialism studies to disrupt binarisms (self/other, Occident/Orient) that often reproduce a Western metropolitan authority. It is in relation to these existing debates that she also employs several idiosyncratic terms (such as the 'contact zone') in discussions of imperialism. 'Contact zones' are, she writes, 'social spaces where disparate cultures meet, clash, and grapple with each other, often in highly asymmetrical relations of domination and subordination'.[10] She points out that the 'contact zone' is often synonymous with the colonial frontier. However, her use of the former term illustrates her effort to avoid the 'European expansionist perspective' associated not only with the latter term but also with studies of the travel genre as well.[11]

Some of Pratt's most important contributions to postcolonial criticism arise out of her discussion of the anti-conquest narrative. Narratives that condemned colonial conquest, she argues, evolved out of the violence and brutality of the contact zone, for these texts were written by Westerners who sought to distance themselves from the violence of imperial expansion. Pratt writes that

■ Anti-conquest [...] refer[s] to the strategies of representation whereby European bourgeois subjects seek to secure their innocence in the same moment as they assert European hegemony. The term 'anti-conquest' was chosen because [...] in travel and exploration writings these strategies of innocence are constituted in relation to older imperial rhetorics of conquest associated with the absolutist era. The main protagonist of the anti-conquest is a figure [...] call[ed] the 'seeing man', an admittedly unfriendly label for the European male subject of European landscape discourse – he whose imperial eyes passively look out and possess.[12] □

According to Pratt, the author of an anti-conquest narrative wants to have it both ways: he or she wants to challenge the 'older imperial rhetorics of conquest' while simultaneously invoking Western superiority and serving the needs of European capitalist expansion. In this analysis, Pratt reveals the seemingly contradictory discourses of science and sentiment to be complementary ways of narrating the anti-conquest. For as she points out, those travel writers who claimed to be 'objective' observers, 'passive' seers or critical voices were often deeply supportive of the European imperialist project.

A fascinating and complex example of this kind of travel narrative is *Travels in West Africa* (1897) by Mary Kingsley (1862–1900). Published only seven years after *In Darkest Africa*, Kingsley's text serves as a counterpoint to Stanley's representation of Africa and its people. Throughout her narrative, Kingsley expresses a negative attitude towards British colonization and sympathy for the peoples of West Africa. Thus, she exemplifies the approach of many nineteenth-century travellers who were not opposed to imperialism or colonization, but who were critical of the abuses engendered by the system. Kingsley, for instance, attacked the European missionaries for attempting to change the people of Africa. She writes about and defends many aspects of African life that had shocked people in England (including polygamy). However, she states that missionary intervention on the West Coast of Africa is turning tribes away from their traditional ways of life and destroying African culture – a situation that will result in a 'seething mass of infamy, degradation and destruction'.[13] Likewise, she denounced those missionaries (and other European travellers) who classified blacks as inferior to whites: she argued that the 'black man is no more an undeveloped white man than a rabbit is an undeveloped hare'. And the African is, she goes on to say, not 'inferior or low', but he has a 'very good form of mind' that is 'different', but equal, to that of a white man.[14]

Kingsley's progressive statements are, however, sometimes undermined in her descriptions of aggressive and intimidating tribes. When she visits the Fan tribe of West Africa, for example, she states that,

> ■ The Fans started selling me their store of elephant tusks and rubber. I did not want those things then, but still felt too nervous of the Fans to point this out firmly, and so had to buy. I made it as long an affair as I could and I gradually found myself the proud owner of balls of rubber and a tooth or so and alas my little stock of cloth and tobacco all going fast. Now to be short of money anywhere is bad, but to be short of money in a Fan village is extremely bad, because these Fans, when a trader has no more goods to sell them, are liable to start trade all over again by killing him, and taking back their ivory and rubber and keeping it until another trader comes along.[15] □

Such a description not only highlights the fact that the Fan cannot understand the principle of fair trade, but also suggests that they are a ferocious and brutal people. This type of characterization, then, runs counter to Kingsley's more progressive critique of European conquest and her debunking of contemporary British stereotypes that characterize Africans as inferior. Instead, this passage panders to an English readership that expects her to depict the tribes as 'uncivilized'. In this, she disseminates the same discourses as those put forward by Stanley, suggesting the African is pre-modern, animalistic and, above all, threatening to the European traveller. Having said this, though, Kingsley follows her description of the threatening tribe with a humorous account of a Fan warrior putting on one of her blouses and a pair of stockings:

> ■ All my trader stuff was by now exhausted, and I had to start selling my own belongings, and for the first time in my life I felt the want of a big outfit. My own clothes I certainly did insist on having more for, pointing out that they were rare and curious. A dozen white ladies' blouses sold well. I cannot say they looked well when worn by a brawny warrior in conjunction with nothing else but red paint and a bunch of leopard tails, particularly when the warrior failed to tie the strings at the back. But I did not hint at this, and I quite realize that a pair of stockings can be made to go further than we make them by using one at a time and putting the top part over the head and letting the rest of the garment float on the breeze.[16] □

By dressing up the African warrior in this way, Kingsley paints a funny portrait that undermines the African ferocity of the previous passage. From a Western perspective, it is difficult to see a man with stockings on his head as particularly threatening. But this image of the Fan warrior in drag also relates to the more general interest in gender that Kingsley explores throughout her narrative. For the masculine tradition of nineteenth-century-European travel writing was considered to reflect public and professional concerns whereas the feminine tradition was considered to fall into the private and domestic sphere. Mary Kingsley's work belies this stereotype, as she weaves together a complex narrative of masculine and feminine attributes. On the one hand, she allied herself with the masculine tradition of producing scientific research by, at times, documenting her travels in an 'objective' and detached style. On the other hand, though, she was well aware of her female authorship and her audience's expectations. Thus, she often adopted a self-deprecating and humorous tone to deflect criticism of inappropriate behaviour on her part. Likewise, her preoccupation with clothing and dress betrays a consciousness that transgressing the boundaries of femininity would not be looked upon kindly. She writes, for instance, that she always wore a dress, and she maintains that she rejected the advice of her peers and did not adopt male garb. On more than one occasion she emphasizes her femininity while stressing the ambiguity of her situation: 'I am a most lady-like old person and yet get constantly called Sir.'[17]

The issues of gender and imperialism in Kingsley's travel narrative are thoroughly explored in Sara Mills's *Discourses of Difference: An Analysis of Women's Writing and Colonialism* (1991). Mills draws on postcolonial theory and feminist criticism to locate Kingsley's text within larger structures of both material and symbolic power in order to stress the importance of the articulations of power, gender and sexuality within travel narratives. Women like Kingsley, Mills suggests, paid attention to different things from their male contemporaries. For instance, Mills writes that Kingsley's descriptions of the landscape are much more detailed and her depictions of the African people are much more sympathetic.[18] However, Mills also points out that Kingsley's status as a white British citizen meant that her travel writing held a certain standing and carried a particular authority. Thus, Kingsley's work must not be read as an eccentric literary product, but as part of a broader discourse about gender, colonialism and travel experience. Indeed, Mills argues that

■ The fact of being a colonial subject, a representative of the colonizing power, enhances one's status as a knowing subject. Even subjects who would have been considered amateur ethnologists and archaeologists were, because of the colonial context, considered to be experts on the colonized country: women travelers became knowledgeable about, for example, the flora and fauna of a colonized country, and they produced scientific accounts of their work, in ways which would have been more difficult for them within the metropolitan culture.

Mary Kingsley had a species of fish named after her, Margaret Fountaine [1862–1940] produced accounts of butterflies, and Marianne North [1830–90] specialized in flowers. Even though the type of knowledge produced by these women was a fairly 'safe' type, the colonial context nevertheless enabled British women to take on a powerful position in relation to knowledge.[19] □

In this passage, Mills highlights the ways in which colonial power enables the production of knowledge. A person from the imperial centre is assumed to be an authority and, as such, she is able to map out the colonial landscape and speak from a position of power. Mills, then, suggests that Kingsley and other British women travellers took advantage of their positions as colonial subjects to gain credibility and power – much more credibility and power than they could have hoped to achieve at home.

The contemporary Indian travel writer and novelist Amitav Ghosh (born 1958) exposes the absurdity of this colonial authority and the subsequent production of knowledge in his travel narratives. In his 1992 book *In an Antique Land*, for instance, Ghosh intertwines the story of Abraham Ben Yiju, a Middle Eastern merchant of the twelfth century, and his Indian slave, Bomma, with Ghosh's own journeys through Egypt during the 1970s and 1980s. In fact, the book's subtitle is 'History in the Guise of a Traveller's Tale', and it is told in the first person by Ghosh (the traveller) who finds himself in Egypt doing anthropological research. Ghosh highlights the fact that he is a non-white traveller in Egypt and, as a result, is seen to lack the cultural authority held by European and American travellers in the region. In this, he exposes the artificial construction of structures of difference, while also calling attention to the fact that he employs a very different gaze from white travellers in Egypt. This is because he is not identified by the Egyptians as coming out of a culture of material wealth and technological advancement. Instead, the Indian traveller in Egypt is treated as irrational and ignorant, a foreigner with no authority.

The literary critic James Buzzard, discussing *In an Antique Land*, says, 'The story delivers a sharp critique of a classic quest – exoticist, anthropological, Orientalist – for pure traditions and discrete cultural differences'.[20] In this, Ghosh's text suggests the impossibility of finding any 'pure' traditions or 'absolute' differences. When he first travels to Egypt, he expects to find in that 'antique land' a settled group of people. But he is wrong. For he discovers that everyone in the village had engaged in extensive travel, and that travelling was an activity that has been done for centuries. Thus, Buzzard notes that in Ghosh's text 'the anthropologist [is] not a worldly traveler visiting local natives, departing from the metropolitan center to study a rural periphery. Instead, his "ancient and settled" fieldsite opens to complex histories of dwelling and traveling, cosmopolitan experiences.'[21]

Ghosh, in short, subverts the colonial travel narrative, uprooting it from its recent past as a tool of Empire. This project is further developed in his 'Foreword' to the anthology *Other Routes* (2006), in which Ghosh writes that, for him, the most successful travel writing is that which does 'not assume a universal order of reality'; nor does it structure the journey into a narrative that 'correspond[s] to teleologies of racial or civilizational progress'.[22] Instead, the most interesting travel narratives are, he suggests, those that express an 'openness to surprise' and an 'acknowledgement of the limits of the knowingness of the witness'.[23] To illustrate his point, he recounts the story of visiting the Cambodian monument Angkor Wat in 1993. Upon reaching the monument, Ghosh tells of how he recalls the account of Henri Mouhot (1826–61) 'discovering' Angkor Wat in 1860: the Frenchman had parted the 'veil of greenery' surrounding the ancient temple and 'found' the abandoned structure that had lain dormant since it was raided by the Thai army in 1431.[24] Ghosh writes,

■ The tale he told was entirely at odds with the tale of [Mouhot's] exploration [and] discovery of Angkor Wat [...] Monks had [in fact] lived in Angkor Wat for centuries before Mouhot's discovery [...] It was only after the monument's 'discovery' by the French that it was truly abandoned: when archeologists took possession of the complex, they forced the monks to move their shrine out of the temple's interior [...] So to whom was the monument 'lost'? Certainly the Buddhist Sangha was well aware of its existence, as were the ruling powers in Thailand and Cambodia [...] It was only to Europeans, then, that Angkor was a 'discovery'.[25] □

Ghosh's description of visiting the Cambodian temple is, among other things, a way for him to illustrate how narratives of travel are linked to power, colonization and the production of knowledge. For Ghosh reveals that in 1860 the European colonial masters re-wrote the complicated narrative of the monument's past. The French travellers and explorers, then, created the narrative of an abandoned site – a lost temple – that Mouhot, the European subject, 'discovered' and brought back to life. But Ghosh's narrative does not end here. For he points out that the European 'discoverers' also tried to recast the actual structure of the temple to fit into their own version of the tale. Thus, the archaeologists attempted to purge the building of all traces of recent human life, forcing the monks out of the temple and compelling them to inhabit the surrounding areas. As a result, Ghosh's postcolonial travel narrative exposes the structures of power and the production of knowledge that lie behind traditional European travel writing.

The postcolonial literary critic and author Tabish Khair (born 1966) confirms Ghosh's assertion. Following Ghosh, Khair notes that

■ in the centuries of European colonization, [...] travel writing [was defined] by the presence of or desire for (colonial) power: In Africa and the East Indies, one can say, there arose the trope of European 'discovery'; in the Middle East, the Holy Land, there arose the trope of European 're-discovery': Palestine, it may be said, was rediscovered by Edward Robinson [1794–1863] in 1841.

In this sense, travel and travel writing were (and are) about the gaze of power. It is this that helps explain how the movements of some (non-European) peoples were effectively frozen under that narrative gaze, even when European travellers noted the presence of non-European travellers in the margins of their texts.[26] ☐

Khair's work on Asian and African travel writing illustrates how it is critical to recognize that 'non-European peoples travelled too', but that the kind of 'general knowledge' that enfolds the travels of Christopher Columbus (1451–1506) or James Cook (1728–79) or Marco Polo (1254–1324) never extends to Asian or African travel narratives.[27] By studying the travel accounts of Ibn Battuta (1304–77) and many others, Khair points to the wealth of writing by African and Asian travellers who left behind fascinating accounts of their journeys. This has enabled scholars to become more aware of travel writings in, for instance, Arabic and Japanese that do not necessarily include the same kind of colonizing gazes that we often find in Western travel texts. Moreover, these non-European travel narratives challenge the assumption that human mobility is, and continues to be, a predominantly European prerogative.

In an age of postcolonialism, the process of writing and reading critically about travel has become much more nuanced and self-conscious. During the era of European colonization, travel narratives were often considered to be transparent, neutral and objective. They were assumed to be the simple descriptions of the places and people which the traveller encountered on his or her journey. As a result, the readers and writers of these texts did not interrogate the language that was used in the text. Nor did they reflect upon how the descriptions were framed or the position that was held by the traveller. Issues such as the traveller's gaze and the site of enunciation and inscription were ignored, and the power dynamics inherent in systems of classification and taxonomy were completely overlooked.

Postcolonial criticism has gone a long way towards helping us see the power dynamics involved in writing and reading about travel. But this is not to say that the entire genre of travel writing should be dismissed as politically problematic. Not at all. In fact, Caryl Phillips (born 1958), the British writer of Caribbean descent, published an article titled 'Necessary Journeys' (2004), in which he championed travel as an important activity in his development as a writer. He states,

■ The gift of travel has been enabling for me in the same way that it has been enabling for those writers in the British tradition, those in the African diasporan tradition, and those in the Caribbean tradition, many of whom have found it necessary to move in order that they might reaffirm for themselves the fact that dual and multiple affiliations feed our constantly fluid sense of self. Healthy societies are ones that allow such pluralities to exist and do not feel threatened by these hybrid conjoinings.[28] □

Here, Phillips speaks as part of the African diaspora, and he points to travel as a significant way of understanding his complex sense of identity as a Black British citizen and writer. Travel enables him to understand the importance of 'reinterpreting' and, if necessary, 'reinventing' himself by exploring ethnicities, national identities and cultural differences. In this article, though, he also mentions, however briefly, the limiting racial assumptions ('the myopia') that characterize European nations (including Britain) – a topic that he explores in depth in his major work of postcolonial travel writing, *The European Tribe* (1987).

Indeed, Phillips's *The European Tribe* chronicles his journey across Europe and his search for a sense of identity. As a Black man raised in a European country, Phillips attempts to come to terms with what it is like for him to feel both part of, and not part of, Europe. 'I wrote *The European Tribe'*, he writes, 'while consumed with the anxieties of knowing that I was a member of the larger European tribe, a member who felt uncomfortable at being such, but who had no viable alternative.'[29] As a European traveller, then, Phillips is simultaneously an insider and an outsider. He has grown up in England, and sees himself as connected to Europe, but his blackness has also disconnected him from his national and European identity. To complicate matters, Phillips states that because of his upbringing in England he did not, as a young man, feel a strong sense of Black identity, or even know much about the black diaspora. 'My ignorance', he writes, 'probably came about as a result of my education [...]. In British schools I was never offered a text that had been penned by a black person.'[30] But when he is travelling in Europe, he is constantly reminded of his blackness. This, then, engenders a keen sense of his racial identity. For regardless of his British background, Phillips learns that he is first a black man in the eyes of the world. In Spain, for instance, he is called 'el senor negro' by the young boys with whom he interacts.[31] Later, in Norway, he is harassed by racist custom agents as soon as he arrives at Oslo airport. Black is black – a transcontinental identity.

Throughout his travels, Phillips gazes back at the European – just as the European traveller had once gazed at people of African descent and recorded the activities of their 'tribal rituals'. Phillips thus turns that paradigm on its head, but with one crucial difference: the Natives of this European tribe gaze back at his black skin and, in so doing, press him into an inferior mould. Indeed, he constantly reminds the reader that his blackness determines the way he is perceived and treated. Thus, during his travels, he surveys the xenophobic sentiments of native white Europeans while making thought-provoking social commentary on the misconstrued state of European race relations. In this, he candidly illustrates the tribal division found in Europe due to its racism, nationalistic views, and an insistence upon creating an external class of non-white Europeans. In the midst of his journey, Phillips draws many conclusions concerning the state of outsider groups in the European countries he visits.

One of the most insightful observations that Phillips makes is that Europe is trapped in its own Eurocentric vision of the world. He writes,

> ■ Europe must begin to restructure the tissue of lies that continues to be taught and digested at school and at home for we, black people, are an inextricable part of this small continent. And Europeans must learn to understand this for themselves, for there are among us few who are here as missionaries.[32] □

This restructuring of thought, through a rejection of Eurocentricism, and a refutation of the lies contained within the metanarratives of European society is, Phillips implies, necessary for Europe to develop. For the stereotypes, assumptions and racism found in European nations are, in the end, destructive not only to minority groups, but also to the nations themselves. This is because Eurocentricism perpetuates discourses of difference and systems of classification and hierarchies that negate the development of a healthy pluralistic society. If this restructuring of thought does not occur, then the nations of Europe will impede the growth of a rich, multiethnic society on the continent.

As we have considered in this chapter, travel writing has been a key genre for interrogating the discourses of empire. On the one hand, travel writing has contributed to the rhetoric of difference that justified and promoted imperial expansion. On the other hand, though, it is a genre that has been used by some postcolonial writers to expose the absurd assumptions and powerful ideologies that are included in traditional travel narratives. In the next chapter, we will observe how a crucial tool of travel – the map – has become a trope and symbol of asymmetrical power relations in postcolonial writing.

representations of the land: it will therefore become the authoritative text that will legitimize the British appropriation of the land.[2] Above all, by redrawing the map, the foreign power reserves the right to add or delete borders, to change the names of places and to determine the law that regulates the jurisdiction. For, as a representation, a map has the power to take away a country's national sovereignty by depicting one nation as coming under the control of another. In this, cartography is not a passive form of colonial administration.

One of the most striking aspects of Friel's play is the fact that the cartographers Anglicize all of the Irish place names: Bun na hAbhann is changed to Burnfoot, Machaire Ban is converted to Whiteplains and Baile Beag is 'translated' into Ballybeg. These changes on the new map correspond to the fact that the British are also establishing new National Schools in Ireland to impose English as the national language. As such, the new map signals the loss of political independence, as well as the death of the Irish language and the implicit loss of cultural and national independence. For the British, language is power and there- fore the map must be composed so that it corresponds to the English tongue. Friel, then, explores how the map both reflects and furthers the imposition of the colonizer's language on the community. Moreover, he suggests that, under the circumstances, it is impossible to resist these processes of colonization. For when the Donnelly twins abduct a British soldier, Yolland, the retaliatory measures taken by the British Army are swift and violent: Captain Lancey announces that his soldiers will begin by killing all of the livestock in the area; after which, if Yolland is still missing, the army will carry out a series of evictions before levelling every house in the district. Mapping is a serious business.

The critic Benedict Anderson (born 1936) argues that the map has been one of the important forms of communication that has shaped the way that countries have imagined their dominion. A map is, after all, thought to illustrate the geography of a nation's domain, the legitimacy of a country's ancestry, as well as the nature of the people ruled over by the state. In his book *Imagined Communities: Reflections on the Origin and Spread of Nationalism* (1983), however, he argues that a nation is noth- ing more than an 'imagined community' made up of people who have never met and do not necessarily have shared interests or outlooks in common. Maps, newspapers, novels and other forms of mass commu- nication became (with the rise of print-capitalism) channels for creating shared cultures, interests and vocabularies within a nation. Maps, then, provide an imagined sense of unity for the diverse people who live in a particular place. But, as Anderson points out, maps are limited, for they only focus on borders and they view the nation from above, filling in the space of the planet with artificially constructed boundaries that make up countries. As a result, maps are totalizing systems that comprise classificatory grids, which are applied to anything under the state's real or imagined control. Still, these bird's-eye-view illustrations of borders and boundaries are important for constructing an imagined sense of community within a nation. For those born within specific borders (within lines on the map) share, at least in principle, a common sense of nationhood and citizenship. It follows from this that the shape of a country becomes a logo that penetrates the national imagination as an emblem of the country. (So, for instance, the boot-like image of Italy on the European map is a striking national symbol.) This contributes to a sense of national belonging: people who have never met can be united by their conceptions of the borders that constitute the nation.

Anderson goes on to discuss the map as an effective tool of empire – a way of dividing up territory and maintaining power. He describes how imperial maps were colour-coded: British colonies were red, the French were blue and the Dutch were yellow. The effect of colour-coding the world in this way made what he calls the 'map as logo'.[3] This practice of representing space served to make these territories highly abstract:

■ Dyed this way, each colony appeared like a detachable piece of a jigsaw puzzle. As this 'jigsaw' effect became normal, each 'piece' could be wholly detached from its geographic context. In its final form all explanatory glosses could be summarily removed: lines of longitude and latitude, place names, signs for rivers, seas, and mountains, neighbours. Pure sign, no longer compass to the world.[4] □

Imperial maps, then, mark the successful abstraction of space where locality and proximity are completely subordinated to the lines of the colonial property. As a result, the experience of the local person – the colonized subject – is lost and the territory becomes defined by an abstract set of boundaries that lie outside of his experience. By extension, these lands are, in Anderson's words, like pieces of a jigsaw puzzle because they have become symbols of Empire. And they are printed and circulated to a mass audience who consume this information in the same way that they consume newspapers.

The poet and novelist Michael Ondaatje (born 1943) often highlights the sense of abstraction, alienation and dislocation associated with the maps of Empire. For example, in the 1982 memoir of his Sri Lankan family, *Running in the Family*, Ondaatje opens with a map of the island. Here, the author chooses to call this Ceylon (even though its name was changed in 1972) as he plots out his return to a now foreign home. 'I spread maps on the floor', he says, 'and searched out possible routes to Ceylon'; eventually, however, he realizes that these are just lines on the page: colours, shapes and words inscribed upon a blank piece of paper.[5] The land to which he wishes to return is no longer there.

His home, like his memory of childhood, has all but disappeared. The ebbs and flows of imperialism have, in other words, produced a drawing and redrawing of the map to reflect the shifts in political power and geographical instability. What Ondaatje comes to realize is that 'Ceylon' has always been mapped out in different ways, and that the 'explorers' of empire have produced a variety of distinct maps. In the following passage he cites a range of cartographers of 'Ceylon': the ancient Egyptian mathematician, astronomer and geographer Ptolemy (2nd century AD); the Flemish geographer and map-maker Gerardus Mercator (1512–94); the Dutch priest and author Francois Valentyn (1666–1727); the Dutch publisher Pieter Mortier (1661–1711); and the German draughtsman and engraver Johann Wolfgang von Heydt (about 1705–after 1750):

■ On my brother's wall in Toronto are the false maps. Old portraits of Ceylon. The result of sightings, glances from trading vessels, the theories of sextant. The shapes differ so much they seem to be translations – by Ptolemy, Mercator, Francois Valentyn, Mortier, and Heydt – growing from mythic shapes into eventual accuracy.[6] □

In this passage, Ondaatje suggests that a map is a form of translation. Indeed, a map attempts to take the physical data of a geographical region and 'translate' it into a figure on the page. In this sense, its lines and colours stand in for the place itself; or, to put this another way, the land morphs into a representation of the region.

But, following Benedict Anderson, it is important to ask how the 'translation' of the map is read by the viewer. Ondaatje reads the map of Ceylon as 'a pendant off the ear of India', a piece of land that 'floats on the Indian Ocean and holds its native mountains'.[7] Here, Ondaatje calls attention to Anderson's assertion that people often identify the shape of a country as a symbol of the nation itself. But unlike the boot of Italy, Ondaatje's reading of this map is highly personalized: we do not generally associate Sri Lanka with an earring that hangs off of the ear of India. In this, Ondaatje calls attention to the fact that a map can be read in many different ways, for it is subject to diverse interpretations based on the position of the viewer. Obviously, Ondaatje reads the maps in ways that are very different from the explorers who created them:

■ The maps reveal rumours of topography, the routes for invasion and trade, and the dark mad mind of travellers' tales appears throughout Arab and Chinese medieval records. The island seduced all of Europe. The Portuguese. The Dutch. The English. And so its name changed, as well as its shape – Serendip, Ratnapida ('island of gems'), Taprobane, Zeloan, Zeilan, Seyllan, Ceilon, and Ceylon – the wife of many marriages, courted by invaders who stepped ashore and claimed everything with the power of their sword or bible or language.[8] □

The history of mapping Sri Lanka is, as Ondaatje points out, inter-twined with the history of colonization. In this history, the shapes, col-ours and names on the maps change. A 'stout rectangle' in one map might transform into a small circle in another; or, a diamond shape in one image might become a triangle in the next.[9] These changes in shapes are accompanied by changes in names (as we have seen in Friel's *Translations*), but it is striking that Ondaatje does not include the island's most recent name in his list. Instead, the name 'Sri Lanka' remains an implied absence: it is never mentioned, but the reader is keenly aware of its presence.

Michael Ondaatje continues to explore these issues in his novel *Anil's Ghost* (2000). At the beginning of the novel, the narrator states that 'the National Atlas of Sri Lanka has seventy-three versions of the island – each revealing only one aspect, one obsession'.[10] And later, as the main character, Anil, waits for her colleague, Sarath, in the Archae-ological Offices in Colombo, she moves from map to map, each depict-ing the island from different perspectives: 'Traits of the country', she wonders, 'are like those of a complex friend.'[11] Sri Lanka has, like so many other colonized countries, an unstable geography. It has a fluid identity that cannot be fixed in one drawing or even a single name. As in Ondaatje's memoir, the lines constituting a map of Sri Lanka engender, for Anil, a process of reterritorialization. She sees the maps as depicting a foreign place that she once called home. A place once familiar, once called Ceylon, has been rendered strange again; a foreignness is thus reincarnated in the formation of the markings on the page, markings which are meant to be mimetic reflections of this at once foreign-familiar place. But now that she is on home ground, she recognizes that it is also in a foreign territory, and, as in *Running in the Family*, Anil's sense of place challenges the reader by asking whether, for any of us, there is a home ground that is not a foreign territory. Is there ever a map that makes perfect sense, or a language fully adequate for the articulation of experience?

Attempts to recapture the past, Ondaatje states, can only take place within the disorienting realm of a new map. Only under the sign of a new geography, one that digs up its own ancestors, can we conceive of the links between the past and a sense of belonging. Anil, for instance, completely remaps traditional conceptions of home, for the narrator tells us that she had always 'courted foreignness, was at ease whether on the Bakerloo line or on the highways around Santa Fe. She felt completed abroad. (Even now her brain held the area codes of Denver and Portland.)'[12] She is only at home when she is abroad. Such a paradoxical state forces Anil to formulate unique geographies of Sri Lanka in her mind. Her childhood home, far from being a place of comfort and security, is a mysterious and unknown place of fear and discomfort.

'She had come to expect clearly marked roads to the source of most mysteries', we are told, 'but here, on this island, she realized she was moving with one arm of language among uncertain laws and a fear that was everywhere'.[13] Like the confusion posed by the multiplicity of maps, Sri Lanka must be approached by Anil with a new language, a new way of seeing and experiencing her surroundings. Old ways of reading are no longer apt in a country where 'information [is] made public with diversions and subtexts – as if the truth would not be of interest when given directly, without waltzing backwards'.[14]

Michael Ondaatje's use of maps to explore complicated relations of power and personalized conceptions of identity is ambivalent. On the one hand, he recognizes the problematic history of mapping as a product of empire but, on the other hand, he sees it as a conceit for articulating the displacement of the colonized subject. Ondaatje's text, then, is a striking example of what the critic Graham Huggan calls,

■ the prevalence of the map topos in contemporary post-colonial literary texts, and the frequency of its ironic and/or parodic usage in these texts [which, according to Huggan,] suggests a link between a de/reconstructive reading of maps and a revisioning of the history of European colonialism.[15] □

Indeed, in his important book *Territorial Disputes: Maps and Mapping in Contemporary Canadian and Australian Fiction* (1994), Huggan argues that maps in literary works may have an ambivalent function, for 'maps may be simultaneously perceived as useful tools and dangerous weapons'.[16] As a result, Huggan outlines the general principles of what he calls 'literary cartography', a way of reading that is suffused with the duelling notions of perception and control. Huggan writes that literary cartography is

■ fundamentally concerned with the process of representation; but whereas the symbolic representation of landscapes in literature is primarily directed towards the question of how the land is perceived, the metaphoric function of maps in literature is addressed first and foremost to the issue of how the land is controlled.[17] □

Huggan goes on to describe literary cartography as a means of exploring 'territorial strategies that are implicitly or explicitly associated with maps'.[18] For the purposes of a postcolonial literary enterprise, the implications of this theory are clear. For postcolonial writers such as Ondaatje articulate a dialectic wherein they come to terms with and tap into the creative sources of a colonized space entirely shaped by stories that have excluded them as well as the realities presented by their physical presence, as they work to 'fashion, explore, and map new [literary] territories'.[19]

When it comes to defining who one is and where one belongs, postcolonial writers often have recourse to the language of cartography, of 'charting' their course in the world, 'mapping' their path.[20] Physical maps give literal direction and practical information, but their constructed nature leads to questions about the constructing consciousness: Who is drawing the map? What are the guiding principles and the selective procedures used in map making? And for whom is the map drawn? As such, map analysis is a postcolonial theorist's delight: behind the lines on the map is a world of unspoken but evident possibilities, silences, absences, powerful discourses and ambiguities. Graham Huggan comments extensively on this 'gap' between what one reads on a map and what lies behind the mapping endeavour. 'Cartographic discourse is', he writes, 'characterized by the discrepancy between its authoritative status and its approximate function, a discrepancy which marks out the recognizable totality of the map as a manifestation of the desire for control rather than as an authenticating seal of coherence'.[21]

The language of maps, then, suggests certainty about where things are, but in fact maps can be read as powerful texts open to interpretation. As Ondaatje suggests, one can read the same map from different angles, depending on one's own 'cultural mapping' or ideological positioning. J. B. Harley, the British geographer, has made this point in a seminal article entitled 'Maps, Knowledge and Power' (1988). Here, he argues that

■ maps are a way of conceiving, articulating, and structuring the human world which is biased towards, promoted by, and exerts influence upon particular sets of social relations. By accepting such premises it becomes easier to see how appropriate they are to manipulation by the powerful in society.[22] □

In this article, Harley calls for the use of discourse analysis to unpack maps' meanings: he argues that we should read maps as a kind of 'literature' and 'consider questions about changing readerships for maps, about levels of carto-literacy, conditions of authorship, aspects of secrecy and censorship, and also about the nature of the political statements which are made by maps'.[23]

Harley's reference to the textual and literary aspects of the map is also present in the literary criticism of the Canadian writer Margaret Atwood (born 1939), who repeatedly refers to literature as a map. 'Literature is', she writes, 'not only a mirror; it is also a map, a geography of the mind. Our literature [in Canada] is one such map, if we can learn to read it as our literature, as a product of who and where we have been.'[24] It is, then, perhaps not surprising that a series of maps appear in Atwood's first novel, *Surfacing* (1973). On the opening pages, for instance, the nameless heroine returns to the region of her youth, and she assumes that she does not need a map because she knows the way. However, she soon gets lost and disoriented, unable to find what she is seeking. Then, upon arriving at a cabin in northern Ontario, she finds a map tacked to the wall, which she attempts to decipher in order to reorient herself and return to a sense of familiar ground. But the map is not fixed or stable; it shifts and changes the landscape to reflect the various appropriations and resettlements of territories and regions arising out of the complexity of this simultaneous postcolonial (in relation to Britain) and neo-colonial (in relation to the USA) space. This doubleness causes the narrator to question her feelings of belonging, for this region is simultaneously her 'home ground' and a 'foreign territory'.[25]

The relationship between home and identity is an important one, and the heroine of Atwood's text needs a map to discover both. As a result, she goes on a search for origins, looking for her vanished father and the Native cave paintings that consumed him. As a guide, she has her father's notes, but these prove to be inadequate and she becomes lost in the maze of the caves. She cannot find the paintings: 'Either I hadn't remembered the map properly', she says, 'or what he'd written on the map was wrong.'[26] This map is, of course, a representation that must be read and interpreted in order to understand the markings of the cartographer. But Atwood's heroine is unable to comprehend the diagonal lines or the shapes that make up the image. Consequently, she becomes, once again, lost in the twists, turns and dead ends of the labyrinth-like structure of the caves.

In his critical analysis of *Surfacing*, David Punter asks if it is possible 'ever to remember a postcolonial map properly, ever to put together a coherent account of a world where histories are mysteriously overlaid?'[27] Indeed, what Punter is calling attention to here is the way in which Atwood's novel connects the heroine's 'lost' state of being to the lost or damaged cultures and histories of Canada's First Nations. The protagonist's search for the Native cave paintings (a project which had also obsessed her father) is part of her attempt to piece together that which has been lost in the wake of European colonization. As her search continues, she begins to decipher her father's maps and notes:

■ The map crosses and the drawings made sense now: at the beginning he must have been only locating the rock paintings, deducing them, tracing and photographing them, a retirement hobby; but then he found out about them. The Indians did not own salvation but they had once known where it lived and their signs marked the sacred places, the places where they could learn the truth. There was no painting at White Birch Lake and none here, because his later drawings weren't copied from things on the rocks. He had discovered new places, new oracles, they were things he was seeing the way I had seen, true vision; at the end, after the failure of logic.[28] □

This passage is, for Punter, an example of how the mapping of a postcolonial space must take place 'under the sign of a new geography, a "radical" geography', which is committed to rediscovering the lost ancestors who have been erased through the history of violence and eradication. The heroine is, for instance, trying to piece together the expression of a Native culture that has suffered under the loss of removal and displacement. Her desire to find the paintings is, then, a way for her to remap the territory, to redraw the borders to correspond to an area that was inhabited long before the arrival of European settlers. Postcolonial maps must, in other words, dig up the past and offer a voice to those who have been silenced by the cartography of colonization.

For Atwood, maps are stories as much about individuals and identity as about the landscape. They reveal changing perceptions of the natural world, as well as conflicts over the acquisition of territories. In her book *Cartographic Fictions: Maps, Race, and Identity* (2002), the postcolonial critic Karen Piper looks at maps in relation to journals, correspondence, advertisements and novels in order to follow the history of cartography through what she identifies as three stages: the establishment of the prime meridian, the development of aerial photography and the emergence of satellite and computer mapping. Throughout these stages, Piper follows the cartographer's impulse to 'leave the ground' as the desire to escape the specificities of those peoples who inhabit the place. Thus, she writes, the cartographer underwrites, ignores and dismisses the racialized or gendered subject. With the distance that the aerial view provides, maps can then be produced 'objectively'; that is, devoid of 'problematic' native interference or input from those who are 'on the ground'. Piper attempts to bring back the dialogue of the 'native informant', demonstrating how maps have historically constructed or betrayed anxieties about race.[29] In so doing, she also tries to bring back to the map key areas of contact between explorer/native and masculine/feminine definitions of space.

Piper thus examines 'the tension between those who map and those who resist or redefine mapping projects'.[30] In this, she goes far beyond the obvious analysis of the modern dependency on maps as spatial instruments to consider the implications of that dependency for the construction of gendered and racial identities within popular culture. For she argues that the inhabitant of modern, western society is a kind of 'cartographic cyborg'; that is, someone so thoroughly intertwined with mapping technologies that it is impossible to say, in terms of knowledge practices, where embodied knowledge ends and technological knowledge begins.

But postcolonial writers also, at times, invoke the process of mapping as a way of representing the power relations that arise within a colonized community. These maps tend to be more conceptual than material, as these texts often investigate who has the power to determine the boundaries and impose borders on a specific space. In the novel *Cereus Blooms at Night* (1996) by Shani Mootoo (born 1958), for instance, the main character, Mala, is driven mad by the restrictions and abuse imposed upon her by her father, Chandin, and the Caribbean community in which she lives. Chandin regulates his two daughters by mapping out the area surrounding his house and fencing it off to confine them within a prison-like structure. 'He fenced off his house crudely with chicken wire,' the narrator says, 'he did not let them out of his sight. He stood guard as they showered in the outdoor bathroom. He waited for them not far from the latrine [...]. He slept in his bed with a child on either side.'[31] As the colonizing tyrant, Chandin polices his victims, determining their movement and limiting their actions. He thus builds a restricted territory in which his children are forced to live. He determines the borders between inside and outside (if only with crude chicken wire) and he builds a garrison to imprison his daughters and prevent his wife from returning. This space then moves from the homely to the unhomely, from a comfortable place where Mala can develop a sense of self to an oppressive and threatening space that destroys her subjectivity. Mala can no longer feel at home in her most familiar environment – she is no longer 'at home' in her father's house. Her sense of place thus becomes inescapably uncanny, not through a spectral sensation in which she glimpses a phenomenal object within this realm, but through a sense of the groundless foundation upon which her home exists. For, paradoxically, the strict policing and limits marked out by the crude borders of Chandin's homely territory do not further a climate of homeliness. Instead, his boundaries create an unstable home that is repressive and destructive.

The relationship between mapping, borders and power is highlighted throughout Mootoo's text. Mala is confronted with further restrictions and limitations on her space when she goes to the playground, where the borders of this public space are also marked off to prevent her from feeling at home. 'Get away from we playground', Walter and the other children shout, 'Get away from us [...]. This park is only for good people.'[32] To illustrate his point, Walter picks up a stick and draws a line between himself and Mala, as if physically to display the border separating what he calls 'good people' from 'bad people'.[33] This line in the sand is a provocation, but it also maps out an image of the land which divides the spaces of centre and margin, privilege and ostracization. Mala and her sister are displaced from the centre, forced onto the margins due to their family's history. As in her father's house, then, Mala's movement is restricted by those who have the power to create borders. In fact, when Walter crosses the line and enters Mala's space, she is powerless to stop him. Even her protest that he remain on his side of the line is met with ridicule: 'Is you who draw the line?', Walter asks, 'Or me?

I draw the line. I go where I want. Who have stick in they hand? You or me? Go home.'[34] Going home, though, is not an option. At home the relationship between space and power is even more oppressive than it is in the playground. But it is here, with these children, that Mala realizes her own powerlessness. For she is unable to confront both a father and a community that determine the territorial divisions between inside and outside, centre and periphery, to which she must submit.

This chapter has traced the many representations of mapping and power in postcolonial literature, demonstrating how the agents of imperialism have drawn maps in order to appropriate the land and subjugate the native population. Often, the postcolonial writer responds to this powerful mode of representation by unearthing what lies beneath the lines and colours of the territories. In so doing, the writer highlights the ideologies of the map and gives voice to those who have been silenced in the so-called objective science of cartography. In the next chapter, we will examine the mapping of the body through a consideration of postcolonial responses to asymmetrical gender relations and the hierarchical divisions between masculinity and femininity in colonial and postcolonial writing.

CHAPTER NINE

Gender

At the beginning of the novel *King Solomon's Mines* (1885) by H. Rider Haggard (1856–1925), the Englishman, Mr. Quartermain, describes a map of Southern Africa which is said to reveal the location of the treasure left by King Solomon. The map, written in the blood of the dying Portuguese explorer, Josés da Silvestra, includes an inscription stating that the treasure can be found by journeying to the 'two mountains named Sheba's Breasts'.[1] Once there, Silvestra continues, the traveller must 'climb the snow of Sheba's left breast till he comes to the nipple' and enter a cave. It is here that 'the countless diamonds stored in Solomon's treasure chamber' will be revealed.[2]

This description of the African landscape and the accompanying map has been used by the postcolonial critic Anne McClintock as an example of how gender often plays an important role in colonial discourse. In her book *Imperial Leather: Race, Gender and Sexuality in the Colonial Conquest* (1995), she describes Haggard's map as a gendered document of conquest. For the treasure can only be revealed once the Englishman has conquered the curves and 'nipple' of 'Sheba's Breasts'; he must mount Sheba and enter her cave before experiencing the delights of her treasure chamber. McClintock begins with Haggard's map for several reasons. First, it illustrates the governing themes of Western imperialism whereby the European subject 'knows' the foreign ground through the technology of the map, enabling him to 'penetrate' into the colony. Second, this 'penetration' results in the extraction of wealth through the exploitation of the colony's natural resources. And, third, it is an example of a patriarchal fantasy that feminizes the colonial territory and, in turn, subjugates it to the imagined dominance of male phallic power. Concerning the latter point, McClintock explains,

■ What sets Haggard's map apart from the scores of treasure maps that emblazon colonial narratives is that it is explicitly sexualized [...]. [I]f the map is inverted, it reveals at once the diagram of a female body. The body is spread eagle and truncated – the only parts drawn are those that denote female sexuality [...]. At the center of the map lie the two mountain peaks called Sheba's Breasts – from which mountain ranges stretch to either side as handless arms. The body's length is inscribed, leading from the threshold of the frozen breasts to over the navel *koppie* straight as a die to the pubic mound [...]. This dark triangle points to and conceals the entrance to the forbidden passages: the 'mouth of treasure cave' – the vaginal entrance into which the men are led.[3] ☐

As McClintock illustrates, the drawing of the map in the form of the female body offers an abstract image of sexuality that is connected to imperialism. For the land is conceived of as part of a masculinist dream wherein the terrain lies open for the Englishmen, offering itself up to the dominance of white male authority.

Such representations of the land link Western imperialism to the transmission of white male power through a control of the feminized colonial landscape. Ania Loomba notes that Renaissance depictions of America, for instance, often conflated gender, sexuality and colonization by depicting the continent as a half-naked woman with a feather skirt or headdress, surrounded by exotic animals and strange beasts.[4] Likewise, Loomba points out that there is a long pictorial tradition that presents the African continent as a woman, and suggests that the region is available for discovery, possession and conquest. Similarly, native women are often described as sexually available, exotic and erotic. Their bodies, then, are linked to the promise and excitement offered by the colonial land, as in the description of the 'wild and gorgeous apparition of a woman' whom the narrator of *Heart of Darkness* (1899) by Joseph Conrad (1857–1924) encounters on the shores of the Congo River:

■ She walked with measured steps, draped in striped and fringed clothes, treading the earth proudly, with a slight jingle and flash of barbarous ornaments. She carried her head high; her hair was done in the shape of a helmet; she had brass leggings to her knees, brass wire gauntlets to the elbow, a crimson spot on her tawny neck; bizarre things, charms, gifts of witch-men, that hung about her, glittered and trembled at every step. She must have had the value of several elephant tusks upon her. She was savage and superb, wild-eyed and magnificent; there was something ominous and stately in her deliberate progress. And the hush that had fallen suddenly upon the whole sorrowful land, the immense wilderness, the colossal body of the fecund and mysterious life seemed to look at her, pensive, as though it had been looking at the image of its own tenebrous and passionate soul.[5] ☐

For Loomba, this passage is representative of how, from the beginning of the colonial period to the present day, female bodies have been used to symbolize the conquered land. She points out that this metaphoric use of the female body varies according to the region and the historical context, but the message is always clear: the power dynamics of colonization are intimately tied to the discourses of patriarchal dominance.

In *Orientalism*, Edward Said argues that the sexual subjugation of the Oriental woman to Western men 'fairly stands for the pattern of relative strength between East and West and the discourse about the Orient that it enabled'.[6] Said goes on to assert that Orientalism develops out of a 'male power-fantasy' that sexualizes a feminized Orient for Western power and possession. In this, sexuality is connected to metaphors about the male power dynamics played out in what Said refers to as a masculinist vision. He writes,

■ Orientalism itself, furthermore, was an exclusively male province; like so many professional guilds during the modern period, it viewed itself and its subject matter with sexist blinders. This is especially evident in the writing of travelers and novelists: women are usually the creatures of a male power-fantasy. They express unlimited sensuality, they are more or less stupid, and above all they are willing.[7] □

Thus, in this male fantasy, the Eastern female body comes to symbolize the 'penetrable' nature of the region and the land that is to be (or has been) conquered. For Said, then, gender and sexuality become important tropes for power relations that are played out in the relationship between the colonizer and colonized. Colonial discourse, for instance, constructs the images of the 'virgin' island and the exotically alluring and passive foreign region whose spoils are open to the Westerner. Discourses of male sexuality, therefore, become a way of articulating asymmetrical power relations on the imperial terrain.

Some postcolonial critics have noted that Said's reading of sexuality only as a metaphor runs the risk of eliding gender as a constitutive dynamic of imperial power. In her book *Gendering Orientalism* (1996), Reina Lewis asserts that Said ignores the participation of women in colonial projects; and, in so doing, he becomes entangled in the same male imperialist view that he criticizes. Lewis writes that

■ For Said, in *Orientalism* at least, Orientalism is a homogeneous discourse enunciated by a colonial subject that is unified, intentional and irredeemably male [...]. In *Orientalism* gender occurs only as a metaphor for the negative characterization of the Orientalized Other as 'feminine' or in a single reference to a woman writer [...]. Said never questions women's apparent absence as producers of Orientalist discourse or as agents within colonial power. This mirrors the traditional view that women were not involved in colonial expansion.[8] □

Here, Lewis calls attention to the absence of women in Said's influential critique of the Western discourses of Orientalism. In so doing, she implies that Said is inadvertently participating in the very discourses of imperialism that he is exposing. For he is, she argues, perpetuating the subplot of a masculinist view of history in which women, if they appear at all, are strictly marginal.

Lewis backs up her claim by illustrating that in *Orientalism* Said only makes a single reference to a women writer, Gertrude Bell (1868–1926). But even in his brief passage on Bell, Lewis points out, Said pays no attention to the possible effects of Bell's gendered position on her texts. As such, the voice of the gendered subject is all but erased from Said's book, and as a corrective Lewis gives voice to the women that Said ignores. For Lewis, 'women did play a part in the textual production that constituted Orientalism and, moreover, gender, as a differentiating term, was integral to the structure of that discourse and individuals' experience of it.'[9] From this perspective, it is important to pay attention to women's role in imperial social and cultural relations in order to develop nuanced and complex accounts of colonization. After all, women have both contributed to and challenged the powerful discourses and power relations of British colonialism. It is therefore crucial to remain aware of a gendered axis of colonial discourse.

Reina Lewis's critique of Said is influenced by Jane Miller's criticism of the masculinist assumptions found in some postcolonial criticism. Miller writes that Frantz Fanon and Edward Said are part of a strand of postcolonial theory that erases women from the discursive and material project of nineteenth-century European imperialism. According to Miller, Said ignores women as participants in imperial power relations:

■ Said [in *Orientalism*] sets out with care and delicacy the parallels and analogies developed in this field between colonial relations and sexual relations, and he shows how illuminating of the reality of the imperial adventure those parallels have been for both West and East. What he does not confront are the sexual meanings on which those illuminations depend. It is possible to feel that within his analysis it is with the distortion of male sexuality [identity and sovereignty] produced by the language of Orientalism that he is chiefly concerned [...]. The question remains: why does such an analysis not entail a concern for women's loss of political and economic status, in itself? [Women's history ...] does not become part of the history which is being rewritten.

In accepting the power and usefulness of an analysis like Said's there is an essential proviso [...] to be made. If women are ambiguously present within the discourses of Orientalism, they are just as ambiguously present within the discourses developed to expose and oppose Orientalism. Their presence in both is as forms of coinage, exchange value offered or stolen or forbidden, tokens of men's power and wealth or lack of them. The sexual use and productiveness of women are allowed to seem equivalent to their actual presence and their consciousness. They are, finally, 'Orientalized' with Said's terms into the perceptions and the language which express, but also elaborate on, the uses men have for women within exploitative societies.[10] □

The fact that Said does not include women's voices in his study is, for Miller, an act of marginalizing women as agents. This lack in *Orientalism* assumes that women are neither writers nor readers, and that women have not played a role in the articulation, dissemination or condemnation of Orientalist discourses.

This eradication of women from scholarship has been critiqued by Gayatri Spivak, especially in her work on the subaltern. The 'subaltern' is a term derived from the writings of the Italian Marxist political philosopher Antonio Gramsci (1891–1937) and adopted by a well-known group of Indian historians to refer to the suppressed or silenced peasantry. The most influential essay to come out of the Subaltern Group has been Gayatri Spivak's 'Can the Subaltern Speak?' Here, Spivak examines the positioning of the subaltern woman, who is most often silenced because of the tendency historically to prioritize men in representations of subaltern agency. A compelling example of such representations is, for Spivak, the documentation of *sati* or widow sacrifice in colonial India. Her interrogation of the abolition of the *sati* in light of Brahmanic codes and texts leads Spivak to claim that between patriarchy and imperialism the figure of the woman disappears. Women are made invisible through the displaced figuration of the 'third world woman' who is caught between tradition and modernization.[11] In her reference to the 'third world woman', Spivak highlights the discursive construction of a particular model of race, class and gender that has been disseminated by, among others, First World feminist theorists. As a result, Spivak critiques a homogenized and systematized vision of female oppression, which can negate the significant differences between women.

An example of subaltern feminist articulation can be witnessed in the founding of the Sistren Theatre Collective. In 1977, Jamaican women formed the collective with the objective of creating theatre by and for Caribbean women. Using the methods developed in Brazil by The Theatre of the Oppressed, Sistren empowered female audiences by seeking solutions to women's issues presented on stage.[12] In the beginning, it was as much a support group as a cultural collective, for it provided a space for urban and rural women to unite and share common political and social concerns. The support, networking and communication successfully empowered many Jamaican women. Between 1977 and 2004, the Collective developed into a highly professional theatre company, performing plays (often based on the personal experiences of the members) to audiences all over Jamaica, as well as Barbados, England, the United States and Canada.

In 1986, Sistren and Honor Ford-Smith (born 1951) published *Lionheart Gal: Life Stories of Jamaican Women*. The book is a collection of first-person testimonies from the Sistren players that were to be turned into plays, but grew and developed into stories that stood alone. The stories are based around the following three questions: How did you first become aware that you were oppressed as a woman? How did that experience affect your life? How have you tried to change it? The Caribbean literary critic Carolyn Cooper writes that in responding to these questions,

> ■ *Lionheart Gal* is impeccably subversive [...]. For its autobiographical form – the lucid verbal flash – articulates a feminist subversion of the authority of the literary text as fiction, as transformative rewriting of the self in the persona of distanced, divine omniscience. *Lionheart Gal*, like much contemporary feminist discourse, does not pretend to be authoritative. Indeed, the preferred narrative mode of many feminist writers is the guise of intimate, understated domestic writing by women: letters, diaries or what Sistren, in an oral/Creole context, simply calls testimony. The simultaneously secular and religious resonances of 'testimony' intimate the potential for ideological development from the purely personal to the political that is the usual consequence of this process of communal disclosure.[13] □

Here, Cooper correctly points out that *Lionheart Gal* does not simply offer a negative critique of male figures or a questioning of masculinist assumptions. Rather, the stories, narratives and testimonials in the text include positive and paradigm-shifting feminist work by proposing alternative approaches to storytelling, aesthetics and politics.

This merger of the personal with the political is also present in the writings of Chandra Talpade Mohanty, a prominent postcolonial theorist, feminist and political activist. Mohanty's most well-known and influential essay, 'Under Western Eyes: Feminist Scholarship and Colonial Discourses', was published in 1986 – an essay that is reprinted in her book *Feminism Without Borders: Decolonizing Theory, Practicing Solidarity* (2003). In the essay, Mohanty articulates a critique of the political project of Western feminism in its discursive construction of the category of the 'Third World woman' as a hegemonic entity. Mohanty states that Western feminisms have tended to gloss over the differences between Southern women, but that the experience of oppression is incredibly diverse and contingent on geography, history and culture.

Feminism Without Borders expands on these ideas by arguing for a bridging of theory and praxis, and the personal and the political. Here, Mohanty addresses issues faced by women in light of the politics of difference, transnational solidarity building and anticapitalist struggle against globalization. Forging vital links between daily life and collective action and between theory and pedagogy, Mohanty highlights the importance of decolonizing and democratizing feminist practice, the crossing of borders and the relation of feminist knowledge and scholarship to organizing and social movements. Mohanty thus offers a sustained critique of globalization and urges a reorientation of transnational feminist practice towards anticapitalist struggles.[14]

One of Mohanty's central endeavours has been to put issues of race and racism at the heart of feminist politics. She thus illuminates how race cannot simply be added onto gender as another cumulative dimension of oppression but that ideologies of masculinity, femininity and sexuality themselves are racialized. In this, she calls for a feminist and postcolonial approach that is geographically and historically specific. For her, the most valuable kind of feminist research is that which avoids specious generalizations about 'Third World Women' or 'Women in Africa' and instead takes the lived experiences of specific women as a basis for understanding and theorizing. In this regard, labels and definitions must never be used unthinkingly because they have the power to produce constructions and understandings of gender and race as well as to reflect them.

Another of Mohanty's goals has been to make explicit and effective the links between scholarship and activism. To do this, she argues, one must acknowledge differences between women (and avoid universalizing narratives) while building coalitions and solidarities. It is possible, she asserts, to build feminist solidarities across national, racial, class and sexual divides, but only if one can understand and theorize how the lives of both privileged and marginalized women are interconnected through global processes. For Mohanty, then, the politics of location matter. That is, she suggests that our personal backgrounds, experiences and the identities we adopt (or have projected onto us) have political and theoretical implications with which we must engage. Thus, she often reflexively explores her multiple identities: she is a member of the secular elite in India, a foreigner in Nigeria and a woman of colour in the USA. In such self-reflexive moments, she illustrates how these identities have informed and continue to inform her feminist politics and scholarship. This is in keeping with Mohanty's constant efforts to place experience at the heart of her work.

Some of these issues are captured in *Nervous Conditions* (1988) by Tsitsi Dangarembga (born 1959), a novel which focuses on how Zimbabwean women can find collective and personal voices in a patriarchal society suffering from the effects of colonization. The title of the novel is taken from the Preface by Jean Paul Sartre (1905–80) to Frantz Fanon's *The Wretched of the Earth* (1963) – 'The Condition of Native Is a Nervous Condition' – in which Sartre writes about the psychosocial effects of colonization.[15] Thus, illness is a pre-existent, thematic condition under which the events of the novel take place. For Nyasha and Tambu, the two young protagonists of *Nervous Conditions*, the nervous condition of nativity results not only from colonization but also from the regulation of women and the restrictions imposed on girls. Their attempts to function in a society that does not allow them socially acceptable verbal or written outlets as educated, African women result in their being punished for inappropriate expressions of dissatisfaction and anger. As such, the effects of colonization permeate the text, which examines a plurality of nervous conditions, especially sexual colonization resulting from the social construction of male privilege within African society. Tambu's coming-of-age story takes place within this context and charts the resistances of various female characters within her extended family to the multiple oppressions of sexism, racism, colonialism and capitalism.[16]

Nervous Conditions is set in Rhodesia in the late 1960s and early 1970s, and it centres around Tambu and Nyasha, two cousins who, until their early teens, lead very different lives. Tambu was raised on her family's farm in Umtali where she was responsible for household chores, gardening and caring for her younger siblings. Tambu's dreams of getting an education are only fulfilled when her brother dies and she becomes next in line for school since she has no other brothers. She is allowed to stay with her aunt and uncle while she attends school at the mission. While there, Tambu shares a room with her cousin, Nyasha, and the girls grow together, although in different ways. These differences arise out of class and economic variations, but also because Nyasha has spent most of her formative years in England while her mother and father were attending university. When she returns to Rhodesia, she realizes the vast differences between European culture and African culture, and she experiences inner turmoil as she tries to come to terms with being a woman in a highly patriarchal society. As we see Nyasha's struggles through the eyes of Tambu, Dangarembga depicts the continuing devastation countries are experiencing as a result of colonization by another culture.

In her important article on *Nervous Conditions*, Pauline Ada Uwakweh argues that 'silence is used as a patriarchal weapon of control'. She further explains how 'voicing is self-defining, liberational, and cathartic' in light of the fact that 'women are treated as second-class citizens'.[17] Dangarembga, Uwakweh argues, takes up issues such as female sub-ordination and its intersection with colonization within the Rhodesian context. Uwakweh explores the theme of male dominance in the text and argues that the character Tambu is the reader's guide to the construction and maintenance of male power in the society. Tambu, as narrator, holds an 'interpretive position', for her point of view offers a perspective that is necessary for the reader's appreciation of the insights she acquires about her experience as a girl in a patriarchal and colonial society.[18]

From this perspective, Uwakweh suggests that Dangarembga's novel belongs to a special category of women's writing that consciously challenges the male hegemony of Zimbabwean society. Dangarembga's use of the autobiographical mode makes her work self-referential and, in so doing, she is able to find a voice in the male-dominated Zimbabwean literary circle. Thus, *Nervous Conditions* explores how women in Zimbabwe must not only liberate themselves from the influences of colonial rule but also fight the effects of patriarchal traditions in the history of their culture. Dangarembga's portrayal of the five women in the novel, then, becomes a striking reminder that Zimbabwean women are under a double yoke when it comes to making their voices heard. In light of these five women, Uwakweh proposes three categories of female characters in the novel: 'the "escaped" females, the "entrapped" females, and the "rebellious" females'.[19] Uwakweh presents Tambu and Lucia as those who have escaped, Tambu's mother and Aunt Maiguru as those who are entrapped, and Nyasha as the rebellious woman. Other critics, though, have questioned whether Lucia has truly 'escaped' because she is still dependent on Babamukuru's money to gain her independence.[20]

The problem of women finding a voice is also the subject of Trinh T. Minh-ha's book *Woman, Native, Other: Writing Postcoloniality and Feminism* (1989). Minh-ha's text offers a feminist perspective on the social status of women (considered as Third World inhabitants) in a post-feminist society by using the concept of writing. Writing the self as a native woman is, for Minh-ha, a way for her to engage in a feminist project that is not defined or regulated by Western academics. She thus pieces together many passages of text (and photographs) alongside her own thoughts and ideas to develop a method of writing that expresses a nuanced liberationist discourse from the perspective of the native woman. Women of colour, she states, must 'write themselves' in the convergence of gender, race, ethnicity, class, displacement and colonization. Consequently, she iterates the importance of

> ■ Writing in the feminine. And on a colored sky. How can you inscribe difference without bursting into a series of euphoric narcissistic accounts of yourself and your own kind? [...] Feminism can be iconoclastic and all the more so when it calls itself Third World. But we have all let ourselves be infected with the leprosy of egoism, which remains the most difficult disease to cure [...]. A distinction needs to be made between 'Write yourself. Write your body' and write about yourself, your body, your inner life, your fears, inhibitions, desires, and pleasures. The first refers to a scriptive act – the emergence of a writing-self – the second, to a consolidation of writing from the self.[21] □

Here, Minh-ha asks how a native woman can 'write the self' while avoiding the navel-gazing process of egotistical and narcissistic reflection. A way of traversing this pitfall is by refusing to write *about* the self and, instead, to develop as an author who writes *from* the self. This distinction is crucial, for a text *about* the self runs the risk of pointless self-analysis, while a text *from* the self draws on personal experience but does so in a contextual and relational framework. To put this simply, writing *from* the self is writing with other people in mind.

Minh-ha therefore suggests that feminist criticism and theory must remain sensitive to the postcolonial processes of cultural hybridization, decentred realities and fragmented selves. In short, she argues that women of colour have multiple identities based on a variety of marginalizations. Thus, the native woman must write about and express those marginal positions in her own voice through a language of rupture. For Minh-ha, then, the challenge of the native woman is to subvert patriarchal and colonizing language, while also paying particular attention to the silences that surround utterances. She writes,

■ Within the context of women's speech, silence has many faces [...]. [S]ilence can only be subversive when it frees itself from the male-defined context of absence, lack, and fear as feminine territories. On the one hand, we face the danger of inscribing femininity as absence, as lack and blank in rejecting the importance of the act of enunciation. On the other hand, we understand the necessity to place women on the side of negativity and to work in undertones, for example, in our attempts at undermining patriarchal systems of values. Silence is so commonly set in opposition with speech. Silence as a will not to say or a will to unsay and as a language of its own has barely been explored.[22] □

Minh-ha makes reference to the complexities of silence in the lives of native women. Silence is, as she points out, one way for the native woman to resist participation in the discourses of patriarchy; in this, silence rejects masculinist modes of expression. However, the native woman who remains silent also runs the risk of being spoken for by the other, so silence can lead to appropriation. This is because her multiple positions of marginalization (woman, native, other) will then be overwritten and spoken for by non-native men and women with their own agendas. In this situation, the issues surrounding native women are potentially erased by the dominant discourses of patriarchy or the counter-discourses of white Western feminism.

As we have seen, postcolonial writing regularly scrutinizes the oppressive effects of discourses of power on native women. This continues to be a highly charged and key facet of the postcolonial project. These debates address the fact that women have sometimes been silenced under colonial rule and have not always gained a voice after liberation. In particular, many postcolonial writers ask how native women can (or should) express themselves in order to be heard. For some, the answer is to develop a new way of writing from the self that merges critical and creative discourses. For others, the answer is to inspect the growth of the self within a particular context.

The following chapter on 'queerness' expands on many of these ideas. We will thus look at criticism that documents the structuring of homophobia by masculinities that become normative in colonial and postcolonial nationalisms. Indeed, as we will see, the rise of queer theory in the academy alongside postcolonial criticism has led to a recent convergence of these two approaches. By informing each other, the combination of these theoretical paradigms has engendered a retracing and reinterpreting of a range of discourses on same-sex love across non-Western cultures. Such criticism, we will note, develops strategies to enable a discussion of same-sex love, desire and sexual relations, especially as these have been reformulated in the colonial and postcolonial periods.

CHAPTER TEN

Queer

Over the past 15 years or so a mode of cultural criticism known as queer theory has gained influence as a perspective that investigates existing categories of sex, gender and sexual desire. Specifically, queer theory highlights ways of thinking about fixed sexual identities like heterosexual and homosexual and essentialist notions of sexuality and genders within Western cultures. As a result, in the words of Peter Brooker, 'queer theory is not [...] a separatist movement claiming an essence of gayness. Rather, it emphasizes the constructedness, plurality and ambivalence of sexual identities'.[1]

In *Postcolonial, Queer: Theoretical Intersections* (2001), editor John C. Hawley suggests that the postcolonial issues of race, nationalism and gender intersect with queer theory on questions of power, oppression and hierarchical relations. In this, Hawley raises important queries about queer subjectivity, as well as the limits and strengths of queer theory, to inform an understanding of same-sex desire, sexuality and sexual expression within a postcolonial context. Queer theory can, Hawley proposes, expand theoretically into the realm of postcolonial studies in order to be more comprehensive in its approach to sexuality. A queer approach can avoid colonizing impulses and begin to unite with postcolonialism to inform a broader discussion about sexualities around the globe. 'Some queer theorists', Hawley writes, 'at times find themselves resistant to the seemingly deeply ingrained homophobia of much postcolonial culture and discourse; many of those in postcolonial studies decry gay/lesbian studies as "white" and "elitist".'[2] Hawley addresses this binarism and identifies the division between these theoretical approaches as limiting, false and mutually destructive.

For Hawley, then, postcolonialism can inform queer theory and thus challenge limited forms of sexual identity politics. In so doing, postcolonial approaches can query uniquely Western conceptions of sexuality and caution against a colonizing 'gay' or 'lesbian' identity that might function to erase global cultural differences. Euro-American concepts of 'gay' and 'lesbian' rights, as they have emanated from the United States, are unique to a specific cultural and national context and, therefore, studies of sexuality in the 'non-western' world cannot assume the presence of gay and lesbian identities as a lens for understanding same-sex relationships around the globe.

Hawley maintains that postcolonial theory can help scholars investigate the discourses that are beginning to emerge in the non-western world around the topic of sexuality. From this perspective, critics can engage in more complex discussions about the ways in which postcolonial studies can connect with queer theory to enhance an ongoing international debate on the interaction between race, class and sexuality. The combination of these two theoretical paradigms can, in other words, help us to understand how sexuality and race are fluid categories of identity with multiple points of contact.

But Hawley also warns against the potential colonizing discourses of queer theory. The study of sexuality in the West can, he asserts, function as a colonizing imperative whereby theorists in North America and Europe judge the level of 'progress' of another country by its advancement of lesbian and gay rights, which are a uniquely Western phenomenon. Within this discourse, the standards of the United States become the benchmark that other countries must live up to, and thus the Western nation is seen to lead the way in the race for a gay and lesbian utopia. Hawley, though, demonstrates how queer theory can join with postcolonial studies so as not to erase global differences and imperial power relations around the issue of same-sex desire. He then shows how emerging subjectivities associated with same-sex desire can address 'the growing need for postcolonial theory to engage with gender theory (and, more specifically, queer theory) to enrich its ongoing consideration of race and class'.[3]

Hawley notes that the convergence of postcolonial and queer theories emerges out of studies that have examined the role of homosexual exploitation in colonial history. In this work, the site of the body has been the focus for some of the criticism that joins postcolonial literary criticism with the study of homosexuality. This is perhaps not surprising when we consider how the body is both racialized and sexualized, but recent critics like Christopher Lane have also explored how the body is 'naturalized' in a heterocentric culture. There are, he argues, powerful discourses that characterize particular uses of the body as 'natural' or 'unnatural', normal or abnormal. In addressing these discourses, some critics have focused on affiliated subjects such as disease and sexual acts, while others have turned to figurative images in which the tropes of the body are explored in detail. Christopher Lane's book *The Ruling Passion: British Colonial Allegory and the Paradox of Homosexual Desire* (1995) is representative of this figurative and tropic approach. Indeed, Lane studies colonial narratives in which homosexuality must 'fall out of representation to allow other meanings to prevail', and thus the body itself, though never absent as a figure, is displaced in favour of colonial mastery.[4]

In his introductory chapter, Lane admits that he could not have written *The Ruling Passion* had he not 'relinquished the fantasy of uncovering or recovering a single and self-evident "colonial homosexuality" in British literature'.[5] Once this fantasy was abandoned, though, Lane states that he was able to examine how colonial factors were brought to bear on the symbolization of masculinity and homosexuality. In this, he argues 'that we miss a crucial element of colonial history when we ignore or dismiss the influence of unconscious identification, fantasy, and conflict on these political events'.[6] Using a psychoanalytic perspective, then, Lane analyses British colonial narratives to highlight the repressed, displaced and 'hidden' in the literary texts. Thus, his purpose is 'to interpret the influence of resistant and generally unassimilable homosexual drives, proposing that sexual desire between men frequently ruptured Britain's imperial allegory by shattering national unity and impeding the entire defeat of subject groups'.[7]

The narratives that Lane reads are diverse and varied, ranging from texts by Rudyard Kipling (1865–1926) and Rider Haggard to E. M. Forster and Ronald Firbank (1886–1926). In his exegesis of Kipling's writing, for instance, he describes how the author asserts the need to restrain all sexual desires in the colonial setting. Such repression, he suggests, leads to a profound distrust of women, and engenders a series of homosocial displacements. In Kipling's 'economy of masculine desire', Lane writes, 'heterosexual desire characteristically disrupts the intimacy that men foster for each other, compelling same-sex friendship (or homophilia) bitterly to engage with the "disloyalty" that cross-gender interest precipitates [...]. Fraternal bonding thus is a redemptive camaraderie against the debilitating influence of women.'[8] This, then, inspires Lane to analyse Kipling's depictions of male attachments as sexually charged and marked by deeply erotic bonds. Likewise, Lane's chapter on Joseph Conrad focuses on the homosocial business relationship between Morrison and Heyst in Conrad's novel *Victory* (1915). Here, Lane sees a homoerotic association linked to Heyst's relationship with his father, and the chapter puts forward the notion that Schomberg's competition with Heyst masks a homoerotic desire. In this, Lane's book uncovers a variety of unique same-sex bonds and, in so doing, the author 'outs' hidden homosexualities in the texts.

Lane's book looks at colonial narratives that are marked by questions of homosexuality and same-sex desire. Such work forms a basis for more recent postcolonial criticism that has explored contemporary literature by authors who incorporate same-sexuality into postcolonial narratives. One such author to attract the attention of both postcolonial critics and queer theorists is the Trinidad-born writer Dionne Brand (born 1953), whose novel *In Another Place, Not Here* (1996) responds politically and poetically to forms of oppression that include homophobia alongside imperialism, racism and sexism. Here, Brand constructs an expressionistic version of selfhood that moves between gendered, sexualized and racialized forms of subjectivity. The novel is set in the Caribbean and Canada and follows two women, Elizete and Verlia, through a series of nomadic movements that include immigration, desire and death. But more important is the fact that Brand composes a lesbian love story that disseminates anti-colonial and anti-racist politics. As a result, the themes of desire, home and colonization are developed through the characters' movements, but as the title indicates the search for a sense of belonging in a particular place is perpetually deferred.

Verlia and Elizete meet while cutting cane on a Caribbean island that is reminiscent of Grenada. The narrative moves back and forth between the Caribbean and Canada, as the characters look for a homely place where they can claim a coherent lesbian subjectivity. But the narrative suggests that this goal cannot be achieved, for the characters are confronted with forms of oppression that displace them from a clearly defined sense of home. All they can turn to is the metaphorical and imaginary home that is created through political struggle and commitment.

Caicou is the cane field where the two women meet and this setting is intimately connected to the growing attraction that Elizete feels for Verlia. The sweetness of the sugar becomes an important symbol for their love and desire, thus connecting both women to the landscape that surrounds them. Elizete describes Verlia in the following way:

■ That woman like a drink of cool water. The four o'clock light thinning she dress, she back good and strong, the sweat raining off in that moment when I look [...] I see she. Hot, cool and wet [...]. See she sweat, sweet like sugar.⁹ □

In this passage, the sensual images of sugar and sweetness combine with the brutal images of sweat and forced labour, reminding us of the history of colonization and slavery. The women, then, are located in the historical frame of the sugar fields (that were once worked by slaves), while this place is also the ground upon which they can develop a loving relationship. For the critic Heather Smyth, Brand's novel 'invokes the Caribbean landscape for at least two purposes: it uses sensual imagery that firmly situates the women's love in Caribbean space; and it links Elizete's body to the landscape to provide a means of fantasizing her resistance'.¹⁰

But after Verlia's death (she is killed during the US invasion of the island), Elizete enters Toronto illegally, seeking a more precise, less haunted, memory of Verlia, and hoping to free herself from the exploitation and slave-like labour practices that she experienced in the Caribbean. But Toronto does not offer the liberation or the sense of belonging that she seeks. Instead, the city is defined by consumerism and materialism – a place where people are exploited and subject to the enslavement of degrading, underpaid work. The ugly hierarchies of Toronto, then, erase any possibility that the city might offer immigrants a comforting embrace or a haven for the dispossessed. 'They were Third World people going to the white man country', explains the narrator. 'That in itself lowered them in their own estimation, they could not hope to look forward to being treated right. Already what affected them was getting an inhuman quality [...]. They felt each morning as someone trundling a wheelbarrow and pulling a donkey as sleek cars whipped by.'[11] The book explores these troubled definitions of Black identity and does so in a way that blurs together forms of identity – national, sexual, racial – and unveils the persistence of Empiric powers that are not limited by borders or territories.

One of the most compelling critics of Dionne Brand's writing is Peter Dickinson, who asserts that Brand's work 'struggles to inscribe her national and sexual experiences in historically defined representational forms'.[12] In fact, throughout his book *Here is Queer: Nationalism, Sexualities, and the Literatures of Canada* (1999), Dickinson synergizes postcolonial and queer theories to analyse Brand and other writers as linking sexuality and politics with a sense of place and nationhood. In his introduction, for instance, Dickinson writes that his criticism seeks 'to juxtapose against the predominantly nationalist framework of literary criticism in this country [Canada] an alternative politics, one propelled by questions of sexuality and, more often than not, homosexuality' (3). With this aim, Dickinson reads a selection of postcolonial texts that challenge binaristic conceptions of sexuality and are deeply rooted in the politics of 'queerness'. Dickinson's analyses of Canadian postcolonial literature push the boundaries of criticism, for he is as much at home using theoretical paradigms to develop his own particular line of inquiry as he is comfortable discussing Canadian writing and its canonization. In responding to the question posed by Northrop Frye (1912–91) about Canadian literature ('where is here?'), Dickinson offers a frank answer: here is queer. This, then, enables him to merge 'different imaginative models of identity', while highlighting the complexities of identity posed by the term 'queer', in an examination of the 'textual dissemination of contemporary Canadian, Québécois, and First Nations literatures' (3). Such an analytical frame incorporates national and sexual notions of self and highlights the sensitivity with which we must treat the various nations – Québec, English Canada and First Nations – within the fragmentary state that is Canada.

Dickinson's *Here is Queer* also unveils the colonizing heterosexist ideologies that underpin conventional literary criticism on Canadian writing. He points out that the rhetoric used by critics has often been both homophobic and misogynistic: words such as 'virile', 'active' and 'masculine' have been used to canonize texts and, in effect, determine literary worth as that which is 'manly' and 'potent'. The essentializing discourses found in this kind of criticism have, Dickinson argues, engendered the canonization of heterosexual male writers and influenced creative production as well as the social construction of literary institutions. This argument is demonstrated in a case study in which Dickinson analyses the critical reception of the gay Québécois playwrights Michel Tremblay (born 1942), René-Daniel Dubois (born 1955) and Michel Marc Bouchard (born 1958). Here, he demonstrates the concord between theories of sexual and national oppression, which foregrounds the centrality of sexuality in nationalist rhetoric as something that is central to the reception of twentieth-century writing. As a result, Dickinson points to the problems arising from adopting a relatively unified notion of the nation when discussing Québécois literature. And thus we are led to query how a playwright's conception of the nation reflects his or her depictions of sexuality.

Such issues, though, range well beyond Québécois or Canadian literature, and they are taken up in Jarrod Hayes's book *Queer Nations: Marginal Sexualities in the Maghreb* (2000), which is largely based on Hayes's analyses of postcolonial Maghrebian novels. (The Maghreb is loosely defined as the region in northwestern Africa colonized by France; it is centred on Algeria, Morocco and Tunisia.) But Hayes's work goes far beyond literary criticism, for he brings together a range of sophisticated theoretical paradigms, including postcolonialism, queer theory, feminism and psychoanalysis. Hayes begins his study by arguing that the dominant discourses and narratives of nationalism frequently depend upon the exclusion of personal stories of sexuality in the Maghreb. In fact, Hayes suggests that national narratives in this region at times depend upon the repression and sublimation of marginal and dissident voices in favour of homogenizing and heterocentric stories. As a corrective, Hayes seeks to recuperate lost voices and, in the process, promote an alternative form of postcolonial nationalism that acknowledges plurality, dissidence and hybridity as vital elements of national histories.

Hayes argues that the recuperation of lost voices and experiences should begin with readings of Maghrebian postcolonial literature. Authors from this region, he suggests, have insisted on telling stories that have been suppressed, including accounts of sexual dissidence, marginal sexualities and gender insubordination. Maghrebian fiction, then, includes counter-discourses that contradict the 'official' dominant discourses of the nation and offer inclusive perspectives that challenge nationalist stories. In this, Hayes demonstrates how novelists can 'queer the nation' by foregrounding the margins and breaking silences in order to question hegemonic social realities within a postcolonial nation. But Hayes also demonstrates how writers such as Tahar Ben Jelloun (born 1944), Tahar Djaout (1954–93) and Assia Djebar (born 1936) do not simply erase the dominant narratives of their nations. Instead, they rearticulate national narratives by recuperating memories, histories and identities that have been dismissed or buried. For Hayes, these novelists present nuanced stories of nationhood – stories that are more complicated and ambiguous than the 'official' national histories.

Breaking the silence is, then, central to the fiction that Hayes analyses. He thus reveals the power of the voice and the repression that is involved in silencing queer identities, marginalized sexual practices and alternative forms of masculinity or femininity. Hayes poses vital questions: How can we hear that which has been silenced? And how can we study silences given the marginalization one must assume is always present in the dominant narrative? Hayes addresses these questions in the openness of his approach. For he refuses overarching metanarratives and he breaks down the divisions between fact and fiction, novel and autobiography, history and memory, the real and the unreal. This, then, sheds light on the political possibilities of queerness; by exposing the queer and the marginal within the nation, Hayes argues that authors can engage in an important movement of historical liberation and emancipation. Such an assertion can only be accomplished by resisting full narrative closure, Hayes suggests, and therefore he avoids imposing a new disciplining and unifying framework by addressing the multiple dimensions of inequality and privilege.

A good example of Hayes's reading practice can be seen in the chapter titled 'Skeletons in the Closet'. Here, he focuses on the writing of Tahar Djaout, a writer who was assassinated in 1993 because of his criticism of both the religious right and the military elite in Algeria.[13] In his novel *Les chercheurs d'os* (*The Bone Hunters*, 1984), Djaout composes an allegorical narrative that exposes cover-ups in the country's recent past and attempts to articulate that which has been silenced. At a crucial moment in the novel, the protagonist unveils national secrets after he digs up the remains of his politically radical brother. However, the nationalist postcolonial authorities fear that this unearthing will threaten the national order, so they force the protagonist to rebury his brother in a much deeper grave. What is clear is that the authorities wish not only to suppress how this man was killed; they also seek to silence his queerness, for he was a gay man who believed in sexual equality. The highly charged symbolism of the act of burying and unburying is present throughout the novel. These images are used to express the political repression of a postcolonial nation that seeks to rewrite history and conceal the past, as well as to police sexuality by forcing gays and lesbians into the closet. Such burials are, the novel suggests, acts of subjugation by a government that wants to consolidate its power.

Djaout's *Les chercheurs d'os* brings hidden skeletons out of the nation's historical closet and reveals how homosexuality and gender are regulated and controlled. In this, the novel depicts violence and oppression as part of the foundations of postcolonial Algeria. But the text also suggests that the repression of marginal sexualities and political dissidence, as well as the postcolonial elite's willingness to consolidate rather than redistribute wealth, will come back to haunt and destabilize the nation. (This is why the skeletons need to be buried deeper.) What is so powerful about Djaout's novel is that the processes of exhumation and reburial are not just fictional or allegorical. For Djaout is referring to the practice of 1960s postcolonial Algerian leaders who unburied and selectively remembered what served their own political projects, while they also buried deeper the threatening aspects of nationalist heroes and their histories. The marginalized and disappeared memories, pasts and peoples – particularly when they are revealed – are dangerous to the nation and its official discourses.

Some of these ideas are also explored in Gayatri Gopinath's *Impossible Desires: Queer Diasporas and South Asian Public Cultures* (2005), which builds on recent criticism by non-Western scholars by merging queer theory with a postcolonial approach. This work is crucial because it questions many of the assumptions and foundations of conventional understandings about same-sex desire in non-Western contexts. By focusing on alternative sexualities in South Asia and beyond, Gopinath and others have begun to challenge the hegemony of Euro-American understandings of same-sex desire. This is a particularly important project, for the processes of globalization are increasingly imposing the Euro-American signifiers of queer desire as a blueprint for same-sex loving individuals across the globe. As the critic Joseph Massad puts it, the 'Gay international' movement in America and Europe channels queer desire through a set of assumptions and expectations that are firmly located in a Western conception of sexuality.[14] For Massad, this leads to a form of cultural imperialism that imposes a prescriptive framework of same-sex desire on cultures outside of the Euro-American axis. These assumptions include the conception of a unified 'gay' identity that is defined as being oppositional: it exists, the prescriptive discourses suggest, in conflict with heterosexuality and finds fulfilment through public visibility and in opposition to heteronormative institutions such as the traditional family and the home. This, then, privileges one particular discourse of same-sex desire and suggests that other articulations of same-sexuality are inferior because they are 'less sophisticated' and 'less developed'. Such a discourse disseminates a colonizing ideology by implying that Euro-American conceptions of non-heterosexual sexualities are more 'evolved' and, as a result, they are conceptions of sexuality that the non-Western culture must 'grow into' through the processes of 'development'.

Gopinath's *Impossible Desires* calls attention to these issues. In so doing, the text queries fixed meanings of non-heterosexual sexualities by foregrounding a 'queer diaspora' framework within the context of South Asian cultures. Thus, Gopinath engages with questions of sexuality alongside concepts such as domesticity, home, family and the interconnectedness of these concepts with the processes and conditions of colonialism, postcolonialism and globalization. The core of her argument revolves around the theorization of queerness, diaspora, impossibility and South Asian public cultures. In the introductory chapter, for instance, she focuses on the notion of diaspora as an analytical tool (a tool developed by postcolonial critics such as Stuart Hall and Paul Gilroy), and suggests that diasporic analyses are particularly relevant for understanding South Asian culture and its relationship to the South Asian 'homeland'.[15] However, Gopinath insists that the concepts of home and nation in this context are often powerfully gendered and sexualized. As a result, in order to understand South Asian nationalisms and the processes of transnationalism, it is necessary to recognize the linkages between conceptions of home and discourses of gender and sexuality.

For Gopinath, though, there is an erasure of queer female diasporic subjectivity in the public cultures of South Asia. This, then, leads to a silencing and denial that results in what she calls the 'impossibility' of women forming a queer diasporic identity. This impossibility is, she argues, intermeshed both with the fetishization of the figure of the (heterosexual) woman in patriarchal and nationalist discourses of the nation and diaspora, and the subordination of the gay male subject. However, ironically, this erasure of queer female subjectivity is a feature not only of patriarchal and heteronormative nationalist and diasporic discourses, but also of some gay male and liberal feminist framings of diaspora. More often than not, she asserts, progressive South Asian diasporic narratives foreclose, deflect or even stigmatize the possibility of the agency of female same-sex desire. As a case in point, Gopinath examines several films, including the diasporic gay male film *Surviving Sabu* (1996) by Ian Rashid (born 1965), to argue cogently that these stories negate any possibility of female queer desire. Thus, even politically progressive discourses of diaspora may inadvertently end up being complicit in conservative agendas.

Although Gopinath refers to the 'impossibility' of queer female subjectivities in such contexts, she does not give up her search. In fact, a vital part of her project is to discover 'evidence of queer diasporic lives and cultures, and the oppositional strategies they enact in the most unlikely of places'.[16] Using what she calls a 'scavenger' approach, she examines zones of cultural debate where tensions and contradictions between national sites and transnational processes are played out. In this, queer diasporic public cultures, she writes, take the form of 'easily recognizable cultural texts such as musical genres, films, videos, and novels that have a specifically transnational address even as they are deeply rooted in the politics of the local'.[17] Moreover, given the elusiveness of queer expressions as far as leaving documentary tracings are concerned, these public cultures extend out to,

■ encompass cultural interventions [...] such as queer spectatorial practices, and the mercurial performances and more informal forms of sociality ... that occur at queer night clubs, festivals, and other community events which allow for sexually and racially marginalized communities [to] reimagine their relation to the past and the present, and thereby, for the rethinking of what constitutes a viable archive of South Asian diasporic cultural production in the first place.[18] □

By taking this approach, Gopinath casts light on queer forms of desire that do not necessarily conform to the oppositional discourses found in Euro-American conceptions of same-sexuality. In the South Asian diasporic context, for instance, she locates expressions of queerness in patriarchal households and conventional families. For Gopinath, queer subjectivity is allowed expression outside of the ideological confines of the Western images of non-heterosexual sexualities. In other words, queer female desire might not create a separate space, for it may not seek to exist outside the domain of patriarchal and heteronormative structures and institutions. But the recognition of this desire and its 'impossibility' underscores Gopinath's challenge to what she calls the 'homonormative' expressions of same-sex desire that are dominant in Europe and North America.

Many of these issues are also taken up in the creative writing of the London author, Hanif Kureishi (born 1954). For instance, Kureishi's screenplay for *My Beautiful Laundrette* (1985) tells the story of a young Pakistani immigrant in London who opens a laundrette with his gay, white lover. The combination of postcolonial and queer issues addressed in the screenplay garnered him a mix of praise and condemnation. Some critics raved that Kureishi had successfully jointed complex questions of ethnicity with sexuality in a nuanced and multifaceted way. One reviewer, Ian Jack, for instance, wrote that this is 'at last a story about immigrants [in England] which shows them neither as victims nor tradition-bound aliens. Kureishi has composed complex characters who have spirit and determination'. However, other critics condemned Kureishi for portraying the London Pakistani community in a negative manner: he was, they argued, depicting immigrants as homosexuals and drug dealers, and thus presenting negative stereotypes of the Pakistani community for British and American audiences. Kureishi has responded to such critiques by saying that he is not an ambassador for a minority community, but that he seeks to depict the sometimes difficult realities of racism, homophobia and class divisions.

Indeed, Kureishi continued to merge representations of queerness and diasporic ethnic identities in his semi-autobiographical novel, *The Buddha of Suburbia* (1990). Here, Kureishi tells the story of the adolescence of Karim Amir, who considers himself 'an Englishman born and bred – almost'. As he grows up in south-east London during the 1970s, Karim is faced with the complex identity of being the son of a mixed Asian-English marriage. Through Karim, Kureishi explores what it means to be Asian in Britain, and engages with the themes of divorce, homosexuality and class membership.

The narrative is told from the perspective of Karim, a sensitive teenager, who is, at the beginning of the text, confused about his sexuality and feeling displaced because of his father's relationship with a mistress. Karim's father, Haroon, is the 'Buddha' of the title, for Haroon has for years been happy to live like an Englishman but now presents himself as a New Age guru. In the opening chapter, Karim meets Eva, his father's English lover. This has major repercussions for Karim, for he becomes infatuated with Eva's son, Charlie, who later gains fame as a singer in a punk band. Eva also introduces Karim to important people in the theatre world. But as an actor Karim is asked to play Indian parts and is persuaded to fake a strong Indian accent, much to his embarrassment. In this, the text captures racial stereotypes and racism, while simultaneously depicting the 'us' and 'them' discourses faced by the immigrant community.

In the next chapter, the emphasis shifts slightly, as we will consider the trope of haunting – a trope that has been extremely prominent in postcolonial writing over the last 30 years. As we shall see, the haunting figures of postcolonial literature mix together two destabilizing and subversive textual traditions: the gothic and the postcolonial. Thus, we will explore the disturbing images of spectral presences, monstrous bodies and lingering traumas.

CHAPTER ELEVEN

Haunting

Toni Morrison's novel *Beloved* (1987) is about the haunting effects of slavery. Sethe, an escaped slave, must deal with this haunted life, from the burning scars on her skin to confronting the spirit of her dead daughter who refuses to rest in peace. For Sethe, slavery does not end when she reaches the free state of Ohio or even after the Emancipation Proclamation (1862) or the American Civil War (1861–5). Instead, it continues to impede her freedom in the ghostly presences that persist throughout her life. Her experiences as a slave have left her deeply wounded – physically, psychologically and emotionally – and she suffers from the traumas of extreme violence and repeated abuse. More importantly, though, when the bond-men arrive in Ohio to force Sethe and her children to return to the Southern plantation, she chooses to murder her daughter, Beloved, rather than allow her child to experience the nightmarish bondage that has been so destructive to Sethe's life.

But the baby ghost of Beloved returns to haunt Sethe, turning her house, 124 Bluestone Road, into a haunted space. The novel opens with a description of this place:

> ■ 124 was spiteful. Full of a baby's venom. The women in the house knew it and so did the children. For years each put up with the spite in his own way, but by 1873 Sethe and her daughter Denver were its only victims. The grandmother, Baby Suggs, was dead, and the sons, Howard and Buglar, had run away by the time they were thirteen years old – as soon as merely looking in a mirror shattered it (that was the signal for Buglar); as soon as two tiny hand prints appeared in the cake (that was it for Howard).[1] □

As this opening passage indicates, Sethe lives in a haunted house. But the reader soon realizes that the haunting does not only arise out of the spectral figure of the murdered child. For Sethe is also haunted by the history of slavery; by the brutality of her life on the Sweet Home plantation, as well as the more generalized legacy of the African American experiences of forced labour, violent repression and the horrors of the Middle Passage. In this, Sethe is haunted by the history of the European colonization of Africa that was fuelled by the buying and selling of Africans in order to maintain the economic profits derived from slavery.

Morrison, then, uses haunting in her novel to explore how the violence of the past continues to exist in the present. As such, she is in line with other postcolonial writers who invoke spectres and ghosts to represent the devastating effects of colonization and slavery. Indeed, the literary critic Liliane Weissberg notes that haunting is a common characteristic of African American and postcolonial literature – a characteristic that Morrison's novel both invokes and furthers. In her article on the 'gothic spaces' of *Beloved*, she writes:

> ■ Introducing Beloved in *Beloved*, Morrison is, indeed, not only restoring Black history via Black folklore, but also reworking the white tradition of Gothic literature in writing the history of its ghosts. But Morrison's use of the gothic does more than that. While treating slaves as invisible spirits, American plantation homes – like 'Sweet Home' – are described as Gothic settings that feature slaves as invisible Blacks. Ghosts, therefore, do not signify the limitations of a white man's power, but a social order that relies on their presence. Morrison's reframing is, therefore, a political one, and it has consequences not only for the contemporary Black novel, but also for a new evaluation of the British literature of the past.[2] □

Weissberg's analysis of the novel is supported by comments made by Morrison in interviews and critical essays. For instance, Morrison asserts that the literary use of haunting offers the possibility of representing 'unspeakable things unspoken'.[3] That is, the spectral can, in some cases, capture that which is beyond language, particularly experiences that are traumatic, psychologically wounding, emotionally scarring or physically harsh.

The horrific experiences of colonization and slavery cannot be easily articulated in a comprehensible language. Racial violence, then, points to the continual eruption of indecipherable languages that attempt to utter the memories of the slave. Indeed, the narrative of infanticide in *Beloved* is just one traumatic event in a history of other traumas. How can these traumatic experiences be spoken within the limitations of language? In order to reveal the aftermath of slavery, Morrison turns to spectrality and has the ghost of Beloved speak in a disjointed and fractured language. For when Beloved speaks, she says,

> ■ I am Beloved and she is mine. I see her take flowers away from leaves she puts them in a round basket the leaves are not for her she fills the basket [...].
>   All of it is now it is always now there will never be a time when I am not crouching and watching others who are crouching too I am always crouching the man on my face is dead his face is not mine his mouth smells sweet but his eyes are locked some who eat nasty themselves I do not eat the men without

skin bring us their morning water to drink we have none at night I cannot see the dead man on my face daylight comes through the cracks and I see his locked eyes I am not big small rats do not wait for us to sleep.[4] □

The ruptures of Beloved's speech signify that which cannot be spoken: her silences are captured through gaps in the utterance, documenting a history of pain and signalling 'unspeakable thoughts, unspoken'.[5] Her words are disembodied, they echo forth from the dead, and as such her speech is broken by a lost syntax that reflects many other losses.

In his Introduction to *The Location of Culture* (1994), Homi Bhabha analyses Beloved's speech and connects it to 'the continual eruption of "undecipherable languages" of slave memory'.[6] In this, Beloved is like the other women in the text, who 'speak in tongues, from a space "in-between each other" which is a communal space'.[7] Bhabha continues,

■ They [Beloved, Sethe and Denver] explore an 'interpersonal' reality: a social reality that appears within the poetic image as if it were in parentheses – aesthetically distanced, held back, and yet historically framed. It is difficult to convey the rhythm and the improvisation of those chapters, but it is impossible not to see in them the healing of history, a community reclaimed in the making of a name.[8] □

Here, the haunting presence of Beloved is read as representing the wounds of the past and the healing of the future. From this perspective, she is both part of a communal trauma and part of the community's recovery from the brutality of colonization and slavery. For Bhabha, then, Beloved extends his explanation of the liminal or interstitial category that occupies a space 'between' competing cultural traditions, historical periods and critical methodologies. He thus utilizes a semiotic and psychoanalytic framework to examine the complexities of the 'ambivalence of colonial rule', suggesting that this ambivalence enables a capacity for resistance. In Morrison's novel, Bhabha seeks out the 'location of culture' in the marginal, haunting and unhomely spaces between dominant social formations.

Bhabha's exploration of representational possibilities of haunting within postcolonial writing is developed by Judie Newman, who connects depictions of haunting to a postcolonial form of the gothic. In her article 'Postcolonial Gothic: Ruth Prawer Jhabvala and the Sobhraj Case', Newman studies 'the ideological consequences of the transfer of a European genre to a colonial environment'.[9] Newman traces the journalistic and television mini-series portrayals of the Indian smuggler and serial killer Charles Sobhraj, and she argues convincingly from this case that

■ The duplicity of Gothic – its propensity for crossing boundaries, violating taboos, transgressing limits, together with its sense of blockage, privation and prohibition against utterance – makes it the perfect means to dramatize the horrors of the relationship between the social group which sanctions its actions by cultural forms, and the excluded from discourse, who speak by deeds [...]. By its intertextual nature [...] it prevents the univocal from holding sway.[10] ☐

Newman asserts that the gothic traits of, among other things, transgression, conflict, fear and anxiety can have political ramifications within postcolonial writing. This is particularly true in postcolonial gothic representations of haunting. After all, to be haunted is, in a sense, to be called upon, for the phantom presence returns to collect an unpaid debt. In postcolonial writing, this unpaid debt often refers back to the imperial dominance and territorial appropriation that forces the voice of the colonized into the unconscious of the imperial subject and thus haunts the colonizer across generations, time and space. Even when the colonized figure is marginalized, shut-up or excluded from dominant political discourses, his or her voice frequently returns as a phantasmic expression, an entity that haunts the colonizer from the margins, the position of Otherness. Such voices are the signifying acts of an affiliative excavation of the ghostly network of traces and hauntings that undermines the essentialist versions of national and regional cultures and enables the postcolonial subject to speak out.

The political implications of these phantoms mean that ghosts are often public figures. Although ghosts are sometimes imagined to be internalized entities, things that haunt our individual psyches, postcolonial writers also speak of collective hauntings, thus framing phantoms as figures that can haunt many of us simultaneously. This is because a community or nation shares certain fears and anxieties that appear before us as ghostly presences. In the postcolonial context, these shared ghosts are often figures of history and power, reminding us of Jacques Derrida's comment that 'haunting belongs to the structure of every hegemony'.[11] In this, Derrida correctly points out that hegemonic power is structured around a series of ghosts, so that the hierarchies of power that structure our lives are themselves ghostly. Power is elusive, imaginary and unreal, but it is also simultaneously material, present and undeniably real. For when we describe hegemonies as socially constructed, we mean that they are built on history, memory, anxiety, fear and desire. As a result, hegemonies mirror ghosts: they both rise out of the same products of our collective imaginations, and because the politics of the national, the racial, the classed and the gendered are the politics of memory and false memory, they are also the politics of spectrality.

In postcolonial writing, then, the body politic is sometimes represented as being haunted by history. By extension, the characters, narrators or authors of a text might be forced to wrestle with a host of phantoms from the past. Derek Walcott's poetic essay 'The Muse of History', for instance, includes the following passage:

■ I say to the ancestor who sold me, and to the ancestor who bought me, I have no father, I want no such father, although I can understand you, Black ghost, white ghost, when you both whisper 'history'.[12] □

This comment is, in a sense, similar to Morrison's *Beloved,* for Walcott's reflections on history lead to claims about the haunting presence of slavery as an historical residue. Thus, Walcott captures the 'psychic contamination' faced by the postcolonial subject who engages with the ghosts of a past that has been physically and psychologically violent.[13] For Walcott, then, a disavowal of the past is part of an assertion of self outside of the sins of the fathers. However, Walcott's words also suggest that disavowal will not work, for the 'whispers' of history are utterances made by disembodied voices that are, like other hauntings, unavoidable and inevitable. The whispers will return to haunt him at every turn.

Haunting also takes centre stage in the novel *Feeding the Ghosts* (1997) by Fred D'Aguiar (born 1960). This non-linear narrative attempts to find ways of telling the traumatic stories of the Middle Passage – stories that can only be told by the disembodied voices of those who haunt back. D'Aguiar's text recounts the history of the slave ship *Zong,* which was the site of a horrific massacre in 1783. Indeed, after its 1783 passage from the West Coast of Africa to the Americas, it emerged that the captain had thrown a large portion of the cargo – 132 slaves – overboard to save, he claimed, the crew and other slaves from disease. D'Aguiar's novel focuses on Mintah, a slave who is cast over the side, but who manages to survive. She is able to climb back into the ship and hide in the storeroom, where she is helped by a member of the crew named Simon. Although she is unable to stop the slaughter, she gives voice to the murdered slaves before she is sold in America and, in the end, journeys to Jamaica where she lives as a free woman.

Mintah's personal trauma, then, merges with the historical traumas of her fellow slaves, the Middle Passage and the institutionalization of slavery. Thus, the narrative resists a linear structure that would relegate pain and suffering to the past. These traumas continue to exist, for they haunt the present. D'Aguiar's narrator states,

■ We were all dead. The ship was full of ghosts [...]. There was no fear nor shame [...]. There was only the fact of the *Zong* and its unending voyage and those deaths that cannot be undone. Where death has begun but remains unfinished because it recurs. Where there is only the record of the sea.[14] □

The slaves, the crew and the historical facts of the *Zong* come back to life in D'Aguiar's novel. Although the factual evidence that the author invokes is open to question, the evidence of such crimes throughout the horrific history of the Middle Passage is solid. Indeed, the genealogy of the Black Atlantic is, in a sense, filled with ghosts. Mintha, then, speaks not only for herself and the victims of the *Zong*, but also for the many other Africans who were lost in transit or in the aftermath of slavery itself.

In dealing with these ghosts, Mintah, who was educated by missionaries, begins to write and carve. Her writing, however, proves to be ineffective, for language cannot articulate the horrors of the past. Still, she composes 'notes for herself' because the,

■ Ghosts needed to be fed. She carved and wrote to assuage their hunger. Her life of feeding the ghosts had slowed to the Sunday school, the occasional howdy from the parents of a child she taught and the odd errand run for her by the other children.[15] □

The hungry spirits need to be fed and, as result, Mintah continues to carve. At first she makes goblets and other functional items, but she soon takes to carving figures that, she states, 'harbour the past' and 'house the souls of the dead'. Although language fails her, Mintah's carving proves to be an effective way of recuperating that which has been lost in the devastation of colonization and slavery. 'These spirits are fed into wood. The ghosts feed on the story of themselves'.[16]

D'Aguiar's use of haunting, then, is connected to the 'postcolonial gothic', which John Thieme identifies with a tradition that explores the 'Gothic trace of colonialism'.[17] Within this tradition, critics like Thieme, David Punter, Justin D. Edwards, Andrew Smith and William Hughes read a series of texts from Joseph Conrad's *Heart of Darkness* (1902) to Amitav Ghosh's *The Calcutta Chromosome* (1996) as depicting the violent history of empire, a history of loss, mourning, melancholy and trauma. Here, the ground upon which the colonized subject encounters the colonizer is a haunted site, a place of spectralization, where we find the recycling of a previous demand that has been inadequately dealt with. This recycling is the basis of an economy in which return and haunting comes into play through the body of the postcolonial subject and a body of postcolonial texts that attempt to gain access to language and desire. Such attempts foreground a phantom presence that rises up out of a dark past and the desire to speak from the position of those who have been dispossessed. Yet though these returns are fundamental to postcolonialism, returns are also crucial to the gothic where haunting usually takes the contractual form of inheritance. From this perspective, the revenant and the ghostly presence are not merely the worn-out conventions of the eighteenth-century gothic. Rather, the trope of the phantom suggests what, on a political and social level, Slavoj Zizek refers to as the 'ideological apparatuses' of the return of the dead, a form of transgenerational haunting that is inherently political.[18]

In a piece titled 'Postcolonial Gothic', Glennis Byron and David Punter consider the relevance of applying the European aesthetics of the gothic to postcolonial writing. They point out that, for some critics, it might be considered problematic to relate the emergence of gothic writing (a phenomenon specifically within European texts) to regions once colonized by Europeans. However, they also argue that distortion, transgression and haunting are central to both European Gothicism as well as 'a form of "postcolonial Gothic" that has become increasingly prevalent since the early 1980s'.[19] During this time, the gothic has seeped into the 'crazed labyrinthine intricacies of Salman Rushdie's architectures' and the 'bizarre and claustrophobic worlds of Margaret Atwood'.[20]

But Byron and Punter also suggest that the postcolonial gothic is often about the haunting effects of a past that cannot be left behind. They argue that,

■ The cultures and histories of colonized nations are shadowed by the fantasized possibility of alternative histories, the sense of what might have been if the violence of colonization had not come to eradicate or pervert the traces of 'independent development' – even if, at the same time, we need to recognize that the notion of 'independence' itself is, politically as well as psychologically, a myth.[21] □

Thus, postcolonial writing is haunted by what might have been *and* what actually happened. For the brutality of imperialism has distorted (and continues to distort) the histories of colonized nations. For Byron and Punter, then, postcolonial narratives deal with history in the forms of phantoms, revenants and ghosts that return from the past to haunt the present. At the same time, though, they observe that the very term 'postcolonial' attempts to distance the formerly colonized nation from the past, for the very word 'post' suggests that which comes 'after' or an 'afterward'. Such an assertion of newness highlights a desire to distance the postcolonial region from the horrors of history and 'exposes itself precisely to the threat of return'.[22] In other words, the attempt to remake the nation in a new form inevitably points to the haunted traces of a past that has been marked by war, exile, forced transportation and brutal domination.

These ideas can be illustrated by a cursory look at postcolonial Canadian literature and criticism. For instance, Margaret E. Turner's *Imagining Culture: New World Narrative and the Writing of Canada* (1995) explores the fragments of the Canadian identity by using gothic discourse. In the first chapter, Turner invokes the expression 'Here there be monsters', a phrase used on the maps of the early Canadian explorers, as an intriguing response to the question that the critic Northrop Frye sees as being at the heart of Canadian writing, 'Where is here?'[23] For Turner, these 'monsters' were not just the 'silent void or fantastical beasts' which were thought to inhabit the new continent; they were physical manifestations of the anxiety arising out of the radical reconceptualization of the 'principles of the universe and of human being'.[24] Indeed, Turner conceives of Canadian space, even during its early conception within the European imagination, as a haunted space that invokes a crisis of selfhood and engenders an anxiety about borders, boundaries and imperial control.

The literary critic Jonathan Kertzer builds upon Turner's reflections concerning Canada's spectral spaces by turning to 'Can. Lit.' by Earle Birney (1904–95), a poem which calls attention to the fact that 'It is only by our lack of ghosts / we're haunted'.[25] In order to write of Canada's 'national ghost', Kertzer turns to gothic discourse as a way to get at a paradox within an imagined English Canadian national literature: 'we are haunted, but only by a palpable absence that marks our peculiar identity crisis'.[26] Although Kertzer, like Turner, is not interested in Canadian gothic narratives in themselves, he spins a frightening yarn by linking gothic discourse to questions of selfhood in the Canadian context. That is, by dismissing attempts to identify Canada's ghost, Kertzer exposes the fact that this spectre, whatever it might be, haunts efforts to define, and even renounce, a postcolonial national literature in Canada. 'The ghost', he writes, 'cannot be captured since it is a spectre of thought, banished by the same reflex that seeks it; but it cannot be exorcised either, even in an age of post-national theory.'[27]

In a postcolonial context, Canadian national unity is an elaborate artifice, the product of an overactive imagination. The Canadian poet and novelist Robert Kroetsch (born 1927), for instance, asserts that Canadian literature is haunted because 'Canadians cannot agree on what their metanarrative is' (Kroetsch 355). Canadians are, in other words, not unified by narratives of origins, national symbols or shared histories. Canada is a country in which most of the citizens (with the important exception of the native population) are from elsewhere. It is a nation in which the majority of people are first or second generation immigrants. It is a nation divided by its colonial ties to the British Commonwealth and the infiltration of American cultural imperialism. It is a nation divided between being a colony and a colonizing power. It is a country separated along linguistic grounds, between the French, English and the many languages of the First Nations. And it is a nation divided by ethnicity and race, between Europeans, Natives and the recently conceived 'multicultural mosaic'. Such fragmentation makes establishing a coherent Canadian identity a difficult, if not impossible, task. For the country's fragmentation leaves it with a lack of shared metanarratives to construct a unified image of the nation.

Indeed, while a national literature has the potential to knit a community together through shared national narratives, the lack of such unifying stories reveals the strain of a pluralist postcolonial society. Canada thus fails to formulate a consensus about its past, present and future. This, then, exposes the nation as an unstable ideological project. In the words of Jonathan Kertzer, 'a careful reading [of Canadian literature] discloses a nervous subtext, a figure in the carpet that reveals how the national fabric was woven'.[28] Existing as it does on the verge of collapse, we can draw a line connecting this 'nervous subtext' in Canadian literature to the doomed stable identity that is central to gothic discourse. For the Canadian splintering of self represents a reconceptualization of identity, not as a stable unified subjectivity, but as vulnerable to ruptures and divisions.

Many of these issues are raised, more generally, in Homi Bhabha's discussion of nationhood in *Nation and Narration* (1990) and his essay 'DissemiNation'. Here, Bhabha points out that the narratives of modern Western nations have often been conceived of as including an erasure of memory, a process of forgetting, that can overcome divisions and lead to national unity. In this, the modern nation is not only based on a shared language, religion, race, etc., but also derived from the repression of migration and conflicts (military, political, imperial) that might threaten national coherence. He writes,

■ The emergence of the later phase of the modern nation, from the mid-nineteenth century, is also one of the most sustained periods of mass migration within the West, and colonial expansion in the East. The nation fills the void left in the uprooting of communities and kin, and turns that loss into the language of metaphor. Metaphor [...] transfers the meaning of home and belonging, across the 'middle passage', or [...] across those distances, and cultural differences, that span the imagined community of the nation-people.[29] □

Metaphors and literary tropes such as 'the nation as one' or 'out of the many one' become important ways of negating difference within a nation and trying to establish a sense of unity and belonging. For Bhabha, the process of 'forgetting' is not the only thing that forges the fiction of nationhood. This is because he argues that the nation also creates a sense of unity by attempting to remember everything. But this attempt to remember everything ultimately leads to an overload that blocks out the past and the present. As such, there is an erasure of both historical moments and the moments of the present. This is because 'that which must be forgotten is not only a diversity of allegiance that existed in moments or centuries before the fusion of the nation into political formation – it is also the diversity that exists synchronically, in the ongoing performance of national identity, and which must be denied by any pedagogical and a priori view of nationhood that attempts to represent the nation as homogeneous and holistic'.[30]

To put this another way, the nation relies on repression to manufacture a homogeneous culture. Bhabha, though, points out that repression always leads to a return of the repressed and that, as a result, the 'unified' nation is haunted by that which has been erased. In this, the desire to deny differences within a nation engenders a move from the homely to the unhomely (the *heimlich* to the *unheimlich*), for the nation is haunted by an uncanny return of the differences that have been denied. From this perspective, the cosy home of the nation becomes a haunted house – a place where the repressed do not remain so, but return in monstrous forms to threaten the myth of the 'many as one'. For Bhabha, then, the nation is haunted by a potential rupture that will reveal national stability and coherence as a mere fiction that is disseminated out of a desire to secure the nation's boundaries against what it perceives to be the Other.

The Australian film *Vacant Possession* (1996), directed by Margot Nash (birthdate unknown), illustrates the unhomely aspects of the nation, focusing specifically on the unsettling aspects of the settler nation. In the film, the white Australian protagonist, Tessa, returns to her childhood home in Botany Bay, an 'original' place of Australian settlement. Upon arrival, Tessa finds the house is in a state of disrepair: boards are broken, paint is peeling and windows need to be replaced. During her visit, the people who live in the area come and go, suggesting that this is a fluid place without fixed boundaries or clearly marked borders. It is here, in this house, that Tessa confronts traumas that return to her in ghostly forms. This haunting arises out of a past that refuses to remain hidden, a history that fuses together personal anguish with the pain of the nation. For we discover that as an adolescent, Tessa had become pregnant after having an affair with Mitch, an Aboriginal youth who had lived not far from the house. In a racist rage, Tessa's father violently murders Mitch and disowns his daughter, banishing her from the family home.

Tessa's return coincides with the return of her father, who simply appears one day out of the blue. As the film works towards its climax, a tempest engulfs the house and traps Tessa, her father, Millie (an Aboriginal girl who lives next door) and a white cat significantly named 'Captain Cook' in the cellar. The storm forces the representatives of a personal conflict (father and daughter) to converge with a national conflict (non-Aboriginal and Aboriginal). In this, they must face each other in the darkness of the cellar as the wind shakes the very foundations of the house. Here, the ghosts of the past cannot be repressed and, as they confront their histories, the house is blown away and the cat is killed.

The ruin of the house and the demise of 'Captain Cook' are read by Ken Gelder and Jane M. Jacobs as representations of 'dispossession' and death that 'signify the successful transition into a suitably postcolonial sensibility'.[31] In fact, in their book *Australian Uncanny: Sacredness and Identity in a Postcolonial Nation* (1998), Gelder and Jacobs identify Nash's film as conjuring up the ghosts of 'Australia itself'. In this, they argue that 'the ghosts of the past unsettle only in order [...] to produce a kind of "subjective immersion"'. That is, by confronting the haunting presences, the characters are led to a reconciliation that,

■ rests on a non-Aboriginal character returning home in order to become *both immersed and dispossessed*: to become homely and homeless at the same time [...]. That is, this non-Aboriginal character is reconciled by becoming 'Aboriginal' in a postcolonial sense: immersed in the landscape, but dispossessed of property. [In the end] everyone finally gets on together, in this ultimately untroubled (the storm finally blows over) fantasy of homely cohabitation through a dispossession everyone can share.[32] □

Gelder and Jacobs explore the unsettling complexities of a settler nation that is haunted by a history of possession and dispossession. By invoking the 'uncanny', the authors highlight a slippage of the homely into the unhomely, an experience that occurs 'when one's home is rendered, somehow and in some sense, unfamiliar; one has the experience, in other words, of being in place and "out of place" simultaneously'.[33] Such a reading underlines the conflicts over land claims, property rights and ownership that continue to haunt settler nations from Australia and New Zealand to Canada and beyond.

As we have seen throughout this chapter, the trope of haunting continues to return in postcolonial writing. It is present in the articulations of traumatic events that cannot be forgotten or ignored. It arises in representations of communities that have been wounded and scarred by violence and domination. And it comes back in the unsettling depictions of settler nations that continue to house a sense of the unhomely at the heart of home – the nation. In the subsequent chapter, we will look at a related topic – memory – and consider how memories play a significant role in the writing and rewriting of postcolonial narratives.

CHAPTER TWELVE

Memory

> Do you know why people like me are shy about being capitalists? Well, it's because we, for as long as we have known you, *were* capital, like bales of cotton and sacks of sugar, and you were the commanding, cruel capitalists, and the memory of this is so strong, the experience so recent, that we can't quite bring ourselves to embrace this idea that you think so much of.[1]

This statement by Jamaica Kincaid is of course about slavery, neo-colonialism and memory. As a citizen of Antigua, Kincaid is part of a legacy of colonization and bondage that has not been forgotten. She thus asserts that the collective memory of this past has caused the people of the Caribbean to shy away from contemporary capitalism. The memory of having been capital – Africans who were bought and sold and traded – lingers on in the present.

And yet memory here is extremely complicated. For the contemporary citizens of this region do not have personal memories of the hardships, exploitation, cruelty and torture of the Middle Passage or of chattel slavery. Instead, they have stories that fill in this past – narratives that help them remember where they come from, how they were brought to the Caribbean and why they were exploited. On the one hand, Kincaid suggests that retaining this memory is important, for it offers a sense of collective identity that links the past with the present. On the other hand, though, Kincaid asserts that Antiguans have a perverted sense of collective memory: they construct an historical narrative of imperialism and slavery that describes 'a pageant full of large ships sailing on blue water, the large ships are filled up with human cargo – their ancestors'.[2] Slavery is, for Antiguans, the story of a dramatic performance, a pageant of costumes and props that is located in the realm of fantasy and false memory. This unreal story, Kincaid states, even extends to emancipation: 'The word "emancipation" is used so frequently, it is as if "emancipation" were a contemporary occurrence, something everybody is familiar with'.[3] For Kincaid, there is a danger in the way in which Antiguans remember slavery: they distance themselves from it by telling a story that moves from the grandness of the ships to the beauty of the sea to the pain of victimization to the simple fact of emancipation. This distancing, then, does not examine the collective memory of slavery in relation to contemporary life on the island. Rather, the story is firmly fixed in the past, so that connections are not made to the present.

In the postcolonial context, memory becomes an important way of uniting the past with the present and engendering a sense of national solidarity. For those nations recently engaged in the processes of political decolonization, the memories of colonization are sometimes painful, unsettling and traumatic. Decolonization, then, sometimes forces the citizens of the emerging nation to remember and articulate the acts of brutality and violence that they experienced during colonial rule. In post-apartheid South Africa, for instance, Desmond Tutu (born 1931) organized the Truth and Reconciliation Commission (TRC) hearings (1996–8), which encouraged victims to remember the violence of apartheid, articulate their pain and confront their victimizers. It also encouraged those responsible for acts of brutality to remember what they had done and offer up a 'confession' to the public and, where possible, the victims themselves. This process of remembering, articulation and confrontation was meant to nurture healing and foster national unity in the aftermath of a traumatic history. While the effectiveness of the *TRC* hearings has been the subject of heated debate, it does serve as a significant example of how memory plays an important role in the postcolonial project.[4]

The postcolonial critic Benedict Anderson has written extensively about this. In the chapter 'Memory and Forgetting' in *Imagined Communities*, Anderson argues that colonial narratives often try to influence collective memory and stories of the past by 'white-washing' the history of conflict, violence and trauma. In the American context, for instance, Anderson writes:

> ■ In 1840, in the midst of a brutal eight-year war against the Seminoles, James Fenimore Cooper [1789–1851] published *The Pathfinder* [...]. Central to this novel, is what Leslie Fiedler called the 'austere, almost inarticulate, but unquestioned love' binding the 'white' woodsman Natty Bumppo and the noble Delaware chieftain Chingachgook (Chicago!). Yet the [...] setting for their bloodbrotherhood is not the murderous 1830s but the lost forgotten/remembered years of British imperial rule.[5] □

Here, Anderson identifies a process of forgetting/remembering in national narratives which engenders 'imaginings of fraternity' and collective memories of coherence. Such a process forgets that the society was, at one time, 'fractured by the most violent racial, class and regional antagonisms'.[6] This forgetting, then, results in a re-remembering, a re-telling of the national tale, that foregrounds an imagined brotherhood and unity. Thus, within the colonial setting, there are 'changes in consciousness' and 'characteristic amnesias' that generate 'oblivions' to 'historical circumstances', making the past 'impossible to remember'.[7]

Part of the postcolonial project has been to resuscitate memories and narratives of the past that have been written over and obscured. If we return for a moment to the writing of Jamaica Kincaid, we find that the retention of memory plays a significant part in the symbolic relationship between the 'mother country' (the imperial power) and the infantilized nation (the colony). For instance, in her book *My Brother* (1997), Kincaid writes that the colonizing figure of her mother 'does not like memory' and, as a result, she teaches her children to 'have no memory'.[8] This process of erasure is a way of controlling and manipulating stories about the past – stories that might challenge the legitimacy of the mother (country) and question the social justice of the dominant power. Kincaid continues to merge the personal and the political in her examination of memory. She writes the following about her mother:

■ When I was a child, I would hear her recount events that we both had witnessed and she would leave out small details; when I filled them in, she would look at me with wonder and pleasure and praise me for my extraordinary memory [...]. As I grew up, my mother came to hate me, because I would remember things that she wanted everybody to forget. I can see clearly even now the moment she turned on me with razor-like ability to cut the ground out from beneath her children, and said I remembered too much [...]. By then it was too late to tell me that.[9] □

Here, Kincaid understands that this particular act of betrayal arises out of her mother's desire to ignore her own transgressions. Like the imperial power, she does not want her daughter to remember things because she does not want to be confronted with the negative aspects of herself. This gives rise to one of Kincaid's harshest critiques of her mother *and* colonization. For according to the symbolic logic of the text, Kincaid condemns the mother (country) for having a selective memory and intentionally forgetting the abuses of the past. By extension, Kincaid maintains that this act of forgetting has a purpose, for it erases abuse and illegitimate power and negates responsibility. Without responsibility, there can be no apology, reparation or forgiveness.

The literary critic Louise Bernard writes that the form of Kincaid's text follows the 'reconstitution of memory' that is 'inextricably tied to Kincaid's immediate identity as a writer'.[10] Bernard also points out that the structure of *My Brother* is non-linear and, as such, it follows the flow of Kincaid's memory. Indeed, the first section begins with Kincaid's description of her visit to the Holberton Hospital, where her brother Devon is dying of AIDS. The narrative then suddenly moves from an account of the circumstances surrounding her brother's death to the events of his birth. Both stages of his life, Kincaid remarks, have taken place in a hospital, for Devon is the only one of Kincaid's siblings to have been born in a hospital ward. This thematic shift from death to life (as sparked by the setting of the hospital) is typical of the way in which the events of the narrative are presented to the reader. In fact, as Louise Bernard suggests, the strange logic of this leap only begins to make sense when we realize that the narrative follows the patterns of Kincaid's memory. As readers, then, we are confronted with the idiosyncratic flow of Kincaid's consciousness. Consequently, the events of the narrative do not always unfold in a rational manner; instead, they take a circuitous route though the processes of remembrance and contemplation. Throughout the text, Kincaid writes about how she has distanced herself from her family. But she also describes how her brother's illness pulls her back into the lives of her mother and brothers. Moreover, Kincaid's return to Antigua and her shifting proximity in relation to her family sparks a plethora of memories, ranging from painful experiences in her youth to her mother's belief in the dangers of obeah practice. In fact, as memories flood back to her, the past is revived and resuscitated.

But what happens when memories of colonization are traumatic? How are these revived? Can they be resuscitated and articulated? After all, the history of imperialism is also, in part, a history of trauma. From this perspective, postcolonial writing often deals with the recollection of traumatic events, sometimes trying to heal the wounds left by colonial rule. Derek Walcott writes about these kinds of wounding memories in 'The Muse of History' when he states that writers in the 'New World',

> ■ reject the idea of history as time for its original concept as myth, the partial recall of race. For them history is fiction, subject to a fitful muse, memory [...]. Their vision of man is elemental, a being inhabited by presences, not a creature chained to the past. Yet the method by which we are taught the past, the progress from motive to event, is the same by which we read narrative fiction. In time every event becomes an exertion of memory and is subject to invention.[11] □

Walcott identifies history as a complex negotiation between memory, forgetting and fiction. This is further explained when he asserts that the traumas of colonization must, in a sense, be forgotten as a means of survival. 'In time', Walcott continues, 'the slave surrendered to amnesia. That amnesia is the true history of the New World. That is our inheritance.'[12]

Memory, trauma and colonization are also examined by the feminist critic Kali Tal. In her book *Worlds of Hurt: Reading the Literatures of Trauma* (1996), Tal notes that the memories of traumatic events often involve cultural–political movements. These movements are fluid, going 'back and forth between the effects of trauma upon individual survivors and the manner in which that trauma is reflected and revised in the larger, collective political and cultural world'.[13] Narratives of trauma, in other words, often move from the memories of the individuals impacted directly by a traumatic experience into communal narratives based on strategies of cultural coping. Traumatic events, then, can begin in the memories of individuals before becoming 'written and rewritten' within a broader community 'until they become codified and narrative form gradually replaces content as the focus for attention'.[14] After this codification has occurred, Tal argues, the 'traumatic experience becomes a weapon in another battle, the struggle for political power'.[15]

Yet the codification of traumatic events can also lead to what Tal calls the 'mythologization' of the painful experience. And this connects directly to Kincaid's critique of the mythologized 'memories' of slavery and emancipation in Antigua. For 'mythologization', Tal writes, 'works by reducing a traumatic event to a set of standardized narratives (twice-told and thrice-told tales that come to represent "the story" of the trauma) turning it from a frightening and uncontrollable event into a contained and predicable narrative'.[16] This relates back to the Antiguan communal memory of what Kincaid calls the 'pageant' of slavery. For in Antigua, she suggests, the traumatic events of bondage are spoken and re-spoken, written and rewritten, until the memory becomes codified and the narrative form replaces the content of the history. Thus, for Antiguans, the pageantry and drama of slavery become a symbol, not for the series of events that have occurred in the past, but for a set of theatrical images that reflect the formal codification of that experience. In this, Kincaid identifies a recognizable set of narrative conventions that come to comprise the memory of slavery in the region. These conventions are so well defined, Kincaid suggests, that they are reproduced in endless recombination to produce a steady stream of memories that fit into a particular narrative framework.

Memory, trauma and power are central to *Obasan* (1981) by the Japanese-Canadian writer Joy Kogawa (born 1935). The novel focuses on the recollections and experiences of Naomi Nakane, a schoolteacher living in the rural Canadian town of Cecil, Alberta. The death of Naomi's uncle, with whom she had lived as a child, leads Naomi to visit and care for her widowed aunt Obasan. Her brief stay with Obasan in turn becomes an occasion for Naomi to revisit and reconstruct in memory her painful experiences as a child during and after World War II.

Naomi's narration thus interweaves two stories, one of the past and another of the present, mixing experience and recollection, history and memory throughout. Naomi's struggle to come to terms with both past and present, confusion and suffering, form the core of the novel's plot. Memories emerge out of Naomi's early traumatic experiences of the Canadian internment of Japanese-Canadians, for the harrowing events of her youth in the detention areas have a dramatic impact on her life and create ongoing problems throughout the story. But it is Obasan who holds the keys to the past, to which Naomi must reconcile herself.[17] Naomi states,

> ■ But we're trapped, Obasan and I, by our memories of the dead – all our dead – those who refuse to bury themselves. Like threads of old spiderwebs, still sticky and hovering, the past waits for us to submit, or depart. When I least expect it, a memory comes skittering out of the dark, spinning and netting the air, ready to snap me up and ensnare me in old and complex puzzles.[18] □

Naomi then goes on to describe Obasan's relation to the past and memory as follows:

> ■ She [Obasan] seems to have forgotten [...]. I notice these days, from time to time, how the present disappears in her mind. The past hungers for her. Feasts on her. And when its feasting is complete? She will dance and dangle in the dark, like small insect bones, a fearful calligraphy – a dry reminder that once there was life flitting about in the weather.[19] □

The literary critic Cynthia Wong calls *Obasan* 'Kogawa's tale of trauma and renewal', a work that mixes painful memories of asymmetrical power relations with the postcolonial themes of territorial dislocation, diaspora and displacement.[20] Likewise, Roy Miki reads Kogawa's novel as an expression of the painful memories of racism and abuse, which is reproduced as a 'Canadianized' postcolonial text that speaks of resolution and universal values, but which refuses to forget the nation's past.[21] Miki, though, follows several other critics (Davey, McFarlane) in criticizing Joy Kogawa for not exploring the historical events that led up to the internment of Japanese Canadians. He asserts that this absence has given way to a normative reading practice that interprets this racist event as a self-contained episode. Although internment and dispersal policies seemed to come as a response to the bombing of Pearl Harbor, there are other aspects of the history that *Obasan* 'forgets'.[22] Indeed, Miki notes that there were social and political factors that had played a prominent role in the discriminatory treatment of Japanese Canadians on the West Coast of Canada and the USA since their arrival. Specifically, the uprooting of Japanese Canadians in 1942 was not an isolated act of racism, but rather the culmination of discriminatory attitudes directed towards them from the early days of settlement. The war itself offered the opportune moment for many powerful politicians and business groups, as well as individuals, in British Columbia to attack the social and economic base of the thriving Japanese Canadian community, under the guise of national security.[23] What is 'forgotten', then, is the fact that internment was not an isolated racist event and that it emerged out of larger socio-cultural relations.

Traumatic memories and diasporic identities are also explored in Smaro Kamboureli's chapter on *Obasan* in *Scandalous Bodies: Diasporic Literature in English Canada* (2000). Here, Kamboureli describes Kogawa's text as an 'allegory of social regulation intended to discipline and manage the movement of diasporic subjects'.[24] But she also argues that gender, sexuality and race are deeply inscribed forces of identification which merge with trauma and memory to constitute Naomi's complicated sense of self. Examining the force of Naomi's discursive agency, Kamboureli focuses on the way her 'historical unconscious' is written into her body as a subtext to her narrative. In addition, she addresses Naomi's silence as a result of traumatic memories and as a form of female hysteria which functions both conservatively and subversively throughout the novel. In short, Kamboureli asserts that Naomi is ignorant of what she represses and this repression, in turn, illuminates the effects of her internalized shame. Rather than interpreting *Obasan* as a text that holds much 'revolutionary' content, Kamboureli contends that Naomi's first-person narration inhabits a thoroughly undecidable social space and should incite readers to remember the history that informs her self-denigration.

Traumatic memories in *Obasan* are, Kamboureli notes, represented through a series of silences that pervade the text: 'Naomi's silence comes from the recesses of her consciousness, but the interiority of her subjectivity, like the wounds that never close, is already open to the world. So her silence may defy language's will to power, but in its elusiveness it is just as articulate as language, if not more so. It lingers on the threshold of words; neither nothingness nor a complement to language, it perpetually agitates the depths as well as the surface of things'.[25] Here, Kamboureli suggests that the text uses silence to represent painful memories in complex ways. For the text constantly refers to hidden speech and silence that covers up what has already been said and done. But, for Kamboureli, this 'silence-as-concealment' resists identity in terms of victimhood and is also motivated by self-preservation and self-protection. However, the knowledge contained by this silence builds up and accumulates weight until the concealed thematic events can no longer be held at bay. In the end, the trauma of violence, displacement and war rises to the surface.

In writing about the relationship between memory and trauma, the literary critic Cathy Caruth points out that a trauma must 'be spoken in a language that is always somehow literary: a language that defies, even as it claims, our understanding'.[26] After all, a trauma is often that which is suppressed within an individual's consciousness, so traumatic material is often difficult, if not impossible, to depict. This point is supported by Judith Lewis Herman, who argues that a trauma is outside of language and, as a result, is unspeakable and unrepresentable.[27] Moreover, traumatic experiences frequently disrupt our notions of the unknown and the knowable: a trauma may exist, unknown to us, within our minds, and to reach toward it is to grasp at something that cannot be spoken. If it can be spoken, if it can be known and put into language, then it might cease to be a trauma. Seen from this perspective, postcolonial writing often tries to speak of the traumatic events of the past. Such attempts not only reconstruct painful memories and document a history of injustice, but also, in their very articulation, seek to overcome the trauma and move on from it. If a trauma can be explained, can be represented in speech or writing, then it sometimes exorcises the trauma that has haunted the subject or the community.

Because the history of imperialism is traumatic, the postcolonial writer 'must be helped to speak the horrifying truth of her past – to "speak the unspeakable"'.[28] Thus, for the critic Ruth Leys, the articulation of a trauma not only has a personal therapeutic effect, but also 'a public collective value'.[29] Leys's comments continue the work on memory and trauma of Paul Antze and Michael Lambek, who assert that the expression of traumatic memories is political, for it includes 'a locus of struggle over epistemological issues'.[30] Indeed, the struggle over lost narratives is a political issue, for it raises several critical questions about ideology and hegemony. What has been erased from the history of colonization? Whose memories are privileged in historical narratives? And whose perspective or point of view is foregrounded in stories about the past?

The novel *Anil's Ghost* (2000) by Michael Ondaatje (born 1943) poses all of these questions by focusing on Anil Tissera, a character who is born in Sri Lanka and trained as a forensic anthropologist in the West. By recovering and reconstructing Sri Lanka's national crimes and murders (the various human-rights violations which the authorities refuse to recognize or remember), Anil attempts to recover part of herself. By going back to Sri Lanka, she faces a genealogy that has been suppressed and forgotten. Now, it seems, she must face it in order to establish her own history and come to terms with a point of origin that will, of course, always recede from her grasp. The text, then, follows her complex process of remembering – of resistance, identification, loss and pain – in relation to parental figures who are unknown, mysterious and absent.

In this narrative of recollection, we witness not an identity that is fixed and given, but improvised, constructed, negotiated in the conditions of danger and trauma.

What Anil finds is that she is still tied to Sri Lanka by her memories of the past. The ground may be unstable, with mystery lurking beneath the surface, but it is also a place that reminds her of family and ancestry. The act of remembering, which is so crucial to Ondaatje's vivid yet unsustainable memories in *Running in the Family* (1982), reappears in Anil's haunted journey. The central question that runs throughout *Anil's Ghost*, a question which remains a ghostly presence, is 'Do you remember?' It is present when Anil avoids reminiscences about her days as a swimming champion. It returns when Anil refuses to speak with Dr. Perera about her father. It is there when Anil is confronted with Leaf's Alzheimer's disease. And it is persistent in the bones of Sailor, as well as in Sarath's archaeological research. This insistent question brings together the personal and the public; it links Anil's journey to the 'secret war' of the nation and the history of Sri Lanka. It shapes Anil's search for connections, for the recovery of lost information or repressed experiences, for the details of great trauma or loss that have receded into the archives of public or private memory. This remembering is often shaded by the fear of the government, often darkened by the dull shades of grief, but in each case it is fundamentally a search for articulation and understanding, for explanations and reasons that will make things cohere and make sense. But it is also a question that is met with silence. And by remaining silent, Ondaatje's text resists the idea that traumatized material can by the mere processes of introspection and self-expression be rearranged into the stuff of causality and linear narrative. Such an ordering, the text suggests, is not possible.

If Ondaatje's *Running in the Family* is a memoir that contributes to the very act of remembering, while simultaneously recognizing itself as a narrative of fiction and fabrication, *Anil's Ghost* is a fiction that uses memory as a subject to explore the complexities of truth. For Anil soon finds that in Sri Lanka the failure of memory is blurred with the art of deception, making truth inaccessible. According to the narrator, for Anil, 'the journey was in getting to the truth. But what would the truth bring [her] into? It was a flame against a sleeping lake of petrol.'[31] As a result, Anil is forced to rethink her ideas about truth. In this place it has been, in the words of Sarath, 'broken into suitable pieces [...]. There were dangers in handling truth [...]. He would have given his life for truth if the truth were of any use'.[32] What is truth worth? Anil must ask. As a forensic anthropologist, she is taught that empirical truth is the ultimate goal. But she is compelled to rethink her training, and search for a new route by which she can enter this country, with a new map to orient herself.

Throughout *Anil's Ghost*, Palipana – the archaeologist and mentor of Sarath – is at home in the shadow of memory and that which has been lost. He thus adopts for himself the identity of 'epigraphist'.[33] Driven by his desire to speak for loss, he is forced into exile and seclusion by a society that does not want to listen. He is left in the darkness of his own blindness with nothing to guide him but the stored-up memories, experiences and histories of the nation. For this man, who has seen the splendour of Sri Lanka's past, the dreadful has already happened. It takes the blind man to see that loss in the past has been painful, and all that can happen now falls under the sign of the repetition compulsion. There is nothing new under the sun; all that can happen has already occurred due to the loss of a great ancient civilization through war and colonization. The sense of personal, historical and national loss that pervades all of the characters is a haunting presence that is tied to fear; a fear that everything bad has already happened and that these bad experiences will continue endlessly to repeat themselves.

As we have seen throughout this chapter, the postcolonial writer who captures memories often does so as a way of bearing witness to the traumatic histories of the past. These acts of remembering are recorded with the hope that abuses of power will not be repeated and that the process of articulation will enable the individual and the community to heal and move on, even though this hope is sometimes presented as fragile. In the next chapter, we will consider another aspect of the merger of cultures under colonization and imperialism – the phenomenon of hybridity.

CHAPTER THIRTEEN

Hybridity

At the end of his poem 'A Far Cry From Africa' (1962), Derek Walcott explores his double consciousness, his combination of African and European cultural identity. He states that he is 'poisoned' by the blood of both and caught between cultures. He thus poses several questions: 'how choose / Between this Africa and the English tongue I love? / Betray them both, or give back what they give?'[1] How can he give up his European language, and how can he turn away from the cries of African liberation?

Literary critics such as Bruce King have pointed out that this poem confronts the poet's ambivalent, anguished responses to the African struggle for independence – in particular, the Kikuyu insurrection in 1950s Kenya.[2] The poet hears the 'far cry from Africa' and cannot fix its meaning or interpret its significance. Does this cry come from the Kikuyu? Does it come from a white Kenyan settler? Or perhaps it comes from both. The source is difficult to determine. But Bruce King argues that this ambiguity, this confusion, also arises out of the fact that Walcott is a Caribbean poet who is the descendant of former slaves and brought up in the former British colony of St. Lucia. Thus, Walcott himself is 'a far cry from Africa' in terms of both geography and culture.[3] The poem, then, struggles to locate a place of ethical certainty from which to respond to Africa's turmoil. It recoils from the brutal violence that often accompanies the break from colonial rule, while also condemning the history of British imperialism in Africa.

It is in this context that Walcott describes himself as 'poisoned with the blood of both' and asks hopelessly, 'Where shall I turn, divided to the vein?' The trauma and bloodshed of the independence struggle presents him with an impossible choice between two versions of self-betrayal: 'How can I face such slaughter and be cool? / How can I turn from Africa and live?' These 'cries' illustrate the dilemma of the postcolonial 'hybrid subject'. For the citizens of postcolonial nations regularly find themselves caught between incompatible cultures or dispersed among multiple cultures. Walcott cannot, for instance, lay claim to a singular, unambiguous and unmixed identity. Walcott's poem, then, follows other postcolonial writers by posing significant questions about the relationship between authenticity and hybridity.

Indeed, one of the projects of postcolonial writing has been to retrieve and re-examine pre-colonial indigenous experience lost under imperialism. But given the fact that colonialism has changed native cultures radically and irredeemably, the postcolonial writer is often left to wonder if it is ever possible (or even desirable) to recreate a culture that has been changed or, in some cases, lost. For even if it were possible to return to an indigenous experience, the question remains: Would this yield an authentic identity? After all, in the Caribbean, for instance, many different cultures have converged, as the islands were settled by the Spanish, Dutch, French and English and largely populated by the descendants of Africans imported as slaves and Indians imported as servants. This diversity is captured by the speaker of Derek Walcott's 1979 poem 'The Schooner Flight' (who has red hair, dark skin and 'sea-green eyes') when he states, 'I have Dutch, nigger, and English in me, and either I'm nobody, or I'm a nation.'[4]

Throughout 'Schooner Flight', Walcott represents hybridity as a challenge to individuality. Hybridity, he suggests, can lead to a sense of dislocation and a lack of belonging that comes out of the diaspora of colonization. Who is the speaker of 'Schooner Flight'? Is he Dutch? English? African? Is he all three? This hybrid form of identity can, the poetic voice indicates, result in conflicting loyalties and identity crises. It can lead to alienation and a situation in which the hybridized subject is always outside of belonging.

But hybridity has also been invoked as an expression of resistance to colonial discourse, which often perpetuates naturalized myths of racial or cultural origin. After all, the myths of racial and cultural purity were disseminated in colonial discourse as a way of establishing and maintaining structures of difference. Hybridity, then, challenges essentialist rhetoric and offers a way of thinking about cultures that moves beyond notions of 'purity' or 'authenticity'. For example, the Australian Aboriginal writer Mudrooroo puts this quite clearly when he writes that 'the Aboriginal writer is a Janus-type figure with a face turned to the past and the other to the future while existing in a postmodern, multi-cultural Australia in which he or she must fight for cultural space'.[5] In this, Mudrooroo embraces his hybridized position not as a 'badge of failure or denigration, but as a part of the contestational weave of cultures'.[6]

Following Mudrooroo, Homi K. Bhabha argues that hybridity is not necessarily a negative by-product of colonization. He writes that 'hybridity is the sign of the productivity of colonial power, its shifting forces and fixities; it is the name for the strategic reversal of the process of domination through disavowal'.[7] Hybridity is, in other words, ambivalent, for it questions the assumptions of authenticity upon which colonial discourse is based. Bhabha continues,

> ■ Hybridity is the revaluation of the assumption of colonial identity through the repetition of discriminatory identity effects. It displays the necessary deformation and displacement of all sites of discrimination and domination. It unsettles the mimetic or narcissistic demands of colonial power but reimplicates its identifications in strategies of subversion that turn the gaze of the discriminated back upon the eye of power. For the colonial hybrid is the articulation of the ambivalent space where the rite of power is enacted on the site of desire, making its objects at once disciplinary and disseminatory.[8] □

Bhabha argues that hybridity and liminality are necessary aspects of the colonial condition, for colonial identities are always marked by flux and transition. To illustrate his claim, Bhabha discusses the transmission of the Bible in colonial India, and the way in which the Book is hybridized as it is taught to the natives.[9] The biblical stories, he observes, were changed to suit an Indian audience, thus questioning the authenticity and purity of the 'original' text. For Bhabha, this suggests how the colonial presence is always ambivalent and split between its appearance as original and authoritative and its repetition as replication and difference.

Bhabha finds a potential site of resistance in the gaps and failures at the heart of colonial discourse. As he explains,

> ■ resistance is not necessarily an oppositional act of political intention, nor is it the simple negation or the exclusion of the 'content' of another culture, as difference once perceived [... but] the effect of an ambivalence produced within the rules of recognition of dominating discourses as they articulate the signs of cultural difference.[10] □

Bhabha, then, locates the subversion of cultural authority in hybridization. Hybridity is therefore the moment in which the discourse of colonial authority loses its coherent grip on meaning and opens itself outward to the trace of the language of the other. Such a definition of hybridity identifies it as 'a problematic of colonial representation [...] that reverses the effects of the colonist disavowal, so that other "denied" knowledges enter upon the dominant discourse and estrange the basis of its authority'.[11] Domination within the colonial situation is, in short, subverted through the hybridity of colonial discourse. This is because hybridity undermines the single voice of cultural authority and foregrounds a double-voicing process that includes the trace of the other.

Hybridity, Bhabha argues, subverts the narratives of colonial power and dominant cultures. The series of inclusions and exclusions upon which a dominant culture is premised are deconstructed by the very entry of the formerly excluded subjects into the mainstream discourse. The dominant culture is contaminated by the linguistic and racial differences of the native self. Hybridity can be seen, in Bhabha's interpretation, as a counter-narrative, a critique of the canon and its exclusion of other narratives.

Hybridity as a form of colonial resistance is stressed in the postcolonial autobiography, *Halfbreed* (1973) by Maria Campbell (born 1940). For Campbell, who is a Métis ('Halfbreed') in Canada, the colonial discourse that authorizes a binary opposition between an authentic 'Nativeness' and 'Whiteness' is undermined in her experience and heritage. Indeed, as a bi-cultural figure, Campbell resists the polarity of ethnic boundaries and her presence provokes inquiries into, and a justification for, the rigid limits of a Canadian construction of ethnic difference. Powerful forces within the nation, then, seek to situate the Métis on the margins of a cultural map of ethnic difference, a map that guards against a disturbance on the smooth surface of a privileged sense of self. In fact, Maria's physical features place her on a continuum of ethnicity that exists in between these imaginary poles of identity:

> ■ My already dark complexion would go almost black during the summer. Black hair was supposed to have, as the story books went, snapping black eyes or sparkling brown ones. Mine were green. My aunts, uncles and cousins all had brown or black eyes and used to tease me for having a dark hair and skin – 'like a nigger' they said – and eyes like a white man. The Indian kids made fun of me and called me names in Cree.[12] □

Where does Maria fit in the imagined categories of 'Whiteness' and 'Nativeness'? She is called a 'nigger' by her Métis relatives; she is not accepted by the Cree children; and her physical features mix together Native and European characteristics. Maria's very presence questions the 'natural' and ontological status of distinct ethnic (and racial) identities. Her body serves as a text that shatters the language of essentialism by bringing into relief the inauthenticity of an 'authentic' sense of self. This engenders the contingency at the heart of identity that produces, in the dominant culture, endless attempts to naturalize its own position by positing the inauthenticity or secondariness of what it will construe as its others. For it is clear that Maria's hybrid ethnicity positions her on the margins of both Native and Euro-Canadian societies. Her Métis identity disqualifies her from the land treaties and official benefits organized by Native groups and the Department of Native Affairs; likewise, her 'Native' features mean that she is forced to suffer the racism of white Canada. As a result, her in-between position and the effects of marginalization become part of her strong sense of Métis identity, which she frames as a cultural construct rather than a racial subjectivity.

Indeed, cultural heritage and political disempowerment is, for Maria, a determinant of Métis experience.

Late in her narrative, Maria considers 'calling [her]self French or Spanish or anything else' that would help her to escape the cycle of poverty and pain inside Métis society.[13] Passing for 'white' is, Maria believes, a way to begin a new life. Indeed, Maria's bicultural heritage offers passing as an option precisely because her features and skin tone are a mixture of Native and European characteristics. But Maria does more than think about passing for European, she also considers passing for Native. 'The Calgary Stampede always needs Indians', Marion tells Maria, 'there's no need to go out and earn a living on the street. We can fix up outfits for ourselves, and go to pow wows, and put on for white people, and get paid.'[14] Maria is shocked to hear that she could perform a minstrel-like show for white audiences who want to see images of Natives in a state of pre-modernity. Campbell's narrative, then, exposes these stereotypes as mere fictions that rely upon performance and acting; they are not, she asserts, essential qualities of Native existence. Ironically, by considering a performance of Native 'authenticity', Maria initiates questions about masquerade and the absurdity of 'true' ethnic categories. And what Maria recognizes is that, within this model of identity, ethnic authenticity is often produced through counterfeit.

The fluidity and transformative aspects of hybridity are also highlighted in Campbell's changes of identity. This arises in performative shifts located on the surface of her body – clothing, hair, skin – to resist searches for 'inner depths' or centred subjects. For instance, when Maria is getting desperate for money, she goes to the Welfare Office dressed in the poverty-stricken clothes of a 'Whitefish Lake squaw'.[15] The welfare worker who meets her instructs her to go to the Department of Native Affairs, and, when she informs him that she is not a 'Treaty Indian, but a Halfbreed', he responds by saying, 'I can't see the difference – part Indian, all Indian. You're all the same.'[16] Here, the voice of the colonizer maintains ethnic essentialism. As a result, the discrete identities that are necessary to a dialectical resurrection of the boundaries of an 'authentic' ethnic self are reinstated in the face of shifting signification.

In his book *Colonial Desire: Hybridity in Theory, Culture and Race* (1995), Robert J. C. Young reminds us that a hybrid is technically a cross between two different species. In botany, for instance, it connotes inter-species grafting, and in the Victorian context, where different races were identified as different species, the term 'hybridization' is loaded with deeply racist assumptions. By tracing its many meanings, Young calls attention to the complexity of the word, identifying its positive and negative connotations. He points out that in current postcolonial studies, the term 'hybridity' refers to the ways in which the Victorian ideologies of race and imperialism are challenged and undermined. Even as imperialist discourses insist upon racial difference, they create cross-overs through a mix of colonial policy and transgression.

But, for Robert Young, there is also a history of negative meanings associated with the word hybridity. He notes how it was influential in imperial and colonial discourse in giving damaging reports on the union of different races. As such, Young argues that at the turn of the century, 'hybridity' was a central part of a colonial discourse of racism. For instance, in Jean Rhys's *Wide Sargasso Sea* to be a Creole or a 'hybrid' was essentially negative. The narrative describes 'hybrids' as lazy, dishonest and always on the verge of reverting to a 'primitive' way of life. In reading Young alongside Rhys, it becomes easy to see the negative connotations that the term once had.

Young, though, goes on to note that in contemporary postcolonial criticism hybridity is often seen as a 'counter-energy'.[17] From this perspective, it challenges the centred, dominant norms of colonial discourse by offering up unsettling perplexities and jarring cultural forms. The term, Young explains, is used in so many different ways that its meaning is not always clear. For instance, writing about the use of the word in contemporary Britain, Young states,

■ Today the notion is often proposed for a new cultural hybridity in Britain, a transmutation of British culture into a compounded, composite mode. The condition of that transformation is held out to be the preservation of a degree of cultural and ethnic difference. While hybridity denotes a fusion, it also describes a dialectical articulation [...]. This doubled hybridity has been distinguished as a model that can be used to account for the form of syncretism that characterizes all postcolonial literatures and cultures.[18] □

Young points out that hybridity is connected to multiculturalism, a discourse that celebrates diversity rather than the hybridized merger of one culture with another. This use of the term differs from its roots, for, in this context, the word does not describe a merger of two things, but instead it describes separate things living alongside one another.

For many postcolonial critics, hybridity is linked to mimicry. Mimicry arises, according to the authors of *The Empire Writes Back*, when the dominant culture, the colonial power, encourages the postcolonial subject to imitate the cultural values of the imperialist. To illustrate their point, Ashcroft, Griffiths and Tiffin analyse *The Mimic Men* (1967) by V. S. Naipaul (born 1932), arguing that the narrator, Kripal ('Cripple') Singh, articulates the 'distinction between the authentic experience of the "real" world and the inauthentic experience of the unvalidated periphery'.[19] In this reading, Naipaul's text explores how the dominating colonial culture privileges particular values and types of experience, while it also denies worth to postcolonial understandings of the world.

The result is that the postcolonial subject is invited to identify with the dominant culture and remove himself from the significant experiences of the postcolonial world. Naipaul's book, they write, 'contrasts the metropolitan centre, which is the location of the power which comes from the control of language but also of order itself, with the periphery of the colonial world, in which only the illusion of power exists and in which disorder always predominates'.[20]

Ashcroft, Griffiths and Tiffin suggest that the cultural hybridity of a Trinidadian writer such as Naipaul leads him to express ambiguous positions concerning mimicry and power. On the one hand, Naipaul unveils the social constructions of power that determine the centre and the margin. And, in so doing, he represents the 'centre of order' as the 'ultimate disorder', thus questioning the centre of reality that is imposed upon the postcolonial subject.[21] On the other hand, Naipaul is drawn to the centre and the illusory power that the dominant culture seems to offer. Ashcroft, Griffiths and Tiffin write that

■ Although Naipaul has one of the clearest visions of the nexus of power operating in the imperial-colonial world, he is paradoxically drawn to that centre even though he sees it constructing the 'periphery' as an area of nothingness. Yet he is simultaneously able to see that the 'reality', the 'truth', and 'order' of the centre is also an illusion.[22] □

Here, the authors call attention to the ambiguity at the heart of *The Mimic Men*. For Naipaul exposes the unjust social construction of power, but he does not completely reject it. Thus, ambivalence arises when he represents the authenticity of the margins. However, for these three critics, this ambivalence is 'by no means disabling, for it provides the tension out of which emerges a rich and incisive reconstruction of post-colonial experience'.[23]

In *The Post-Colonial Studies Reader* (1995), Bill Ashcroft revisits the notion of hybridity and reasserts its positive attributes. According to Ashcroft, most postcolonial writing has focused on the hybridized nature of post-colonial culture as a strength rather than a weakness. It is not a case of the oppressor obliterating the oppressed or the colonizer silencing the colonized. In practice, it stresses the mutuality of the process. The clash of cultures can impact as much upon the colonizer as the colonized. Even under the most potent form of oppression, distinctive aspects of the culture of the oppressed can survive and become an integral part of the new formations which arise. Ashcroft explores how 'hybridity and the power it releases may well be seen as the characteristic feature and contribution of the post-colonial, allowing a means of evading the replication of the binary categories of the past and developing new anti-monolithic models of cultural exchange and growth'.[24]

Homi Bhabha's analysis of Naipaul's *Mimic Men* further explores how hybridized forms of mimicry disrupt the colonial discourse by doubling it. For Bhabha, the simple presence of the colonized Other within the textual structure is enough evidence of the ambivalence of the colonial text, an ambivalence that destabilizes its claim for absolute authority or unquestionable authenticity. The text's disruption of essentialism, Bhabha suggests, discloses the contradictions inherent in colonial discourse in order to highlight the colonizer's ambivalence with respect to his position towards the colonized Other. As such, Bhabha shifts the superlative certainty of the colonizer and the strategic effectiveness of the postcolonial subject's political intentions into an alarming uncertainty. Naipaul's mimic men, he asserts, destabilize colonial subjectivity because they are authorized versions of otherness. This makes the characters 'part-objects of a metonymy of colonial desire [who end up emerging] as "inappropriate" colonial subjects … [and who], by producing a partial vision of the colonizer's presence', unsettle its authoritative centrality, and corrupt its discursive purity.[25] He goes on to write that mimicry 'repeats rather than re-presents', and in that very act of repetition, originality is lost, and centrality de-centred.[26] What is left is the trace, the impure, the artificial and the second-hand.

Bhabha's writing on hybridity is groundbreaking in that he illustrates how the colonizer and colonized are not independent of each other. However, some critics have pointed out that Bhabha's ideas tend to universalize and generalize the colonial encounter. That is, his notion of the hybrid colonized subject could exist anywhere in the colonial world, thus universalizing the colonial subject and making him homogeneous. This tendency is at odds with the concepts of ambiguity and liminality that Bhabha ascribes to the colonial experience. To put this another way, how can the colonial subject be both ambiguous and universal? Or, how can he be simultaneously liminal and homogeneous? In Bhabha's formulation, the colonial subject is internally split and antagonistic, but undifferentiated by gender, class or location.

The postcolonial critic Benita Parry has called attention to these problems in Bhabha's theory of hybridity. In her detailed critique of his work, Parry argues that he reduces all colonial dynamics to a linguistic interchange. 'What he offers us', Parry writes, 'is The World according to The Word.'[27] This word, by extension, lies with the colonizer and it is treated with notable uncertainty. From this perspective, the complexities of hybridity can only be traced through an examination of the mutations of European culture and Western colonial discourse. It does not, in other words, leave room to examine the nuances that are necessarily present in the convergence of cultures. This means that Bhabha's theory of hybridity is housed in the West, for its in-betweenness cannot be understood without reference to the ideological and institutional structures of colonization.

Furthermore, Benita Parry suggests that Bhabha's theory of hybridity removes the astringent conflicts and strains between colonizer and colonized. In this, the celebration of hybridity has the potential to gloss over the violence of the past and therefore erase key aspects of the anticolonial struggle. Struggles for independence were fuelled by injustice and marginalization that cannot be understood in the context of positive theories of hybridity. In fact, the binary opposition between colonizer and colonized was necessary for many liberation movements that succeeded in gaining independence and seizing power from the clutches of empire. From this perspective, positive theories of hybridity are potentially apolitical, for they erase the terrain upon which political action can take place.

An altogether different view of hybridity is articulated by Paul Gilroy, who links hybridity with the history of black diaspora. Indeed, in *The Black Atlantic: Modernity and Double Consciousness* (1993), Gilroy discusses the development of colonial hybridity in terms of the political and intellectual cross-fertilizations that have resulted from the black diaspora. For Gilroy, the 'movements of black people' from Africa to Europe and the Americas not only resulted in 'slavery and exploitation', but also led to the creation of groups involved in 'struggles towards emancipation, autonomy, and citizenship'.[28] Hybridity, then, becomes an important aspect of what Gilroy calls a 'black Atlantic', which he defines as an 'intercultural and transnational formation' and which 'provides a means to re-examine the problems of nationality, location, identity, and historical memory'.[29] Gilroy illustrates the cross-pollinations between African American, European and Caribbean cultures, showing the extent to which they influence one another as well as the metropolitan cultures with which they interact. New identities, Gilroy asserts, arise out of black diasporas, and these hybridized cultures must be analysed in complex ways. After all, if there is no authentic or uncorrupted white European culture, then the black subject must also be seen as a product of historical, political and cultural forces. This means that the word 'ethnicity' cannot connote stable identities or a given essence; instead, it must be viewed to be a constructed process, not a fixed entity. As a result, the contemporary black identities in Britain emerge from the 'cut and mix' process of 'cultural *diaspora-ization*'.[30]

Diasporic identities have also given rise to forms of cultural hybridity that have developed out of postcolonial migrancy. In fact, literary migration in postcolonial writing has generated the intersection and intertwining of various cultures, so that we are forced to question the very nature of what was once called 'English Literature'. Elleke Boehmer writes that

■ For different reasons, ranging from professional choice to political exile, writers from a medley of once-colonized nations have participated in the late twentieth-century condition of migrancy. We might mention the St. Lucian writer Derek Walcott, now a commuter between Boston and Trinidad; the Bombay-born Salman Rushdie; the Antiguan resident in New York, Jamaica Kincaid; the Black British writer of Caribbean descent, Caryl Phillips; the Nigerian Londoner Ben Okri [born 1959]; the now Canadian, once Trinbagonian poet Nourbese Philip [born 1947]; Amitav Ghosh, Indian but based in the United States; the South African exile in London, Lauretta Ngcobo [born 1931]; Vikram Seth [born 1952], who writes about Delhi and San Francisco with equal facility.[31] □

Boehmer suggests that the postcolonial writer is, more often than not, a cultural traveller, moving between countries and cultures. Such migrations foster connections and further develop the hybridity that was present in the era of European imperialism. 'If the postcolonial text generally is', Boehmer continues, 'a hybrid object, then the migrant text is that hybridity writ large and in colour. It is a hybridity, too, which is form-giving, lending meaning to the bewildering array of cultural translations which migrants must make'.[32]

This position is critiqued in Tabish Khair's book *Babu Fictions: Alienation in Contemporary Indian English Novels* (2001). Khair, who is a poet and novelist as well as a postcolonial literary critic, notes that expressions of postcolonial hybridity are 'based on the best of intentions', for such theories constitute a valid unveiling of the divisions within the constructed subject.[33] However, he points out that hybridity has been theorized by privileged Indian writers (Rushdie) and Indian critics (Bhabha) who celebrate hybridity within the discourse of a cosmopolitan multiculturalism. In this, hybridity is part of a valorization of plurality and heteroglossia that offers the privileged writer/critic a sense of belonging. Khair writes,

■ '[I]t is part of my contention that hybridity as a theoretical position serves not just to obscure certain Indian and global realities but is, in itself, an attempt — determined or not — by highly Westernized Indian English academics and intellectuals to escape the negative connotations of being described as alienated.[34] □

Khair notes that hybridity is defined from the centre in order to save the Indian intellectual in the West from falling into the void of alienation. In this, hybridity is 'always a familiar, self-congratulatory construct' because definitions of hybridity are always limited to the convergence of colonizer and colonized. As a result, Khair notes that the Indian whose father is Maharashtrian Hindu and mother is Bengali Muslim 'appears to be less hybrid (or even not-hybrid) simply because that kind of hybridization is not privileged in postcolonial discourse or familiar to most westernized postcolonial theorists'.[35]

For Khair, then, hybridity is a Westernized theory that privileges the centre over the margin. This idea is explored in his poem 'Unhybrid', which mixes a playful use of language with serious political issues. The second half of 'Unhybrid' includes the following stanzas:

> If you throw hard words at us like 'hybrid',
> The literate among us will hear 'hai bread'
> (The illiterate call bread 'pauroti' which
>
> Is their lost Portuguese to your learnt English —
> So they will hear nothing till others publish
> This lament for bread by a suited-booted Babu) [...]
>
> Hybrid's not really the word for them. They don't
> Attach much importance to what other people say
> In tongues strange and so funny. If they had their way
>
> Language would not overflow with meanings. You see
> Most of us have not grown up with any language — only,
> It seems, many languages have grown up with us.[36]

The title of the poem and its sentiments focus on those who are left outside of the 'official' Westernized celebrations of hybridity. In so doing, Khair's poem is in dialogue with his own criticism, particularly his theoretical claim that conventional notions of hybridity obscure the question of power. This poem, then, reinvigorates a politics of 'unhybridity' by suggesting that hybridity tends to absolve its postcolonial adherents of the need to develop strategies of political resistance. As a result, Khair's tribute to the 'unhybrid' foregrounds 'the degree to which the notion of power is obscured by most hybrid discourses', and it also signals the fact that 'only certain identities (such as the westernized postcolonial one) are perceived as hybrids or more hybrid'.[37]

In this chapter, we have looked at the many meanings and debates over hybridity. Some critics and writers celebrate hybridity as a challenge to essentialism and problematic ideas about purity or authenticity. Others, however, see theories of hybridity as potentially apolitical and monolithic. Still others argue that discourses of hybridity are voiced from the privileged metropolitan centres of the West and, as such, are detached from the rural communities of India, South Africa, Jamaica and elsewhere. In the next chapter, we will examine critical and literary responses to a topic related to hybridity – diaspora – and observe how writers have identified diasporic cultures as central topics in postcolonial studies.

CHAPTER FOURTEEN

Diaspora

The term 'diaspora' is etymologically derived from the ancient Greek word '*diaspeirein*', from *dia-*, 'across' and *-speirein*, 'to sow or scatter'. In this sense, diaspora can refer to people who have been dispersed, displaced or dislocated from their homeland due to exile, forced migration, immigration or resettlement. The second edition of the 1989 *OED* states that the origins of the word 'diaspora' can be traced back to its appearance in the Old Testament (Deuteronomy 28:25). Here, the *OED* calls attention to the 'dispersal' of the people of Israel across the world. According to this definition, the Jews were the first diasporic people, but not the last. For, as the 1993 edition of the *Shorter Oxford Dictionary* makes clear, the word 'diaspora' can refer to 'any body of people living outside of their homeland'.

Diaspora, then, is a word used in postcolonial studies to describe groups of people who have been removed or displaced due to territorial disputes, war, forced migration or immigration. It is in this context that Robin Cohen writes of 'global diasporas' as a way of articulating the many experiences, contexts and histories that the word 'diaspora' has come to connote.[1] In fact, for Cohen, the word is on the verge of becoming over-determined because it runs the risk of being too inclusive and thus simultaneously meaning everything and nothing. After all, Cohen writes, there is an overarching commonality that unites all forms of diaspora: diasporic peoples are those who are forced to inhabit a place outside of their 'natal (or imagined natal) territories'.[2] The experience of these people is necessarily similar in that they are displaced from a homeland that is connected to language, religion and a sense of cultural belonging. Cohen locates the origins of diaspora in the Jewish experience, but he also argues that we must take other diasporic experiences into account to understand fully the word. Thus, Cohen identifies several different kinds of diasporic experience: victim diasporas, labour diasporas, imperial diasporas, trade diasporas, 'homeland' diasporas and cultural diasporas. Such taxonomies are necessary, Cohen states, for recognizing the different causes of migration, displacement and movement. For instance, the contemporary Mexican diaspora in the United

States may be seen as a product of labour diasporas – a form of migration that is fuelled by a neocolonial system that demands cheap workers. But it must also be noted that these categories of diaspora are not mutually exclusive. The African diaspora, for example, can be seen as a result of the institutionalization of chattel slavery and the subsequent victimization of Africans due to aggressive transmigrational policies that supported European imperialism.

Cohen points out that the word 'diaspora' is now used as much as 'globalization' as a way of trying to make sense of the movement and diversity of postmodern nations and cultures. Paul Gilroy's influential and insightful book, *The Black Atlantic: Modernity and Double Consciousness*, has played a major role in this shift. For Gilroy has redirected attention away from nation-based analyses towards the consideration of multiple diasporic formations, travelling cultures and travelling theories. Gilroy's theorization of 'the Black Atlantic as a counterculture of modernity' based on diaspora echoes a general shift in postcolonial studies towards privileging mobility, movement and the shattering of borders.[3] As Gilroy states,

■ The Black Atlantic can be defined, on one level, through [a] desire to transcend both the structures of the nation-state and the constraints of ethnicity and national particularity. These desires are relevant to understanding political organizing and cultural criticism. They have always sat uneasily alongside the strategic choices forced on black movements and individuals embedded in national political cultures and nation-states in America, the Caribbean and Europe.[4] □

For Gilroy, the diasporic dimensions of 'the Black Atlantic' circumvent the limitations of cultural nationalisms that insist upon clean breaks between races, cultures and nations. Gilroy foregrounds the fluid movement of peoples within the 'Black Atlantic' to avoid the ethnic essentialism that often characterizes cultural nationalism. The 'Black Atlantic', then, is a transnational space of traversal, cultural exchange and belonging that spans several continents and connects people through its history of diasporic paths. Throughout the history of colonization, the Atlantic was a contact zone where European setters and traders were not isolated from the Native American, African and Asian people whom they exploited. If, as Gilroy suggests, modernity is characterized by colonist expansion, slavery, genocide and indenture, then the connections between cultures present in the 'Black Atlantic' offer a counterculture to modernity.

From this perspective, the concept of diaspora is very appealing for Black British writers such as Caryl Phillips, who states that 'for people of the African Diaspora, "home" is a word that is often burdened with a complicated historical and geographical weight'.[5] This being the case, travel has been important, for it has provided African diasporic people with a means of clarifying their own unique position in the world. The literary critic James Procter writes that Phillips is 'a diasporic writer, whose work rejects the investment in national belonging'. For Procter, Phillips's texts privilege the 'border spaces of the black Atlantic' and underscore what Phillips sees as 'the gift of displacement' and the 'high anxiety of belonging'.[6] Phillips's meditations on belonging are not surprising when we consider his birth in St. Kitts and his early removal to England soon thereafter. Indeed, his writing depicts an African diaspora and the residue of colonization in order to offer insights into the diversity of diasporic experiences, noting that the discourses of displacement are far from monolithic. As he observes in *The Atlantic Sound* (2000), the Ghanaian understanding of the dispersal of Africans due to the slave trade is, for instance, very different from the ways in which African Americans conceive of this displacement.

Several of Phillips's novels touch on this very issue. The disparate understandings of African diasporas in the wake of the Atlantic slave trade are, for example, addressed in his Caribbean-based works such as *The Final Passage* (1985), *A State of Independence* (1986) and *Cambridge* (1991). His first novel, *The Final Passage*, tells the story of a woman who leaves the Caribbean to live with her husband and baby in London, and *A State of Independence* addresses the Caribbean islands' growing dependency on the United States and other nations within the Americas. *Cambridge* focuses on a young woman from England visiting her father's plantation in the Caribbean, and two of Phillips's non-fiction texts, *The European Tribe* (1987) and *The Atlantic Sound* (2000), are travel narratives that specifically address the subject of African diasporas. Throughout this latter work, Phillips documents the dispossession and exile in order to meditate on the complexities of postcolonial history, recognizing his impressions of displacement, diaspora and homelessness. Reflecting on his birth in St. Kitts, for instance, Phillips retraces the first transatlantic journey he made with his mother in the late 1950s, by 'banana boat' from the Caribbean to the grey shores of England – 'the Mother Country'.[7] He also visits three cities central to the African slave trade: Liverpool, Elmina in Ghana and Charleston in South Carolina. Finally, in Israel, he finds a community of 2,000 African Americans who have lived in the Negev desert for 30 years.

Phillips, then, meditates on the meanings of home and homelessness in the context of an African diaspora. In this, he shuffles between the identities of insider and outsider, between the son of Caribbean immigrants and a high-profile English intellectual and writer. He writes,

■ West Indian Immigrants such as my parents [...] traveled in the hope that the mother country would remain true to her promise, that she would protect the children of her empire. However, shortly after disembarkation the West Indian immigrants of the fifties and sixties discovered the realities of this new world were likely to be more challenging than they had anticipated. In fact, much to their dismay, they discovered that the mother country had little, if any, desire to embrace her colonial offspring.[8] ☐

Here, Phillips criticizes Britain for misleading her 'colonial offspring' during the massive increase in Caribbean emigration to England in the 1950s and 60s.

But Phillips also resists the discourses that would romanticize an ideal African home. He does this by demystifying 'the Afrocentric dream that exalts the roots of displaced blacks' and dismissing the essentialist ideas that often inform Afrocentricity.[9] By contrast, Phillips charts the diversity of cultures that exist within the topography of the black Atlantic world. Commenting on this aspect of Phillips's writing, Bénédicte Ledent asserts that

■ Unlike earlier thinkers who, influenced by Pan-Africanism and Negritude, regarded Africa as an iconic model, Phillips shows enough critical distance to avoid giving a romantic view of the continent and the dispersal of its people, a view which is central to *The Atlantic Sound*. The diaspora he depicts is marked from its very origins by paradox.[10] ☐

Ledent points out that unity does not underlie Phillips's depiction of the African diaspora. Instead, paradox, contradiction, juxtaposition and difference are represented as disrupting any search for a universal black culture.

For Phillips, then, the African diaspora is an important access route into the complicated matrix of his identity. By calling attention to this diasporic culture, Phillips resists the urge to essentialize the Black British subject or experience, but rather unpacks how both 'Blackness' and 'British-ness' are culturally constructed for themselves and for the dominant culture. In this, he is doing more than simply re-staging the narratives of an English culture that the British state has used to define itself. His texts are intended not simply to invert the axis of political discrimination by installing the excluded term at the centre. Rather, Phillips attempts to disrupt the narratives forged to define the dominant culture, to hybridize the discourse, to reconfigure the concept of all cultural identities as fluid and heterogeneous. Instead of seeking recognition from the dominant culture or addressing specific instances of political injustice, his writing tries to reconfigure the relations of dominance and resistance, to reposition both the dominant and the marginalized on the stage of cultural discourse, and to challenge the static borders of national and cultural identity.

In their book *Key Concepts in Post-Colonial Studies* (1998), Ashcroft, Griffiths and Tiffin share the *OED*'s definition of 'diaspora', but they relate the term directly to the process of European colonization. For them, diaspora is 'the voluntary or forcible movement of peoples from their homelands to new regions', but under colonialism, diaspora is a multifarious movement that involves several key features.[11] For instance, Western imperialism has led to the 'temporary or permanent' migration of Europeans across the globe. This was, of course, responsible for European settlements in the colonies and, in some cases, the displacement of indigenous peoples. One diaspora begets another, and the economic exploitation of 'settled' areas necessitated labour that could not be satisfied by the local population. This, then, led to the diaspora of Africans resulting from enslavement and relocation to the European colonies.[12]

Ashcroft, Griffiths and Tiffin further note that diasporas are of importance to postcolonial studies because the descendants of slaves and indentured labourers have produced highly unique cultures that both maintain and build upon their original cultures. One example of this is the contemporary Indian diaspora, which constitutes an important, and in some respects unique, force in world culture. This diaspora is often depicted by the postcolonial writer Sunetra Gupta (born 1956), who was born in India but grew up in Africa, Britain and the USA. Diaspora is, for Gupta, central to her sense of identity and belonging. As a result, when asked in a recent interview about the subject of 'home' and displacement, Gupta stated that

■ We have to accept that we are going to be perpetually wandering [...]. That's the kind of crisis that we're in now, that we're forced to be in a state of perpetual wandering, so we can't be at home.[13] □

For Gupta, even when a person sits at home, she is forced to travel, just because of what is going on around her. We must, she continues, be comfortable with this notion, for one's cultural identity does not necessarily come from 'home' but it is located wherever an individual is rooted (or rooted in).

Gupta's comments on home and wandering are echoed in her novel, *The Glassblower's Breath* (1993). The characters of this story live transnational lives that disrupt conventional notions of home and belonging. Indeed, the protagonists move fluidly from London to Paris to Calcutta to New York without ever expressing a sense of rootedness in one particular place. In this flux, the characters' birthplaces are not necessarily identified as their homelands. Instead, they are at home in movement, shifting between cityscapes, and always simultaneously connected to and detached from the places where they are temporarily residing. Throughout the text, these urban wanderers attract fellow wanderers to form a community of people who are united through their movement and commitment to transnational fluidity. Upon arriving in London, for instance, the narrator considers leaving: 'London is a city I would say I both hate and love, if the large part of our relationship were not indifference.' When her acquaintance replies that he hates London, her response is simply, 'When I get tired of London, I go to Paris.'[14]

This form of migration is, of course, made possible by the privileged economic positions held by the characters of Gupta's text. Because they have the money for plane tickets, hold Western passports and work in flexible professions, the characters can embrace mobility as a challenge to the traditional narratives that locate home and belonging in the modern nation-state. By contrast, the writing of Hanif Kureishi does not represent the South Asian diaspora of London as holding the same economic advantages. In *The Black Album* (1995), for example, the main character – Shahid – gains a sense of belonging in the multi-ethnic and multi-cultural area of London where he grows up. Although his parents are from Pakistan, he feels no connection to his family's homeland. Karachi is, for Shahid, distant and unfamiliar, whereas the streets of London are part of his earliest memories and play a significant role in his development. Thus, as a non-white Londoner born in Britain, he does not see his homeland as a distant place. Instead, the issue that he grapples with is how he and his first-generation contemporaries will construct identities in a Britain that refuses to recognize them as embodiments of its culture.

Shahid's view of the South Asian diaspora in England is very different from that of his parents. In fact, his mother and father identify Karachi as their 'home', and they pay annual visits to Pakistan. Shahid's father attempts to instil a sense of Pakistani identity in his son, explaining to Shahid that the British Empire transformed Pakistan by creating new borders and displacing many people. However, for Shahid, Pakistan is a restrictive nation marked by poverty and crime: 'The place enraged him: the religion shoved down everyone's throats; the bandits, corruption, censorship, laziness, fatuity of the press; the holes in the roads, the absence of roads, the roads on fire.'[15] (89). These negative aspects of Pakistan are, according to Shahid's father, a direct result of colonial rule and the aftermath of imperialism. For Papa and Uncle Asif, the British must be held responsible for the problems faced by Pakistan. They describe a time (however romanticized) before the forced migration of Pakistanis – a time when the country was a comforting homeland rather than a nation scarred by crime, poverty and religious intolerance.

The distinct diasporic experiences described by the different generations in *The Black Album* suggest that any study of migration must take into account historical and cultural specificities. As we have seen, diasporas are all different and, as a result, any movement of people must be placed within its specific context. This is confirmed by the critics Jana Evans Braziel and Anita Mannur, who argue that

■ Theorizing diaspora offers critical spaces for thinking about the discordant movements of modernity, the massive migrations that have defined this century – from the late colonial period through the decolonization era to the twenty-first century. Theorizations of diaspora need not, and should not, be divorced from historical and cultural specificity. Diasporic traversals question the rigidities of identity itself – religious, ethnic, gendered, national; yet this diasporic movement marks not a postmodern turn from history, but a nomadic turn in which the parameters of specific historical moments are embodied and – as diaspora itself suggests – are scattered and regrouped into new points of becoming.[16] □

Braziel and Mannur note that recent theorizations of diasporas have sought to remain sensitive to the myriad of experiences and diverse communities that have been marked by migrations. After all, diasporic communities develop their own particular forms of hybridity and heterogeneity in specific cultural, linguistic, ethnic and national contexts.

Heterogeneity is, for many diasporic writers, also foregrounded in representations of gender and sexuality. In *Funny Boy* (1994), a novel by the Canadian–Sri Lankan writer Shyam Selvadurai (born 1965), the upper-middle class Tamil narrator, Arjie, reflects upon his childhood and adolescence in the context of the Tamil–Sinhalese riots of 1983 and his family's migration to Canada. This migration is the focal point of the novel and Arjie contemplates the meanings of home through the removal and the reminiscences of his adolescent homosexual awakening. In the ultimate section of the novel, for instance, Arjie imagines 'home' in terms of a 'queer diasporic memory'.[17] Here, Arjie has sex with his first lover – Shehan – before taking the plane to Toronto. This memory becomes an important image of belonging for Arjie, for the smell of Shehan remains on his clothes. Shehan's odour is described as 'a final memento', not just of Arjie's first homoerotic affair, but of his imagined home in Sri Lanka.[18]

The postcolonial critic Gayatri Gopinath reads this final section of *Funny Boy* as 'queering' the homely space of Sri Lanka by 'disrupting the logic of nationalism which consolidates "the nation" through normative hierarchical sexual and gender arrangements that coalesce around the privatized, bourgeois domestic space of "home" as a site of sanitized heterosexuality'.[19] In this, Gopinath explores how Selvadurai depicts the desire to belong to a home (or nation) as inseparable from identities of gender and sexuality. Gopinath writes that

■ *Funny Boy* lays claim to both the space of 'home' and the nation by making both the site of non-heteronormative desire and pleasure in a nostalgic diasporic imaginary. Such a move disrupts nationalist logic by forestalling any notion of queer or non-heteronormative desire as insufficiently authentic. *Funny Boy* thus refuses to subsume sexuality within a larger narrative of ethnic, class, or national identity, or to subsume these other conflicting trajectories within an overarching narrative of 'gay' sexuality.[20] □

Indeed, the text positions Arjie's voice from his new home in Canada and articulates the notion of belonging through nostalgia and desire. This retrospective novel, Gopintha suggests, offers possibilities for thinking about how diaspora and the nation (where home is read as an emblem of the nation) are re-imagined within a queer framework. Because queer subjects are often erased from the traditional images of the nation, Arjie must renegotiate ways of belonging to the nation. Thus, Gopinath argues that Arjie – the queer diasporic subject – utilizes images of nostalgia to imagine a form of belonging to spaces such as the home and nation that have traditionally cast him as invisible.

This exploration of queer postcolonial narratives once again challenges monolithic notions of diaspora. In this way, Gopinath intervenes in contemporary discourses of diaspora, suggesting that questions of belonging in a nation-state and the desire to belong are complicated for South Asian subjects who must negotiate a path that includes same-sexuality alongside their identities as diasporic national subjects.

This focus on diversity and difference is also foregrounded by Stuart Hall, whose influential essay, 'Cultural Identity and Diaspora' (1990), draws upon the Derridean notion of *différance* (see CHAPTER TWO of this Guide) to describe the heterogeneous nature of diasporic identities. Here, Hall distinguishes between two forms of cultural identity. The first is a form of identity that arises out of a collective, shared sense of belonging due to a common history and mutual ethnic or racial heritage. While this identity might be fixed, Hall argues that the second form of cultural identity is defined by instability, juxtapositions, tensions and contradictions. It is this latter form of cultural identity that Hall likens to Derrida's theoretical play of difference, pointing to Caribbean cultural identities as heterogeneous composites arising out of diasporic histories. Hall writes,

■ The diaspora experience [...] is defined, not by essence or purity, but by the recognition of a necessary heterogeneity and diversity; by a conception of 'identity' which lives with and through, not despite, difference; by *hybridity*.

Diaspora identities are those which are constantly producing and reproducing themselves anew, through transformation and difference.[21] □

To illustrate this point, Hall turns to the Caribbean, arguing that the cultural presences in this region cannot be reduced to the simple binaries of black/white, centre/periphery or colonizer/colonized. Instead, the different heritages of the Caribbean islands make it a unique cultural composite with African, European and American influences. The '*Présence Africaine*, *Présence Européen* and the [...] *Présence Américaine*', Hall writes, combine with 'the many other cultural "presences" that constitute the complexity of Caribbean identity (Indian, Chinese, Lebanese, etc.)'[22]

Hall's tale of diaspora, then, holds a subversive resonance when contrasted with that of the nation-state. For embedded in his tale is a revolt against the limits of national identity by foregrounding transnational notions of selfhood with little regard for national boundaries. Thus, Hall asserts that within diasporic identities there can be no absolute return to a fixed site of origin. He states,

■ Cultural identities are the points of identification, the unstable points of identification or suture, which are made within the discourses of history and culture. Not an essence, but a positioning. Hence, there is always a politics of identity, a politics of position, which has no absolute guarantee in an unproblematic, transcendental 'law of origin'.[23] □

Here, Hall describes the importance of establishing a discourse of positionality in a diasporic context. This is particularly significant because many diasporic peoples have to articulate relations between place/nation and transnational identifications. This situation places the individual in an ambiguous relationship to both the strictures of the nations and the cultural identities that he or she experiences.

These ideas are echoed in Arjun Appadurai's important essay 'Disjuncture and Difference in the Global Cultural Economy' (2003). Appadurai argues that it is no longer valid to reduce the new global economy to the simplistic spatial paradigms of centre and periphery. Instead, he writes that diaspora, migration and the transnational flow of capital across the world force us to rethink the basic principles that govern the global cultural economy. As a way of understanding the mechanisms by which this new cultural economy functions, Appadurai describes five different 'scapes'. He writes,

■ I propose that an elementary framework for exploring such disjunctures is to look at the relationship between five dimensions of global cultural flow which can be termed: (a) ethnoscapes; (b) mediascapes; (c) technoscapes; (d) financescapes; (e) ideoscapes. The suffix -*scape* allows us to point to the fluid, irregular shapes of these landscapes, shapes which characterize international capital as deeply as they do international clothing styles.[24] □

For Appadurai, the term 'ethnoscape' describes people who move between nations, such as tourists, immigrants, exiles, guestworkers and refugees. 'Technoscapes' is a word used to describe the global spread of new technologies, usually through the markets that are created by multinational corporations. This is, of course, connected to 'financescapes', which expresses the global flow of capital through large corporations, currency markets and stock exchanges. 'Mediascapes' highlights the international movement of information through electronic sources made possible by satellites, televisions, mobile phones and the Internet. These new electronic technologies, in turn, act as powerful tools for disseminating 'ideoscapes', which Appadurai defines as official state ideologies and counter-ideologies.

Finally, we must stress that Appadurai's work is central to diaspora studies in that it theorizes the relocation of people alongside the movement of products, capital, technology, culture and ideas. In this theorization, we can glimpse the connections between the study of diasporas and analyses of globalization. We will return to many of these ideas in the next chapter on globalization.

CHAPTER FIFTEEN

Globalization

In November 1999, approximately 70,000 anti-globalization protestors congregated in Seattle, Washington to campaign against the neo-liberal policies that were being promoted by the World Trade Organization (WTO). In the crowd was an improbable mix of trade unionists, environmental activists, intellectuals, teachers, homemakers, children and the industrial working class of the developed world. The diverse crowd was united in voicing their opposition to environmental despoliation and the economic ravages in the under-developed world, as well the policies of the International Monetary Fund (IMF), the World Bank (WB) and the WTO. It was a protest against the poverty and inequality perceived to be caused by globalization – the intensifying global reach of capitalism and the market.[1]

The demonstration in Seattle paralyzed the scheduled meetings of delegates and led to the partial abandonment of the proceedings. It also raised awareness about the existence of a movement against globalization and neo-liberal economic policies. Here was evidence that the spread of global capitalism was not being passively received and accepted. This, then, provided inspiration and unity for traditional parties and groups of the left: here was a single issue that united them all. As a result, the protest in Seattle was only the beginning, for the anti-globalization movement spread in strength and sophistication. Tom Hickey and Anita Rupprecht record that the protests 'traverse[d] the globe and all five continents': 40,000 protested against the IMF in Quito, Ecuador; 20,000 against the World Bank in Prague; 10,000 against the Asia–Europe summit in Seoul, South Korea; 20,000 against the Asia–Pacific summit in Melbourne, Australia; and 300,000 against the G8 summit in Genoa, Italy, to name but a few.[2]

All of these protests voiced concern that the forces of globalization were increasingly bringing the world's economies into a single system. The new technologies, new media and new political landscape (following the fall of the Soviet Union), protestors said, enabled multi- and transnational companies to enter global markets outside of the established markets of the West. This expansion has led to outsourced manufacturing, call centres and other business deals in any country that is poor and reasonably politically stable. For many of the protestors, then, globalization encouraged dependency, disenfranchisement and disempowerment deriving from Coca Cola-ization and McDonaldization that eroded cultural differences. Protestors also expressed outrage that multinational companies based in the West were increasingly controlling the world's natural resources and local economies and regulating spending power.

The economic effect of large multinational companies and the existence of high levels of debt in developing countries have maintained a version of economic colonial power. In this, wealthier western powers can call the shots in poorer countries, thus undermining the independence of the poor nation. This point is made, more generally, in Edward Said's *Culture and Imperialism*. Looking at the 'empire imperative' in political and social discourse, Said argues that imperialism remains a 'compellingly important' and significant 'configuration in the world of power and nations'.[3] Imperialism, he insists, is not about a moment in history; it is about a continuing interdependent discourse between subject peoples and the dominant discourses of those in power.

From a postcolonial perspective, one of the most powerful forces fuelling imperialism is globalization, a term which has become a buzzword in the mouths of managerial elites, political activists, cultural workers and intellectuals. For some, the term signifies an unprecedented degree of cultural homogenization and Americanization; for others it implies an increasingly unequal relationship of power between the North and South and the uneven distribution of global wealth. Historically, the term can be considered alongside the various histories of colonialism, and in recent years, postcolonial studies has engaged in a critical analysis of the ways in which globalization reshapes literature and the construction of cultural and political discourses of social change. Such an examination considers globalization as a set of multiple processes that impact the relationship between the local and the global, between historical ruptures and continuities and the construction of new global subjects and identities.

Supporters of the economic practices that contribute to globalization claim that the wealthy countries profit from cheap labour and raw materials while, in return, the developing nation gets employment and technology that boosts modernization. Such arguments, though, tend to gloss over the fact that the majority of jobs created in developing nations are low-paid, with very few benefits, and that modernization is often destructive for indigenous cultures, local ways of life and the environment. Multinational corporations rarely, if ever, enrich the overall population in underdeveloped countries. Instead, they tend to generate unsustainable development and perpetual underdevelopment; a dependency that cultivates reservoirs of cheap labour and raw materials, while restricting the poor country's access to advanced production techniques that would develop its own economy. Anne McClintock substantiates many of these points in her excellent essay 'The Angel of Progress' (1992):

■ The US 'development' myth has had a grievous impact on global ecologies. By 1989, the World Bank had $225 billion in commitments to poorer countries, on condition that they, in turn, endure the purgatory of 'structural adjustment', export their way to 'progress', cut government spending on education and social services (with the axe falling most cruelly on women), devalue their currencies, remove trade barriers, and raze their forests to pay their debts.[4] □

What McClintock makes clear is that wealthy Western countries maintain a powerful presence in developing economies, especially through the exploitation of raw materials. This form of domination is fuelled by international financial institutions such as the IMF and the WB, both of which exert decisive forms of control through the choice to grant or refuse loans to developing regions. In order to qualify for loans or economic aid, the IMF and WB often force poor countries to make 'structural adjustments' – to take steps favourable to the financial interests of the granting institutions, but detrimental to the economy of the underdeveloped nation because they increase rather than alleviate poverty.

Global exploitation, then, can function without formal colonies (as in United States imperialism today) but nevertheless exercise domination and control. The result of these economic practices is to maintain a system of imperial control that is 'unofficial' in political terms, but plays itself out on the economic terrain. Ania Loomba puts this quite clearly when she writes that 'Direct colonial rule is not necessary for imperialism in this sense, because economic (and social) relations of dependency and control ensure both captive labour as well as markets for European industry as well as goods. Sometimes the words "neo-imperialism" or "neo-colonialism" are used to describe these situations.'[5]

In postcolonial fiction, Fidelis Odun Balogun (born 1952) in *Adjusted Lives: Stories of Structural Adjustments* (1995) captures the stress and agony in the lives of Nigerians as they daily grapple with the economic woes resulting from their country's adoption of measures dictated by the IMF and the WB. In Balogun's text, the 'Structural Adjustments' imposed upon Nigeria as a requirement for loans and debt relief have generated a free market economy that has opened up Nigerian markets to global trade. This has meant cuts to food subsidies and health care, the privatization of public services and decentralization, resulting in more poverty and greater economic disparities between rich and poor. Balogun describes the result of these measures: 'The middle class rapidly disappeared, and the garbage heaps of the increasingly rich few became the food table of the multiplied population of abjectly poor [...]. The result was the massive failure of businesses, an incredible inflation in the cost of living, mass unemployment, hunger, increased crime and political instability.'[6] Throughout the text, the narrator and the characters make direct references to 'the SAP', the IMF-mandated Structural Adjustment Programme (SAP) instituted throughout the 1980s. 'After their mysterious laughter', the narrator states, 'they quickly changed the topic to other things. How were people back home surviving sap?'[7] The answer is clear: people are not surviving, for it is described as the equivalent of a great natural catastrophe, destroying forever the heart of Lagos and 're-enslaving' Nigerians.

Balogan describes how SAP policies of 'privatizing in full steam' have left Nigerians 'more hungry by the day'. His descriptions thus detail how the IMF and WB used the leverage of debt to restructure the economy in favour of global trade policies that benefited multinational corporations located in North America and Europe. His stories, then, illustrate the violence of 'adjustments' that have increased the slums of Nairobi and Lagos, immersing many Nigerians in poverty. The SAP is, in Balogun's view, part of an imperialist agenda that has led to a social crisis in Kenya. For 'Adjusted lives' is, in his work, a metaphor that brings home the result of global restructuring (usually discussed in technocratic terms) and the very direct changes in everyday conditions of living and survival for the majority of Kenyans, with multiple personal and social ramifications. In his writing, the lived experience of the urban poor is one of permanent insecurity, of ill-health, hunger and malnutrition, cramped and dirty living conditions and unemployment. In short, the structural violence of this neoliberal reform is a form of violence that adjusts people's lives.

Balogun's stories also point to the fact that contemporary forms of imperialism have, in some cases, motivated community-based resistance. This and other depictions of inequity are taken up in Jamaica Kincaid's *A Small Place*, her 80-page essay about how colonization, slavery, tourism and globalization are intimately intertwined. Kincaid suggests that North Americans and Europeans perpetuate the power dynamics that were established in the past, but which continue to have negative effects upon the residents of Antigua, the Caribbean and the developing world. More importantly, though, the text calls attention to how these inequities destroy both the wealthy *and* the impoverished. For the poor nation suffers from exploitation, poverty and marginalization, while the powerful country is caught up in perpetuating a vicious cycle of greed and consumption that causes a profound disconnect in their lives, displacing those at the centre of power from ethics, morality and humanity.

The Caribbean island of Antigua, Kincaid states, suffers from contemporary forms of imperialism because it is controlled by the global tourist industry. She thus illustrates the way in which the experience of the tourist is intimately tied to a global economic system promoted by the North American or European metropolis that the tourist calls home. This global economy is foregrounded in the very food that is eaten by the tourist while he is on the island. Addressing the white tourist directly, Kincaid writes,

> ■ When you sit down to your delicious meal, it's better you don't know that most of what you are eating came off a plane from Miami. And before it got on a plane from Miami, who knows where it came from? A good guess is that it came from a place like Antigua first, where it was grown dirt-cheap, went to Miami, and came back.[8] □

Kincaid emphasizes the complex artifice of presenting the illusion of a local culture for the tourist. The 'authentic' Antiguan food might or might not be produced in a developing economy (for which the local people would be paid very poorly) before it moves through global economic channels. Perhaps the food is grown in the Caribbean, but then it is processed in North America before it is sent back to Antigua to be consumed by tourists. The transnational movement of food turns it into an expensive commodity – a commodity that the local people of Antigua cannot afford to buy. What lies behind Kincaid's comments, then, is a cutting irony: the local people cannot afford the very food that they grow.

In *Understanding Jamaica Kincaid* (2007), I argue that Kincaid urges the citizens of Antigua to examine the past. For it is through an awareness of the history of colonization that one can understand contemporary imperialism in Antigua.[9] Tourism, that is, can only be understood in the context of a background of economically driven external intervention. For the colonial projects of the nineteenth century are linked to the economic institutions of the late twentieth century. And the exploitation of Antigua is part of the driving force of trade that has always stimulated the growth of European and American capital. Kincaid uses the contemporary example of Barclays Bank in order to illustrate her point:

> ■ The Barclay Brothers, who started Barclays Bank, were slave-traders. That is how they made their money. When the English outlawed the slave trade, the Barclay brothers went into banking. It made them richer. It's possible that when they saw how rich banking made them, they gave themselves a good beating for opposing an end to slave trading.[10] □

Kincaid thus connects the establishment and growth of a multinational bank to the nineteenth century spread of slavery and British colonization of the Caribbean. Barclays Bank is, of course, an important financial institution in contemporary Antigua. But it is also one of the largest banks in the world, generating enormous annual profits for its executives and shareholders. In 2004, for instance, the worldwide pre-tax profits reported by Barclays Bank exceeded 6 billion US dollars, more than nine times as much as the annual GNP of Antigua in that same year.[11]

The adaptation of *A Small Place* for the narrative of the film *Life and Debt* (2001) illustrates the ways in which Kincaid's text addresses globalization.[12] The film, a critique of global capitalism and multinational companies, uses *A Small Place* to highlight the continuing forms of imperialism that are perpetuated by lending agencies (such as the IMF), the tourist industry and unequal terms of trade. The Caribbean is, according to *Life and Debt*, controlled by a world increasingly dominated by the United States and US-based corporations, further complicating the dynamics of place and global relations. In this, the film indicates that the Caribbean youth, in particular, are continuing an unhealthy pattern of inferiority and dominance that now locates the centre of imperialism in North America. The message is clear: the power relations of the past are repeated in the present.

Exploitation and other aspects of present-day imperialism are taken up in Michael Hardt and Antonio Negri's *Empire* (2000). The contemporary definition of 'Empire' is, for Hardt and Negri, neither a figure of speech nor a form of imperialism. Rather, it is 'a decentred and deterritorializing apparatus of rule that progressively incorporates the entire global realm within its open, expanding frontiers'.[13] This would seem to be a radicalized version of current understandings of 'globalization'. Indeed, with a vision of a 'postmodernized global economy', Hardt and Negri do not believe that any nation-state (even the US) can act as the centre for an existing imperialist project. They write,

■ Along with the global market and global circuits of production has emerged a global order, a new logic and structure of rule – in short, a new form of sovereignty. Empire is the political subject that effectively regulates these global exchanges, the sovereign power that governs the world [...]. The United States does not, and indeed no nation-state can today, form the center of an imperialist project. Imperialism is over. No nation will be world leader in the way modern European nations were.[14] □

Transformations of the new global order make the emerging Empire quite different from previous eras of imperial dominance and capitalist expansion, opening new spaces for political projects seeking to construct a truly democratic global society. The shift from modernity to postmodernity, or from imperialism to Empire, has generated an economic system 'composed of a series of national and supranational organisms united under a single logic of rule'.[15] As such, sovereignty is made up of regulatory frameworks that create the transnational figure called 'Empire' out of a new conception of space. For Empire is characterized by a lack of boundaries, and thus its rule has no limits: 'the spatial divisions of the three Worlds (First, Second, and Third) have been scrambled so that we continually find the First world in the Third, the Third in the First, and the Second almost nowhere at all. Capital seems to be faced with a smooth world – or really, a world defined by new and complex regimes of differentiation and homogenization, deterritorialization and reterritorialization.'[16]

Hardt and Negri insist that the construction of Empire is 'a step forward in order to do away with any nostalgia for the power structures that preceded it and refuse any political strategy that involves returning to that old arrangement, such as trying to resurrect the nation-state to protect against global capital'.[17] Localist opposition to globalization may be politically well intentioned but, according to them, it rests on false assumptions and is therefore damaging. It assumes that the local is 'outside' of globalization, that it represents difference as against the homogenization of the latter. It also misidentifies 'the enemy' insofar as the production of locality is also an effect of the globalization processes. The local cannot represent a stable barrier against the new accelerated global capital flows; only an internationalist strategy of resistance can counter-hegemonize or at least seek to democratize capital's globalization project.

But there is, they suggest, room for optimism. For they argue that the paradox of this new power is that while it unifies every element of social life, it leads to resistance no longer being marginal as it becomes active in the very centre of a society that opens up in networks. The multitude (their word for the people) can also globalize and fight back:

■ The Empire we are faced with wields enormous powers of oppression and destruction, but [...] [t]he passage to Empire and its processes of globalization offer new possibilities to the force of liberation [...]. The creative forces of the multitude that sustain Empire are also capable of autonomously constructing a counter-Empire, an alternative political organization of global flows and exchanges.

The struggles to contest and subvert Empire, as well as those to construct a real alternative, will thus take place on the imperial terrain itself – indeed, such new struggles have already begun to emerge. Through these struggles, and many more like them, the multitude will have to invent new democratic forms and a new constituent power that will one day take us through and beyond Empire.[18] □

The 'post-modernized global economy', far from being all-powerful, contains the seeds of its own destruction and, they argue, the political climate has never been more favourable for an uprising by the multitude. Thus, *Empire* sees possibilities for creation and liberation: 'The multitude, in its will to be against and its desire for liberation, must push through Empire to come out on the other side.'[19]

But critics of Hardt and Negri suggest that they reproduce a colonial modernist mode of producing knowledge. Lisa Rofel, for instance, argues that by adopting a Eurocentric approach to history, narrative and philosophy, Hardt and Negri inadvertently reinscribe the notion that 'the universal Idea is the driving force of social life'. Their pursuit of 'Empire' as a 'concept' requiring a philosophical approach and their focus on Europe and Euro-America ignores 'the rest of the world and tells a Eurocentric tale of everyone else's histories'. Within this paradigm, Europe is the only place that is 'theoretically knowable'; all other places and histories are 'matters of empirically fleshing out the European theoretical subject'.[20]

Rofel points out that Hardt and Negri assume a 'master imperial logic' that places Europe at the centre of thought, history and being. Thus, they do not 'decenter' the rule of European supremacy or 'provincialize Europe'.[21] Instead, 'the political unconscious of *Empire* is the European subject looking out'. This is a problem. For 'viewing the world order from other perspectives might offer a method for taking seriously the experiences and world views of those "Others" who exist not merely to construct a European subject but have multiple relationships with multiple non-European others (e.g., China with Southeast Asia)'.[22] For Rofel, contemporary critiques of capitalism and globalization must leave behind the European discourses of modernity. Such critiques must focus on the cultural production of capitalism and the transformations currently taking place in this production. Above all, Rofel thinks we must emphasize 'the culturally, geographically, and historically specific and uneven manifestations of these processes'. We should also, she continues, treat 'discourses of global capitalism and globalization as, themselves, elements within this cultural production that require critical scrutiny not only regarding their accuracy but also, more importantly, regarding the kinds of work to which they are being put'.[23]

Many of these ideas are echoed by the Indian novelist and political activist, Arundhati Roy (born 1961): 'The only thing worth globalising', she states, 'is dissent.'[24] Roy, the author of the Booker-Prize winning novel *The God of Small Things* (1997), often critiques the processes whereby individual lives and local communities are effected by economic and cultural forces that operate worldwide. As an outspoken public figure in India's anti-globalization movement, Roy has criticized the privatization and corporatization of India's essential infrastructure.[25] This economic process is, for Roy, part of the on-going imperialist relationship between the First and Third World. In her depictions of globalization, she highlights a new form of imperialism that has arisen in the wake of the period of rapid decolonization that followed World War II. This new form has transmuted the old politics of imperialism into the supra-national operation of economics, communication and culture. Globalization is not, she posits, about the eradication of world poverty. Rather, it is a mutated form of colonialism that is remote-controlled and digitally operated from the metropolitan centres of the First World.

Roy's work, then, envisions continuity between the history of colonial rule in India and the current domination of Indians by Western economic policies. *The God of Small Things* contains a detailed, though indirect, exploration of this historical continuity through an illustration of the cultural and economic transactions that take place between the local and global culture. According to the literary critic Julie Mullaney,

> ■ *The God of Small Things* is concerned with the resemblances between how individuals, groups, or local communities engage with the forces of globalization and how they might have engaged and appropriated the forces of imperial dominance historically. More generally, Roy's engagement with the politics of globalization offers us an interesting overview or case study of the ways in which certain national governments along with international organizations like the World Bank and the IMF (International Monetary Fund) are complicit in the organization, execution, and maintenance of new imperialisms.[26] □

Indeed, throughout the novel, the reader finds instances in which India's subjugation to the demands of transnational corporate interests and global networks affects the day-to-day lives of the average Indian citizen. In one of the most powerful images in the book, the once vibrant Meenachal River is depicted as suffering a long and painful death through unsustainable development. The river, which was once the livelihood of many people, has been damaged by environmental changes brought on by industries that have reduced its energetic flow to a tepid trickle of factory effluents and waste from a five-star hotel chain. The powerful flow of the great river has been undermined and replaced by the powerful flow of capital – an economic system that consumes everything in its path.

The novel also plays out the relationship between past and present forms of imperialism through Roy's depiction of Ayemenem, a town in the southern state of Kerala, India. Ayemenem is a place where the continuity of history exposes the fact that little has changed; the imperial rule of the past has been replaced by the new global economy. For the transatlantic flow of goods, money and labour that defined 'the British colonial enterprise' continues despite the 'ostensible dismantling of Empire with independence'.[27] Perhaps the structures that control India's relation to the world have changed slightly, but for those who inhabit the edge of the dominant order, life is the same as it ever was. The poor of Ayemenem can only sit and watch as houses fuelled by the 'Gulf-money' of those who have worked in faraway places are planned and constructed throughout the area. Likewise, those same occupants of Ayemenem watch as the land and water become polluted and begin to 'smell like shit, and pesticides bought with World Bank loans'.[28] The worst affected by these changes are the fisherman of the region, whose ancestors have lived off the Meenachal River for centuries. Once the lifeblood of the area, the river has been diverted and polluted by various economic policies so that the lives of people have been disrupted and transformed. Thus, 'the keys to the region's many pasts are being disrupted, erased, elided, and displaced in its troubled transactions with the managers of the global economy'.[29]

David Punter's reading of *The God of Small Things* stresses Roy's depiction of the 'terror of history' – a terror that combines with the fear of abandoning 'historical and geographical coordinates'.[30] This fear is represented in the character Baby, who gives up her passionate gardening project, which captures the historical complexities behind India's cultural plurality, in favour of satellite TV. Indeed, by replacing history and tradition with global television, Baby becomes robbed of life and energy: she spends all of her time sitting in front of the box, consumed and zombified by American programmes like *The Bold and the Beautiful*, *Santa Barbara*, *Prime Bodies* and *Wrestling Mania*. In this, the cultural diversity of India's history is lost, and the forces of globalization and postmodernity disseminate a homogeneous form of popular culture. As Punter points out, Roy's text illustrates how the homely local site is threatened by a globalized culture that seeks to control the characters' engagement with the world. Global culture is shaping India and, as a result, the relations between definitions of home and the rest of the world need to be reconfigured. The expansion of global networks and transnational communication systems begets new kinds of negotiations of space and place. New maps are being drawn and new, yet similar, configurations of power are exerting control over Indian territories.

Punter's reading of Roy's text is part of his larger examination of postcolonial literature in the age of Empire. In analysing texts by, among others, Naipaul, Rushdie, Coetzee and Achebe, Punter sees a continuity between imperial expansionism and capitalist resource exploitation – a continuity that he identifies as a 'neocolonial web' that is 'seamless and complete'.[31] For instance, in the context of a brief passage on *The Marabou Stork Nightmares* (1995) by Irvine Welsh (born 1958), Punter pauses to pose an important question:

■ The question thus raised is one that strikes at the very heart of the postcolonial, namely, whether it is politically accurate or helpful to use the term 'postcolonial' at all in a world where the ending of formal colonial status has in most cases succeeded only in prolonging economic subjugation and indeed in many cases in intensifying economic differences between the industrialized nations and those other parts of the world for which there is, indeed, not even an agreed-upon name.[32] □

From this perspective, postcolonial writing is, for Punter, engaged in a continuous battle. Not the battle to overpower colonist forces or the fight with those who control so much of the former European colonies. Rather, it is combating a discourse that maintains the inevitability of succumbing to the forces of globalization and homogenization. The postcolonial writer, then, must disseminate a counter-discourse, an alternative, to those who preach the impossibility of resisting global norms.

Punter thus warns against the pitfalls of the study of postcolonial literature becoming complicit in globalization. That is, the process of writing about postcolonial literature and the 'development' of post-colonial theory can, in effect, take on the ideologies and practices of consumption, development, progress, abstraction and elitism that are institutionalized in the very discourses of imperialism and globalization.

Conclusion

The interest in postcolonial literature and criticism, as we have seen in this Guide, shows no sign of abating. As noted in Chapters ONE, FOURTEEN and FIFTEEN the growing awareness of globalization, diaspora and contemporary imperialism continues to generate heated debates in postcolonial studies. In fact, over the last 30 years, postcolonial writing has asserted an irresistible attraction, with works by Michael Ondaatje, Arundhati Roy, Toni Morrison, Derek Walcott and many others attracting international acclaim. Likewise, as more postcolonial authors keep winning major literary awards such as the Nobel prize (Coetzee, Morrison, Walcott) and the Booker prize (Ondaatje, Roy, Atwood), the literary works by authors from former European colonies will further attract audiences across the globe.

From the critical material contained in this Guide, it is possible to see that what might seem at first to be an easy and unproblematic category – postcolonial literature – is one that is fraught with controversy and argument. As an area of study, postcolonial literature needs to be analysed with reference to its shifting nature; by its context and by the way it has been interpreted and reinterpreted in recent decades. For each new generation of writers, critics and theorists, the significance attached to postcolonial literature, and the cultural and political values associated with it, have been in a process of transition. These changing perceptions of postcolonial writing have, of course, been informed by shifts in power, political ideologies and social change, yet they have also been informed by changes in aesthetics and literary techniques and transformations in criticism.

We have considered, throughout this Guide, how often postcolonial writers have challenged the structures of difference and the discourses of essentialism. These ideas are reinforced on many levels in postcolonial texts through the exposure of lost historical narratives and the unveiling of traumas from the past. We have also noted that this type of writing is often closely followed by political strategies that attempt to stress the unethical power relations perpetuated by colonization and imperialism. The references to a wide range of postcolonial writing and theory in this Guide demonstrate that no one view of postcolonial literature has been accepted as inevitable or incontestable, even though some prominent critical trends can be identified during the last 30 years.

In future, postcolonial writing will extrapolate from the current issues discussed herein and explore new areas. It will, for instance, continue to critique and expose the terrain of modernity, which disseminates the discourses of 'progress' and the geopolitical exclusions and markings of difference. By questioning the assumptions of modernity, postcolonial critics will continue to decentre or provincialize Europe. Such questioning will avoid replicating Eurocentric assumptions and teleologies. Thus, postcolonial studies will lead in several related directions: focusing on the contemporary cultural production of economics and power; emphasizing geographically and historically specific literatures and cultures in context; treating global capitalism and globalization as elements within cultural production that require scrutinizing; and analysing the universalizing category of 'human rights' as a terrain that highlights an interconnected world that is also based on exclusions.

This Guide has attempted to provide an overview of some of the main concepts and key approaches that have characterized postcolonial writing. It has also attempted to expose, rather than obscure, the divergent and sometimes contradictory meanings that have been draw out of postcolonial literature by critics. While, as we have seen, postcolonial writing is charged with political commitment and liberationist assertions, it is, at the same time, still very much available to be restructured and reinvested with significance: by the next novelist, the next critic or perhaps, inevitably, by the next empire.

Notes

CHAPTER ONE

1 Venessa Allen, 'Prince Charles' Hong Kong Fury', *The Mail*, 23 February 2006, p. 2.
2 Chinua Achebe, *Things Fall Apart* (London: Heinemann, 1958), p. v. Here, Achebe, Nigerian novelist, quotes W. B. Yeats's 1921 poem 'The Second Coming', which includes the lines, 'Things fall apart; the centre cannot hold; / Mere anarchy is loosed upon the world'. Yeats's poem is, among other things, a meditation on Irish independence. See Yeats, 'The Second Coming', in *Norton Anthology of Modern Poetry*, ed. Richard Ellman (New York: Norton, 1988).
3 Bill Ashcroft, Gareth Griffiths and Helen Tiffin, *The Empire Writes Back: Theory and Practice in Post-Colonial Literatures* (London: Routledge, 1989), p. 2.
4 Ania Loomba, *Colonial/Postcolonialism* (London: Routledge, 1998), pp. 7–8.
5 Bart Moore-Gilbert, *Postcolonial Theory: Contexts, Practices, Politics* (London: Verso, 1997), p. 11.
6 Elleke Boehmer, *Colonial and Postcolonial Literature* (Oxford: Oxford University Press, 1995), p. 3.
7 Edward Said, *Culture and Imperialism* (London: Vintage, 1993), p. 15.
8 Benedict Anderson, *Imagined Communities: Reflections on the Origin and Spread of Nationalism* (London: Verso, 1983), p. 12.
9 Aijaz Ahmad, *In Theory: Classes, Nations, Literatures* (London: Verso, 1992), p. 18.
10 Mary Louise Pratt, *Imperial Eyes: Travel Writing and Transculturation* (New York: Routledge, 1992), pp. 10–15.
11 Pratt (1992), p. 5.
12 Ann McClintock, *Imperial Leather: Race, Gender, and Sexuality in the Colonial Context* (New York: Routledge, 1995), p. 5.
13 McClintock (1995), pp. 5–6.
14 David Punter, *Postcolonial Imaginings: Fictions of a New World Order* (Edinburgh: Edinburgh University Press, 2000), p. vi.
15 Michael Hardt and Antonio Negri, *Empire* (Cambridge, MA: Harvard University Press, 2000), pp. 222–4.
16 Michael Hardt and Antonio Negri, *Multitude: War and Democracy in the Age of Empire* (New York: Penguin, 2004), p. xiv.

CHAPTER TWO

1 David Malouf, *Remembering Babylon* (London: Vintage, 1993), p. 3.
2 Jacques Derrida, 'Signature, event, context', *Glyph* 1 (1977), pp. 20–5.
3 Jacques Derrida, *Writing and Difference*, trans. A. Bass (London: Routledge, 1978), pp. 33–9.
4 Gayatri Spivak, *The Spivak Reader* (New York: Routledge, 1996), p. 28.
5 Spivak (1996), pp. 26–8.
6 Edward Said, *Orientalism* (New York: Vintage, 1978), p. 12.
7 Said (1978), p. 14.
8 Said (1978), pp. 204, 273.
9 C. S. Byron, 'Legacies of Darkness: Neocolonialism, Joseph Conrad, and Taleb Salih's *Season of Migration to the North*', *Ariel* 30 (October 1999), p. 7.

10 Tayeb Salih, *Season of Migration to the North* (London: Heinemann, 1969), pp. 20, 28.
11 Salih (1969), pp. 120, 25, 34.
12 Said (1978), p. 71.
13 Said (1978), p. 71.
14 Said (1978), p. 4.
15 Henry Louis Gates, ed., *'Race', Writing and Difference* (Chicago: Chicago University Press, 1987), p. 5.
16 Gates (1987), p. 6.
17 Gates (1987), p. 7.
18 Having said this, it must be said that the history of black–white relations in the United States is quite different from that in England or other European nations. In the US, whites imported blacks from Africa as slaves, whereas the English confined slavery to their colonies in the Caribbean, Africa and other colonies. But while the dynamics of racial and cultural politics are different, some of the effects are the same.
19 Ashcroft et al. (1989), p. 2.
20 June Jordan, *Civil Wars* (Boston: Beacon, 1981), p. 114.
21 Jordan (1981), pp. 115–17.
22 June Jordan, 'Poem About My Rights', in *Norton Anthology of Modern Poetry*, ed. Richard Ellman (New York: Norton, 1988), p. 1468.
23 A. Deveaux, Interview with June Jordan, *Essence Magazine*, 12 January 1981, p. 12.

CHAPTER THREE

1 Ken Saro-Wiwa, *Sozaboy: A Novel in Rotten English* (New York: Longman, 1985), p. 1.
2 William Boyd, Introduction, *Sozaboy: A Novel in Rotten English* (New York: Longman, 1985), p. I.
3 Boyd (1985), pp. iii–iv.
4 Frantz Fanon, *Black Skin, White Masks*, trans. C. L. Markmann (London: Pluto Press, 1986), pp. 18–22.
5 Fanon (1986), p. 18.
6 Fanon (1986), p. 18.
7 In addition to writing groundbreaking postcolonial literary criticism, Ngugi's English-language novels include: *Weep Not, Child* (1964), *A Grain of Wheat* (1967), *The River Between* (1965) and *Petals of Blood* (1978), as well as a memoir of the time he spent detained by the Kenyan government, *Detained* (1981). Since turning to Gikuyu, Ngugi has written a play, *I Will Marry When I Want* (with Ngugi wa Mirii, 1977), and novels such as *Devil on the Cross* (1980) and *Matigari* (1987).
8 Ngugi wa Thiong'o, *Decolonising the Mind: The Politics of Language in African Literature* (Trenton, NJ: Africa New World Press, 1986), p. 16.
9 Ngugi wa Thiong'o (1986), pp. 15–16.
10 By contrast, Chinua Achebe contends that African writers must write in a European language to capture a wide readership – with the qualification that the author need not stick to the 'Queen's English'. The writer can, instead, develop forms of English that are appropriate in an African context.
11 Ngugi wa Thiong'o, Taban Lo Liyong and Henry Owuor-Anyumba, 'On the Abolition of the English Department', *Norton Anthology of Theory and Criticism*, ed. Vincent B. Leitch (New York: Norton, 2001), p. 2093.
12 Ngugi expands on these ideas in his book *Writers in Politics* (London: Heinemann, 1981).
13 For an interesting discussion of this, see J. Joyce, 'African-centered Scholarship: Interrogating Black Studies, Pan-Africanism and Afrocentricity', in *Decolonizing the Academy: African Diaspora Studies*, ed. C. Davies (Trenton, NJ: Africa New World Press, 2003), pp. 125–47.
14 Jamaica Kincaid, *A Small Place* (New York: Farrar, Straus and Giroux, 1988), p. 31.

15 For more on this metaphor, see Diane Simmons's *Jamaica Kincaid* (New York: Twayne, 1994), pp. 138–40.
16 Kincaid (1988), p. 43.
17 Kincaid (1988), pp. 42–3.
18 E. K. Brathwaite, *History of the Voice: The Development of Nation Language in Anglophone Caribbean Poetry* (Boston: Beacon Press, 1984), pp. 5–6.
19 Brathwaite (1984), p. 8.
20 Brathwaite (1984), p. 7.
21 Brathwaite (1984), p. 8.
22 Derek Walcott, 'What the Twilight Says: An Overture', in *Dream on Monkey Mountain and Other Plays* (New York: Farrar, 1970), p. 30.
23 Walcott (1970), p. 31.
24 W. Baer, ed., *Conversations with Derek Walcott* (Jackson: University Press of Mississippi, 1996), p. 28.
25 Walcott (1970), p. 33.
26 James Kelman, *How Late It Was, How Late* (London: Vintage, 1994), p. 3.
27 Punter (2000), p. 114.
28 *Daily Telegraph*, 13 October 1994, p. 9.
29 James Kelman, 'Booker Prize Acceptance Speech', *Scotland on Sunday*, 16 October 1994, p. 12.
30 C. Wright, 'Scotched', *Boston Phoenix*, 15 May 1997, p. 5.
31 Kelman (1994), p. 12.
32 Quoted in E. Kelly, 'Multi-Ethnic Scotland: Race, Religion and Language', *Scottish Affairs* 26 (Winter 1998), p. 85.

CHAPTER FOUR

1 Quoted in Elleke Boehmer, *Colonial and Postcolonial Literature* (Oxford: Oxford University Press, 1995), pp. 218–19.
2 Eric Michaels, 'Constraints on Knowledge in the Economy of Oral Information', *Current Anthropology* 26.4 (1985), p. 17.
3 Michaels (1985), p. 21.
4 Marshall McLuhan, *Understanding Media* (London: Routledge, 1964), p. 36.
5 Jeff Lewis, *Cultural Studies: The Basics* (London: Sage, 2000), p. 384.
6 Penny van Toorn, 'Aboriginal Writing', *The Cambridge Companion to Canadian Literature* (Cambridge: Cambridge University Press, 2004), p. 24.
7 Maria Campbell, 'Preface', *Achimoona* (Saskatoon, SK: Fifth House, 1985), p. x.
8 Emma LaRocque, 'Here Are Our Voices – Who Will Hear?', in *Writing the Circle: Native Women of Western Canada*, ed. J. Perrault (Edmonton: NeWest, 1990), p. xx.
9 LaRocque (1990), p. xvii.
10 Bill Ashcroft, Gareth Griffiths and Helen Tifflin, eds, *The Post-Colonial Studies Reader* (London: Routledge, 1995), p. 322.
11 Thomas King, *Green Grass, Running Water* (Toronto: Harper, 1999), p. 1.
12 Thomas King, 'Godzilla vs. Post-Colonial', *World Literature Written in English* 30.2 (1990), p. 11.
13 King (1990), p. 3.
14 King (1990), p. 4.
15 King (1990), p. 5.
16 Terry Goldie, *Fear and Temptation: The Image of the Indigene in Canadian, Australian and New Zealand Literatures* (Montreal: McGill-Queen's University Press, 1989), p. 125.
17 Walter Ong, *Orality and Literacy: The Technologizing of the World* (London: Methuen, 1982), p. 27.
18 Ong (1982), p. 29.

19 Mudrooroo, 'White Forms, Aboriginal Content', in *Aboriginal Writing Today*, ed. J. Davis and B. Hodge (Canberra: Australian Institute of Aboriginal Studies, 1985), p. 20.
20 Boehmer (1995), p. 229.
21 Mudrooroo, *Doctor Wooreddy's Prescription for Enduring the Ending of the World* (Melbourne: Hyland House, 1983), p. 196.
22 Boehmer (1995), p. 232.
23 Mudrooroo, *Writing from the Fringe: A Study of Modern Aboriginal Literature in Australia* (Melbourne: Hyland House, 1990), p. 24.
24 E. R. Knudsen, *The Circle and the Spiral: A Study of Australian Aboriginal and New Zealand Maori Literature* (Amsterdam: Rodopi, 2004), p. xiv.
25 Knudsen (2004), p. xi.
26 Patricia Grace, *Collected Stories* (Auckland: Penguin, 1987), p. 11.
27 J. Bardolph, 'A Way of Talking: A Way of Seeing: The Short Stories of Patricia Grace', *Commonwealth: Essays and Studies* 12.2 (1990), p. 32.
28 Grace (1987), p. 14.
29 Grace (1987), p. 14.
30 Grace (1987), p. 14.

CHAPTER FIVE

1 Derek Walcott, *Omeros* (New York: Farrar, Straus and Giroux, 1990), p. 233.
2 Homer is the name given to the author of the early Greek poems the *Iliad* and the *Odyssey*. It is now generally believed that they were composed orally in the period from the 8th to 7th century BC. These poems are epics, which is a broadly defined genre of narrative poetry, characterized by great length, multiple settings, large numbers of characters and a long time span.
3 *Beowulf* is an Old English epic poem composed during the Early Middle Ages. Traditionally, the poem's date of composition has been estimated as approximately 750–800 AD. But some estimates place it close to 1000 AD.
4 John Thieme, *Postcolonial Con-texts: Writing Back to the Canon* (London: Continuum, 2001), pp. 1–3.
5 Thieme (2001), p. 1.
6 Thieme (2001), p. 2.
7 Ashcroft, Griffiths and Tiffin (1989), p. 189 [or Ashcroft et al.]
8 Judie Newman, *The Ballistic Bard: Postcolonial Fictions* (London: Arnold, 1995), p. 24.
9 Gayatri Spivak, 'Three Women's Texts and a Critique of Imperialism', *Critical Inquiry* 12 (1986), p. 244.
10 Spivak (1986), p. 261.
11 Spivak (1986), p. 253.
12 Benita Parry, 'Problems in Current Theories of Colonial Discourse', *Oxford Literary Review* 9.1 (1987), p. 30.
13 Parry (1987), p. 30.
14 Parry (1987), p. 34.
15 Parry (1987), p. 35.
16 Peter Hulme, 'The Locked Heart: The Creole Family Romance of *Wide Sargasso Sea*', in *Colonial Discourse/Postcolonial Theory*, ed. Baker, Hulme and Iverson (Manchester: Manchester University Press, 1994), p. 72.
17 Newman (1995), p. 15.
18 Newman (1995), p. 15.
19 For instance, J. M. Coetzee's 1986 novel *Foe* (a rewriting of Defoe's *Robinson Crusoe* from the perspective of Friday) is completely dependant on the reader having knowledge of Defoe's text. *Foe* cannot stand on its own; it exists as a corollary or even an appendix to Defoe's 1719 novel.

20 Ruth P. Jhabvala, *Heat and Dust* (London: Penguin, 1975), p. 73.

21 Jhabvala (1975), p. 43.

22 Richard Cronin, '*The Hill of Devi* and *Heat and Dust*', *Essays in Criticism* 36 (1986), p. 157.

23 Newman (1995), p. 2.

24 Edward Said, *The World, the Text and the Critic* (London: Faber, 1984), pp. 171–6.

25 Thieme (2001), p. 9. See also Tabish Khair, *Babu Fictions: Alienation in Contemporary Indian English Novels* (Delhi: Oxford University Press, 2001), p. 286.

26 Salman Rushdie, *Midnight's Children* (London: Picador, 1981), p. 258.

27 Said (1993), pp. 100–16.

28 Said (1993), p. xx.

CHAPTER SIX

1 Aimé Césaire, *Discourse on Colonialism*, trans. J. Pinkham (New York: Monthly Review Press, 1972), p. 9.

2 Césaire (1972), pp. 11, 21.

3 J. M. Coetzee, *The Narrative of Jacobus Coetzee*, in *Dusklands* (London: Vintage, 1974), p. 59.

4 Coetzee (1974), p. 58.

5 Dominic Head, *J. M. Coetzee* (Cambridge: Cambridge University Press, 1997), p. 34.

6 Head (1997), p. 38.

7 Coetzee (1974), pp. 79–80.

8 Rosemary Jolly, *Colonization, Violence, and Narration in White South African Writing* (Athens, OH: Ohio University Press, 1996), p. 117.

9 Loomba (1998), p. 54.

10 Gayatri Spivak, 'Can the Subaltern Speak?', in *Marxism and the Interpretation of Culture*, ed. Nelson and Grossberg (Basingstoke: Macmillan, 1988), p. 279.

11 For more on Subaltern Studies, see Dipesh Chakrabarty's *Habitations of Modernity: Essays in the Wake of Subaltern Studies* (Chicago: University of Chicago Press, 2002).

12 Gayatri Spivak, *A Critique of Postcolonial Reason: Toward a Critique of the Vanishing Present* (Cambridge, MA: Harvard University Press, 1999), p. 144.

13 Spivak (1988), p. 306.

14 Spivak (1988), p. 306.

15 Scholars interested in subaltern studies have recently been drawn to Dalit literature of India. Dalit refers to a person who is oppressed or broken, an untouchable or an outcaste. It was used in the 1930s as a Hindi and Marathi translation of 'depressed classes'. In the 1970s, the 'Dalit Panthers' revived the term and expanded its reference to various social groups, including poor peasants, women and people who are exploited politically or economically. Dalit has become a symbol of change and revolution. See Arjun Dangle's *Poisoned Bread: Translations from Modern Marathi Dalit Literature* (Stosius Inc/Advent Books Division, 1992).

16 Patricia Grace, *Baby No-Eyes* (London: Women's Press, 1999), p. 38.

17 Grace (1999), p. 38.

18 Grace (1999), p. 37.

19 Michelle Keown, *Postcolonial Pacific Writing* (London: Routledge, 2005), pp. 168–9.

20 Keown (2005), p. 164.

21 Frantz Fanon, *The Wretched of the Earth*, trans. C. Farrington (London: Penguin, 1986), p. 43.

22 Fanon (1986), p. 69.

23 Fanon (1986), p. 70.

24 Fanon (1986), p. 71.

25 Shimmer Chinodya, *Harvest of Thorns* (London: Heinemann, 1989), p. 115.

26 Chinodya (1989), p. 162.

27 Ranka Primorac, 'Shimmer Chinodya', *The Literary Encyclopedia*, 21 March 2002, The Literary Dictionary Company, 6 July 2006. http://www.litencyc.com/php/speople.php?rec=true&UID=863.
28 Toni Morrison, *The Bluest Eye* (London: Vintage, 1999), p. 31.
29 Morrison (1999), p. 32.
30 Morrison (1999), p. 31.
31 Toni Morrison, Afterword, *The Bluest Eye* (London: Vintage, 1999), p. 172.
32 Punter (2000), p. 22.

CHAPTER SEVEN

1 Kincaid (1988), p. 35.
2 Kincaid (1988), pp. 34–6.
3 Patrick Holland and Graham Huggan, *Tourists with Typewriters: Critical Reflections on Contemporary Travel Writing* (Ann Arbor: University of Michigan Press, 1998), p. 48.
4 Henry Morton Stanley, *In Darkest Africa* [1890] (Santa Barbara, CA: The Narrative Press, 2001), p. 35.
5 Stanley (2001), p. 77.
6 David Spurr, *The Rhetoric of Empire: Colonial Discourse in Journalism, Travel Writing and Imperial Administration* (Durham, NC: Duke University Press, 1993), pp. 76–7.
7 Douglas Ivison, 'Travel Writing at the End of Empire: A Pom Named Bruce and the Mad White Giant', *English Studies in Canada* 29.3–4 (December 2003), pp. 200–1.
8 Pratt (1992), p. 5.
9 Pratt (1992), p. 5.
10 Pratt (1992), p. 4.
11 Pratt (1992), p. 7.
12 Pratt (1992), p. 7.
13 Mary Kingsley, *Travels in West Africa* [1897] (New York: Dover, 2003), p. 278.
14 Kingsley (1897), p. 121.
15 Kingsley (1897), p. 362.
16 Kingsley (1897), p. 363.
17 Kingsley (1897), p. 502.
18 Sara Mills, *Discourses of Difference: An Analysis of Women's Travel Writing and Colonialism* (London: Routledge, 1991), pp. 153–75.
19 Mills (1997), pp. 115–16.
20 James Buzzard, *Routes: Travel and Translation in the Late Twentieth Century* (Cambridge, MA: Harvard University Press, 1997), p. 5.
21 Buzzard (1997), p. 2.
22 Amitav Ghosh, 'Foreword', in *Other Routes: 1500 Years of African and Asian Travel Writing*, Khair, Leer, Edwards and Ziadeh, eds (Oxford: Signal Books, 2006), p. ix.
23 Ghosh (2006), p. ix.
24 Ghosh (2006), p. x.
25 Ghosh (2006), p. xii.
26 Tabish Khair, 'Introduction', in *Other Routes: 1500 Years of African and Asian Travel Writing*, Khair, Leer, Edwards, Ziadeh, eds (Oxford: Signal Books, 2006), pp. 6–7.
27 Khair (2006), p. 7.
28 Caryl Phillips, 'Necessary Journeys', *The Guardian*, Saturday 11 December, 2004. http://books.guardian.co.uk/review/story/0,,1370289,00.html.
29 Caryl Phillips, *The European Tribe* (London: Picador, 1987), p. x.
30 Phillips (1987), p. 1.
31 Phillips (1987), p. 29.
32 Phillips (1987), p.129.

CHAPTER EIGHT

1 Brian Friel, *Translations* (London: Faber and Faber, 1980), p. 31.
2 Friel (1980), p. 31.
3 Benedict Anderson, *Imagined Communities: Reflections on the Origin and Spread of Nationalism* (London: Verso, 1983), p. 175.
4 Anderson (1983), p. 175.
5 Michael Ondaatje, *Running in the Family* (New York: Norton, 1982), p. 22.
6 Ondaatje (1982), p. 63.
7 Ondaatje (1982), p. 63.
8 Ondaatje (1982), p. 64.
9 Ondaatje (1982), p. 63.
10 Michael Ondaatje, *Anil's Ghost* (Toronto: McClelland and Stewart, 2000), p. 39.
11 Ondaatje (2000), p. 146.
12 Ondaatje (2000), p. 54.
13 Ondaatje (2000), p. 54.
14 Ondaatje (2000), p. 55.
15 Graham Huggan, 'Decolonizing the Map: Post-Colonialism, Post-Structuralism and the Cartography Connection', *Ariel* 20.4 (1989), p. 123.
16 Graham Huggan, *Territorial Disputes: Maps and Mapping in Contemporary Canadian and Australian Fiction* (Toronto: University of Toronto Press, 1994), p. 31.
17 Huggan (1994), p. 31.
18 Huggan (1994), p. 31.
19 Huggan (1994), p. 57.
20 Huggan (1994), p. 58.
21 Huggan (1989), p. 127.
22 J. B. Harley, 'Maps, Knowledge, Power', in *The Iconography of Landscape*, Cosgrove and Daniels, eds, (Cambridge: Cambridge University Press, 1988), p. 278.
23 Harley (1988), p. 278.
24 Margaret Atwood, *Survival* (Toronto: Oxford University Press, 1972), p. 19.
25 Margaret Atwood, *Surfacing* (Toronto: McClelland and Stewart, 1973), p. 5.
26 Atwood (1973), p. 121.
27 Punter (2000), p. 30.
28 Atwood (1973), p. 139.
29 Karen Piper, *Cartographic Fictions: Maps, Race, and Identity* (New Brunswick, NJ: Rutgers University Press, 2002), p. 7.
30 Piper (2002), p. 16.
31 Shani Mootoo, *Cereus Blooms at Night* (Toronto: McClelland and Stewart, 1996), p. 70.
32 Mootoo (1996), p. 93.
33 Mootoo (1996), p. 92.
34 Mootoo (1996), p. 93.

CHAPTER NINE

1 H. Rider Haggard, *King Solomon's Mines* (London: Dent, 1885), p. 74.
2 Haggard (1885), p. 118.
3 McClintock (1995), p. 3.
4 McClintock (1995), p. 151.
5 Joseph Conrad, *Heart of Darkness* (London: Penguin, 1975), p. 87.
6 Said (1978), p. 6.
7 Said (1978), p. 207.
8 Reina Lewis, *Gendering Orientalism: Race, Femininity and Representation* (New York: Routledge, 1996), p. 18.

9 Lewis (1996), p. 18.

10 Jane Miller, *Seductions: Studies in Reading and Culture* (London: Virago, 1990), pp. 118–20.

11 Spivak (1988), p. 308.

12 The Theatre of the Oppressed was founded in Brazil by Augusto Boal (born 1931). Boal was an innovative and influential theatrical director, writer and politician who developed a political theatrical form originally used in radical popular education movements and influenced by the book *Pedagogy of the Oppressed* (1968) written by Paulo Freire (1921–97).

13 Carolyn Cooper, *Noises in the Blood: Orality, Gender and the Vulgar Body of Jamaican Popular Culture* (London: Macmillan, 1993), p. 87.

14 Chandra Talpade Mohanty, *Feminism Without Borders: Decolonizing Theory, Practicing Solidarity* (Durham, NC: Duke University Press, 2003), pp. 148–62.

15 Jean Paul Sartre, 'Preface', in Frantz Fanon, *The Wretched of the Earth* [1961], trans. R. Philcox (New York: Grove Press, 2004), p. xliii.

16 Tsitsi Dangarembga, *Nervous Conditions* (London: Women's Press, 1988), pp. 10–24.

17 Pauline Ada Uwakweh, 'Debunking Patriarchy: The Liberational Quality of Voicing in Tsitsi Dangarembga's *Nervous Conditions*', *Research in African Literatures* 26.1 (Spring 1995), pp. 75–80.

18 Uwakweh (1995), p. 78.

19 Uwakweh (1995), p. 79.

20 For more on this debate, see M. Vizzard, '"Of Mimicry and Woman": Hysteria and Anti-Colonial Feminism in Tsitsi Dangarembga's *Nervous Conditions*', *SPAN: Journal of the South Pacific Association for Commonwealth Literature and Language Studies* 36 (1993) and Deepika Bahri, 'Disembodying the Corpus: Postcolonial Pathology in Tsitsi Dangarembga's *Nervous Conditions*', *Postmodern Culture* 5.1 (1994).

21 Trinh T. Minh-ha, *Woman, Native, Other: Writing Postcoloniality and Feminism* (Bloomington: Indiana University Press, 1989), p. 28.

22 Trinh T. Minh-ha, 'Not You/Like You: Post-Colonial Women and the Interlocking Questions of Identity and Difference', *Inscriptions* 3–4 (1988), http://humwww.ucsc.edu/cultstudies/PUBS/Inscriptions/vol_3-4/v3-4top.html.

CHAPTER TEN

1 Peter Brooker, *A Concise Dictionary of Cultural Theory* (London: Arnold, 1999), p. 182.

2 John C. Hawley, *Postcolonial, Queer: Theoretical Intersections* (Albany: SUNY Press, 2001), p. 1.

3 Hawley (2001), p. 9.

4 Christopher Lane, *The Ruling Passion: British Colonial Allegory and the Paradox of Homosexual Desire* (Durham, NC: Duke University Press, 1995), p. 232.

5 Lane (1995), p. xi.

6 Lane (1995), p. 3.

7 Lane (1995), p. 41.

8 Lane (1995), p. 21.

9 Dionne Brand, *In Another Place, Not Here* (Toronto: Vintage, 1996), pp. 3–4.

10 Heather Smyth, 'Sexual Citizenship and Canadian-Caribbean Fiction: Dionne Brand's *In Another Place, Not Here* and Shani Mootoo's *Cereus Blooms at Night*', *Ariel* 30.2 (April 1999), p. 153.

11 Brand (1996), p. 167.

12 Peter Dickinson, *Here is Queer: Nationalisms, Sexualities, and the Literatures of Canada* (Toronto: University of Toronto Press, 1999), p. 157.

13 Jarrod Hayes, *Queer Nations: Marginal Sexualities in the Maghreb* (Chicago: University of Chicago Press, 2000), p. 96.

14 Joseph Massad, 'Re-orienting Desire: The Gay International and the Arab World,' *Public Culture* 14 (2002), p. 362.

15 Gayatri Gopinath, *Impossible Desires: Queer Diasporas and South Asian Public Cultures*

(Durham, NC: Duke University Press, 2005), pp. 6–7.
16 Gopinath (2005), p. 22.
17 Gopinath (2005), p. 21.
18 Gopinath (2005), p. 21.

CHAPTER ELEVEN

1 Toni Morrison, *Beloved* (New York: Signet, 1987), p. 3.
2 Liliane Weissberg, 'Gothic Spaces: The Political Aesthetics of Toni Morrison's *Beloved*', *Modern Gothic: A Reader,* ed. Sage and Smith (Manchester: Manchester University Press, 1996), pp. 115–16.
3 Weissberg (1996), p. 116.
4 Morrison (1987), p. 259.
5 Morrison (1987), p. 245.
6 Homi Bhabha, *The Location of Culture* (London: Routledge, 1994), p. 15.
7 Bhabha (1994), p. 17.
8 Bhabha (1994), p. 17.
9 Judie Newman, 'Postcolonial Gothic: Ruth Prawer Jhabvala and the Sobhraj', *Modern Gothic: A Reader*, ed. Sage and Smith (Manchester: Manchester University Press, 1996), p. 171.
10 Newman (1996), p. 185.
11 Jacques Derrida, *Specters of Marx: The State of the Debt, the Work of Mourning, and the New International*, trans. by Peggy Kamuf (New York: Routledge, 1994), p. 37.
12 Derek Walcott, 'The Muse of History', in *Is Massa Day Dead?*, ed. Orde Coombs (New York: Anchor, 1974), p. 67.
13 David Punter (2000), p. 64.
14 Fred D'Aguiar, *Feeding the Ghosts* (London: Chatto and Windus, 1997), p. 229.
15 D'Aguiar (1997), p. 222.
16 D'Aguiar (1997), p. 230.
17 Thieme (2001), p. 91.
18 Slavoj Zizek, *Looking Awry: An Introduction to Lacan through Popular Culture* (Cambridge, MA: MIT Press, 1991), p. 44.
19 David Punter and Glennis Byron, *The Gothic* (Oxford: Blackwell, 2004), p. 54.
20 Punter and Byron (2004), p. 55.
21 Punter and Byron (2004), p. 54.
22 Punter and Byron (2004), p. 55.
23 Margaret Turner, *Imagining Culture: New World Narrative and the Writing of Canada* (Montreal: McGill-Queen's University Press, 1995), p. 22.
24 Turner (1995), p. 4.
25 Earle Birney, 'Can. Lit.', in *Oxford Book of Canadian Poetry,* ed. Margaret Atwood (Toronto: Oxford University Press), p. 116.
26 Jonathan Kertzer, *Worrying the Nation: Imagining a National Literature in English Canada* (Toronto: University of Toronto Press, 1998), pp. 37–8.
27 Kertzer (1998), p. 38.
28 Kertzer (1998), p. 119.
29 Homi Bhabha, 'DissemiNation: Time, Narrative and the Margins of the Modern Nation', in *The Location of Culture* (London: Routledge, 1994), p. 139.
30 A. Trevorson, 'The Number of Magic Alternatives: Salman Rushdie's 1001 Gothic Nights', in *Empire and the Gothic: The Politics of Genre*, ed. Smith and Hughes (Basingstoke: Palgrave Macmillan, 2003), p. 209. In this essay, Trevorson offers an interesting reading of what he calls 'Bhabha's Gothic' and, by extension, the spectres that haunt the notion of national unity.
31 Ken Gelder and Jane M. Jacobs, *Uncanny Australia: Sacredness and Identity in a Postcolonial Nation* (Melbourne: Melbourne University Press, 1998), pp. 36–7.

32 Gelder and Jacobs (1998), p. 37.
33 Gelder and Jacobs (1998), p. 23.

CHAPTER TWELVE

1 Kincaid (1988), pp. 36–7
2 Kincaid (1988), p. 54.
3 Kincaid (1988), p. 55.
4 This debate over the effectiveness of the TRC hearings has been fuelled by, among others, J. M. Coetzee. His 1999 novel *Disgrace* does not depict the articulation of painful memories or the submission of confessions as enacting liberation from the past. Instead, Coetzee avoids the confessional mode to suggest that South Africans must come to terms with their memories and the diminished possibilities bequeathed by history and one's participation in the crimes of the past. J. M. Coetzee, *Disgrace* (London: Vintage, 1999). For more on this these issues in South African literature (although not specifically on Coetzee), see M. Heyns, 'The Whole Country's Truth: Confession and Narrative in Recent South African Writing', *Modern Fiction Studies* 46.1 (2000), pp. 42–66.
5 Anderson (1983), pp. 202–3.
6 Anderson (1983), p. 203.
7 Anderson (1983), p. 204.
8 Jamaica Kincaid, *My Brother* (New York: Farrar, Straus and Giroux, 1997), p. 74.
9 Kincaid (1997), p. 75.
10 Louise Bernard, 'Countermemory and Return: Reclamation of the (Postmodern) Self in Jamaica Kincaid's *The Autobiography of My Mother* and *My Brother*', *Modern Fiction Studies* 48.1 (2002), p. 132.
11 Derek Walcott, 'The Muse of History', in *Is Massa Dead? Black Moods in the Caribbean*, ed. Orde Coombes (New York: Doubleday, 1974), p. 64.
12 Walcott (1973), p. 66.
13 Kali Tal, *Worlds of Hurt: Reading the Literatures of Trauma* (Cambridge: Cambridge University Press, 1996), p. 5.
14 Tal, p. 6.
15 Tal, pp. 6–7.
16 Tal, p. 6.
17 Joy Kogawa, *Obasan* (Toronto: Penguin, 1981), pp. 12–36.
18 Kogawa (1981), pp. 30–1.
19 Kogawa (1981), p. 31.
20 Cynthia Wong, *Reading Asian American Literature* (Princeton: Princeton University Press, 1993), p. 19.
21 Roy Miki, *Broken Entries: Race Subjectivity Writing* (Toronto: Mercury Press, 1998), p. 8.
22 Miki (1998), p. 9.
23 Roy Miki and Cassandra Kobayashi, *Justice in Our Time: The Japanese Canadian Redress Settlement* (Vancouver: Talonbooks, 1991), p. 17.
24 Smaro Kamboureli, *Scandalous Bodies: Diasporic Literature in English Canada* (Toronto: Oxford University Press, 2000), p. 186.
25 Kamboureli (2000), p. 227.
26 Cathy Caruth, *Unclaimed Experience: Trauma, Narrative, and History* (Baltimore: Johns Hopkins University Press, 1996), p. 5.
27 Judith Herman, *Trauma and Recovery* (New York: Basic Books, 1992), p. 1.
28 Ruth Leys, *Trauma: A Genealogy* (Chicago: Chicago University Press, 2000), p. 109.
29 Leys (2000), p. 110.
30 Paul Antze and Michael Lambek, 'Introduction', in *Past Tense: Cultural Essays in Trauma and Memory* (New York: Routledge, 1996), p. xxvi.

31 Michael Ondaatje, *Anil's Ghost* (Toronto: McClelland and Stewart, 2000), p. 156.
32 Ondaatje (2000), p. 157.
33 Ondaatje (2000), p. 79.

CHAPTER THIRTEEN

1 Derek Walcott, 'A Far Cry from Africa' [1962], in *Norton Anthology of Modern Poetry* (New York: Norton, 1988), p. 1368.
2 Bruce King, *Derek Walcott: A Caribbean Life* (Oxford: Oxford University Press, 2000), pp. 274–5.
3 King (2000), pp. 292–3.
4 Derek Walcott. 'The Schooner Flight' in *Collected Poems 1948–1984* (New York: Farrar, Straus and Giroux, 1986), pp. 360–1.
5 Mudrooroo, *Writing from the Fringe: A Study of Modern Aboriginal Literature* (Melbourne: Hyland House, 1990), p. 24.
6 Mudrooroo (1990), p. 24.
7 Homi Bhabha, *The Location of Culture* (New York: Routledge, 1994), p. 112.
8 Bhabha (1994), p. 112.
9 Bhabha (1994), pp. 117–22.
10 Bhabha (1994), p. 153.
11 Bhabha (1994), p. 156.
12 Maria Campbell, *Halfbreed* (Toronto: McClelland and Stewart, 1973), p. 83.
13 Campbell (1973), p. 120.
14 Campbell (1973), p. 133.
15 Campbell (1973), p. 133.
16 Campbell (1973), p. 133.
17 Robert J. C. Young, *Colonial Desire: Hybridity in Theory, Culture and Race* (London: Routledge, 1995), p. 22.
18 Young (1995), pp. 22–3.
19 Ashcroft et al. (1989), p. 88.
20 Ashcroft et al. (1989), p. 89.
21 Ashcroft et al. (1989), p. 90.
22 Ashcroft et al. (1989), p. 90.
23 Ashcroft et al. (1989), p. 91.
24 Ashcroft et al. (1995), p. 183.
25 Bhabha (1994), p. 88.
26 Bhabha (1994), p. 89.
27 Benita Parry, 'Signs of Our Times: Discussion of Homi Bhabha's *The Location of Culture*', *Third Text* 28/29 (Autumn/Winter 1994), p. 9.
28 Paul Gilroy, *The Black Atlantic: Modernity and Double Consciousness* (Cambridge, MA: Harvard University Press, 1993), p. 16.
29 Gilroy (1993), p. 16.
30 Stuart Hall, 'New Ethnicities', in *Stuart Hall, Critical Dialogues in Cultural Studies*, Morley and Chen, eds (London: Routledge, 1996), p. 447.
31 Boehmer (1995), p. 233.
32 Boehmer (1995), p. 234.
33 Tabish Khair, *Babu Fictions: Alienation in Contemporary Indian English Novels* (Delhi: Oxford University Press, 2001), p. 78.
34 Khair (2001), p. 79.
35 Khair (2001), p. 80.
36 Tabish Khair, 'Unhybrid', in *When Parallel Lines Meet* (Delhi: Penguin, 2000), pp. 32–3.
37 Khair (2001), p. 80.

CHAPTER FOURTEEN

1 Robin Cohen, *Global Diasporas* (London: UCL Press, 1997), p. v.
2 Cohen (1997), p. ix.
3 Gilroy (1993), p. 32.
4 Paul Gilroy, 'The Black Atlantic as a Counterculture of Modernity', in *Theorizing Diaspora*, Braziel and Mannur, eds (Oxford: Blackwell, 2003), p. 66.
5 Phillips (2004).
6 James Procter, *Dwelling Places: Postwar Black British Writing* (Manchester: Manchester University Press, 2003), p. 97.
7 Caryl Phillips, *The Atlantic Sound* (London: Faber and Faber, 2000), p. 15.
8 Phillips (2000), p. 15.
9 Bénédicte Ledent, *Caryl Phillips* (Manchester: Manchester University Press, 2002), p. 8.
10 Ledent (2002), p. 126.
11 Bill Ashcroft, Gareth Griffiths and Helen Tiffin, *Key Concepts in Post-Colonial Studies* (London: Routledge, 1998), p. 68.
12 Ashcroft et al. (1998), pp. 69–70.
13 Sunetra Gupta, 'Interview with Bronwyn Williams', February 1996. http://social.chass.ncsu.edu/jouvert/v3i3/willia.htm.
14 Sunetra Gupta, *The Glassblower's Breath* (London: Orion, 1993), p. 107.
15 Hanif Kureishi, *The Black Album* (London: Faber and Faber, 1995), p. 89.
16 Jana Evans Braziel and Anita Mannur, 'Nation, Migration, Globalization: Points of Contention in Diaspora Studies', in *Theorizing Diaspora*, Braziel and Mannur, eds (Oxford: Blackwell, 2003), p. 3.
17 Gayatri Gopinath, 'Nostalgia, Desire, Diaspora: South Asian Sexualities in Motion', in *Theorizing Diaspora*, Braziel and Mannur, eds (Oxford: Blackwell, 2003), p. 270.
18 Shyam Selvadurai, *Funny Boy* (Toronto: McClelland and Stewart, 1995), p. 121.
19 Gopinath (2003), p. 270.
20 Gopinath (2003), p. 275.
21 Stuart Hall, 'Cultural Identity and Diaspora', in *Identity: Community, Culture, Difference*, ed. Rutherford (London: Lawrence and Wishart, 1990), p. 234.
22 Hall (1990), p. 230.
23 Hall (1990), p. 226.
24 Arjun Appadurai, 'Disjuncture and Difference in the Global Cultural Economy', in *Theorizing Diaspora*, Braziel and Mannur, eds (Oxford: Blackwell, 2003), p. 31.

CHAPTER FIFTEEN

1 The World Trade Organization is an international organization designed to supervise and liberalize international trade. The organization deals with the rules of trade between nations at a global level; it is responsible for negotiating and implementing new trade agreements. The International Monetary Fund oversees the global financial system by observing exchange rates and balance of payments, as well as offering financial and technical assistance under certain conditions. The World Bank was intended to aid developing countries and promote sustainable growth through investment. Critics argue that it promotes the economic interests of wealthy nations.
2 Tom Hickley and Anita Rupprecht, 'Anti-globalisation Movements', in *A Historical Companion to Postcolonial Literatures in English*, ed. Poddar and Johnson (Edinburgh: Edinburgh University Press, 2005), p. 39.
3 Edward Said, *Culture and Imperialism* (London: Vintage, 1993), p. 35.
4 Ann McClintock, 'The Angel of Progress: Pitfalls of the Term "Post-colonial"', *Social Text* 21 (1992), p. 95.
5 Loomba (1998), pp. 5–6.

6 Fidelis Balogun, *Adjusted Lives: Stories of Structural Adjustments* (Trenton, NJ: Africa New World Press, 1995), p. 100.

7 Balogun (1995), p. 81.

8 Kincaid (1988), p. 14.

9 Justin D. Edwards, *Understanding Jamaica Kincaid* (Columbia, SC: University of South Carolina Press, 2007), p. 98.

10 Kincaid (1988), pp. 25–6.

11 For the financial information on Barclays Bank, see James Anyanzwa's 'Big Banks, Big Trouble', *Financial Standard*, 17 August 2005, p. 5. For more information on the GNP for Antigua and Barbuda, see the United Nations Statistics Division, Department of Economic and Social Affairs, http://unstats.un.org/unsd/snaama/.

12 *Life and Debt*, Director, Stephanie Black, Tuff Gong Pictures, 2001. This film is a feature-length documentary which addresses the impact of the Inter-American Development Bank, the International Monetary Fund and current globalization policies on developing countries such as Jamaica.

13 Michael Hardt and Antonio Negri, *Empire* (Cambridge, MA: Harvard University Press, 2000), p. xii.

14 Hardt and Negri (2000), p. xi.

15 Hardt and Negri (2000), p. xii.

16 Hardt and Negri (2000), p. 42.

17 Hardt and Negri (2000), p. 43.

18 Hardt and Negri (2000), p. 46.

19 Hardt and Negri (2000), p. 218.

20 Lisa Rofel, 'Modernity's Masculine Fantasies', in *Critically Modern: Alternatives, Alterities, Anthropologies*, ed. Knauft (Bloomington: Indiana University Press, 2002), p. 183.

21 D. Chakrabarty, *Provincializing Europe: Postcolonial Thought and Historical Difference* (Princeton: Princeton University Press, 2000), pp. 6–17.

22 Rofel (2002), p. 184.

23 Rofel (2002), p. 182.

24 Quoted in Julie Mullaney, *Arundhati Roy's The God of Small Things: A Reader's Guide* (New York: Continuum Press, 2002), p. 14.

25 Arundhati Roy's comments on the negative effects of globalization can be found in her non-fictional works, especially *The Cost of Living* (London: Flamingo, 1999) and *Power Politics* (Cambridge, MA: South End Press, 2001).

26 Mullaney (2002), p. 16.

27 Mullaney (2002), p. 49.

28 Arundhati Roy, *The God of Small Things* (London: Flamingo, 1997), p. 13.

29 Mullaney (2002), p. 50.

30 Punter (2000), p. 86.

31 Punter (2000), p. 183.

32 Punter (2000), p. 18.

Bibliography

POSTCOLONIALITY

Achebe, Chinua, *Things Fall Apart* (London: Heinemann, 1958).

Ahmed, A., *In Theory: Classes, Nations, Literatures* (London: Verso, 1992).

Allen, Venessa, 'Prince Charles' Hong Kong Fury', *The Mail*, 23 February 2006.

Anderson, Benedict, *Imagined Communities: Reflections on the Origin and Spread of Nationalism* (London: Verso, 1983).

Ashcroft, Bill, Griffiths, Gareth and Tiffin, Helen, *The Empire Writes Back: Theory and Practice in Post-Colonial Literatures* (London: Routledge, 1989).

Boehmer, Elleke, *Colonial and Postcolonial Literature* (Oxford: Oxford University Press, 1995).

Hardt, Michael and Negri, Antonio, *Empire* (Cambridge, MA: Harvard University Press, 2000).

Hardt, Michael and Negri, Antonio, *Multitude: War and Democracy in the Age of Empire* (New York: Penguin, 2004).

Loomba, Ania, *Colonial/Postcolonialism* (London: Routledge, 1998).

McClintock, Ann, *Imperial Leather: Race, Gender, and Sexuality in the Colonial Context* (New York: Routledge, 1995).

Moore-Gilbert, Bart, *Postcolonial Theory: Contexts, Practices, Politics* (London: Verso, 1997).

Pratt, Mary Louise, *Imperial Eyes: Travel Writing and Transculturation* (New York: Routledge, 1992).

Punter, David, *Postcolonial Imaginings: Fictions of a New World Order* (Edinburgh: Edinburgh University Press, 2000).

Said, Edward, *Culture and Imperialism* (London: Vintage, 1993).

FURTHER READING

Ashcroft, Bill, Griffiths, Gareth and Helen Tiffin, *Post-Colonial Studies: The Key Concepts* (London: Routledge, 2000).

Childs, P. and Williams, P., *An Introduction to Post-Colonial Theory* (Hemel Hempstead: Prentice Hall, 1997).

Ghandi, Leela, *Postcolonial Theory: A Critical Introduction* (New York: Columbia University Press, 1998).

Thieme, John, *Postcolonial Studies* (London: Edward Arnold, 1989).

Thieme, John, *The Arnold Anthology of Post-Colonial Literatures in English* (London: Edward Arnold, 1989).

Tiffin, C. and Lawson, A., *De-scribing Empire* (London: Routledge, 1994).

Wisker, Gina, *Postcolonial and African American Women's Writing: A Critical Introduction* (Basingstoke: Macmillan, 2000).

Young, Robert, *Postcolonialism: An Historical Introduction* (Oxford: Blackwell, 2001).

DIFFERENCE

Bhabha, Homi, 'On the Irremovable Strangeness of Being Different', *PMLA* 113.1 (January 1998).

Byron, C., 'Legacies of Darkness: Neocolonialism, Joseph Conrad, and Taleb Salih's *Season of Migration to the North*', *Ariel* 30 (October 1999).

Derrida, Jacques, 'Signature, event, context', *Glyph* 1 (1977).

Derrida, Jacques, *Writing and Difference*, trans. A. Bass (London: Routledge, 1978).

Deveaux, A., Interview with June Jordan, *Essence Magazine*, 12 Janurary 1981.

Ellman, R., ed., *Norton Anthology of Modern Poetry* (New York: Norton, 1988).

Gates, Henry Louis, ed., *'Race', Writing and Difference* (Chicago: Chicago University Press, 1987).

Jordan, June, *Civil Wars* (Boston: Beacon, 1981).

Jordan, June, 'Poem About My Rights', in Richard Ellman, ed., *Norton Anthology of Modern Poetry* (New York: Norton, 1988).

Malouf, David, *Remembering Babylon* (London: Vintage, 1993).

Said, Edward, *Orientalism* (New York: Vintage, 1978).

Salih, Tayeb, *Season of Migration to the North* (London: Heinemann, 1969).

Spivak, Gayatri, *The Spivak Reader* (New York: Routledge, 1996).

FURTHER READING

Currie, Mark, *Difference* (London: Routledge, 2000).

Chrisman, L. and Williams. P., eds, *Colonial Discourse and Post-Colonial Theory* (Hemel Hempstead: Prentice Hall, 1993).

Hulme, Keri, *Te Kaihau/The Windeater* (Brisbane: University of Queensland Press, 1986).

Lee, R., ed., *Other Britain, Other British: Contemporary Multi-cultural Fiction* (London: Pluto, 1995).

Plasa, C., *Textual Politics from Slavery to Postcolonialism: Race and Identification* (Basingstoke: Macmillan, 2000).

Young, Robert, *White Mythologies: Writing, History and the West* (London: Routledge, 1990).

LANGUAGE

Baer, W., ed., *Conversations with Derek Walcott* (Jackson: University Press of Mississippi, 1996).

Boyd, William, "Introduction", *Sozaboy: A Novel in Rotten English* (New York: Longman, 1985).

Brathwaite, K., *History of the Voice: The Development of Nation Language in Anglophone Caribbean Poetry* (Boston: Beacon Press, 1984).

Fanon, Frantz, *Black Skin, White Masks*, trans. C. L. Markmann (London: Pluto Press, 1986).

Joyce, Joyce B., 'African-Centered Scholarship: Interrogating Black Studies, Pan-Africanism and Afrocentricity', in C. Davies, ed., *Decolonizing the Academy: African Diaspora Studies* (Trenton, NJ: Africa World Press, 2003).

Kelly, E., 'Multi-Ethnic Scotland: Race, Religion and Language', *Scottish Affairs* 26 (winter 1998).

Kelman, James, 'Booker Prize Acceptance Speech', *Scotland on Sunday* 16 October 1994.

Kelman, James, *How Late It Was, How Late* (London: Vintage, 1994).

Kincaid, Jamaica, *A Small Place* (New York: Farrar, Straus and Giroux, 1988).

Punter, David, *Postcolonial Imaginings: Fictions of a New World Order* (Edinburgh: Edinburgh University Press, 2000).

Saro-Wiwa, Ken, *Sozaboy: A Novel in Rotten English* (New York: Longman, 1985).

Simmons, Diane *Jamaica Kincaid* (New York: Twayne, 1994).

Thiong'o, Ngugi wa, *Decolonising the Mind: The Politics of Language in African Literature* (Trenton, NJ: Africa New World Press, 1986).

Thiong'o, Ngugi wa, Liyong, T. and Owuor-Anyumba, H., 'On the Abolition of the English Department' in *Norton Anthology of Theory and Criticism*, ed. Vincent B. Leitch (New York: Norton, 2001).

Walcott, Derek, 'What the Twilight Says: An Overture', in *Dream on Monkey Mountain and Other Plays* (New York: Farrar, 1970).

Wright, E., 'Scotched', *Boston Phoenix* (15 May 1997).

FURTHER READING

Bennett, L., 'Colonialism in Reverse', in *Jamaica Labrish* (Kingston: Sangsters Books, 1966).

Brathwaite, Kamau, *Other Exiles* (Oxford: Oxford University Press, 1975).

Dirks, N., *Colonialism and Culture* (Ann Arbor: University of Michigan Press, 1992).

Fanon, Frantz, 'On National Culture' (1961), in *Literature in the Modern World*, ed. D. Walker (London: Edward Arnold, 1967).

Mukherjee, M., *The Perishable Empire: Essays on Indian Writing in English* (New Delhi: Oxford University Press, 2002).

Ngugi wa, Thiong'o, *A Grain of Wheat* (London: Heinemann, 1967).

Ngugi wa, Thiong'o, *Moving the Centre* (London: Heinemann, 1993).

Philip, Marlene N., *She Tries Her Tongue Her Silence Softly Breaks* (London: The Women's Press, 1989).

Talib, I., *The Language of Post-Colonial Literatures: An Introduction* (London: Routledge, 2002).

Zabus, Chantal, *The African Palimpsest: Indigenization of Language in the West African Europhone Novel* (Amsterdam: Rodopi, 1991).

ORALITY

Ashcroft, Ben, Griffiths, Gareth and Tiffin, Helen, eds, *The Post-Colonial Studies Reader* (London: Routledge, 1995).

Bardolph, J., 'A Way of Talking: A Way of Seeing: The Short Stories of Patricia Grace', *Commonwealth: Essays and Studies* 12.2 (1990).

Campbell, Maria, *Achimoona* (Saskatoon: Fifth House, 1985).

Goldie, Terry, *Fear and Temptation: The Image of the Indigene in Canadian, Australian and New Zealand Literatures* (Montreal: McGill-Queen's University Press, 1989).

Grace, Patricia, *Collected Stories* (Auckland: Penguin, 1987).

King, Thomas, 'Godzilla vs. Post-Colonial', *World Literature Written in English* 30.2 (1990).

King, Thomas, *Green Grass, Running Water* (Toronto: HarperCollins, 1999).

Knudsen, Eva, *The Circle and the Spiral: A Study of Australian Aboriginal and New Zealand Maori Literature* (Amsterdam: Rodopi, 2004).

LaRocque, Emma, 'Here Are Our Voices – Who Will Hear?', in *Writing the Circle: Native Women of Western Canada*, ed. J. Perrault (Edmonton: NeWest, 1990).

Lewis, J., *Cultural Studies: The Basics* (London: Sage, 2000).

McLuhan, Marshall, *Understanding Media* (London: Routledge, 1964).

Michaels, E., 'Constraints on Knowledge in the Economy of Oral Information', *Current Anthropology* 26.4 (1985).

Mudrooroo, *Doctor Wooreddy's Prescription for Enduring the Ending of the World* (Melbourne: Hyland House, 1983).

Mudrooroo, 'White Forms, Aboriginal Content', in *Aboriginal Writing Today*, ed. Davis and Hodge (Canberra: Australian Institute of Aboriginal Studies, 1985).

Mudrooroo, *Writing from the Fringe: A Study of Modern Aboriginal Literature in Australia* (Melbourne: Hyland House, 1990).

Ong, Walter, *Orality and Literacy: The Technologizing of the World* (London: Methuen, 1982).

Toorn, Penny, 'Aboriginal Writing', *The Cambridge Companion to Canadian Literature* (Cambridge: Cambridge University Press, 2004).

FURTHER READING

Armstrong, Jeanette, *Slash* (Penticton, BC: Theytus Books, 1996).

Brodber, E., *Jane and Louisa Will Soon Come Home* (London: New Beacon Books, 1980).

Cooper, Carolyn, *Noises in the Blood: Orality, Gender and the Vulgar Body of Jamaican Popular Culture* (London: Macmillan, 1993).

Duff, Alan, *Once Were Warriors* (New York: Vintage, 1990).

Duff, Alan, *Maori: The Crisis and the Challenge* (Auckland: HarperCollins, 1993).
Johnson, Linton Kwesi, *Mi Revalueshanary Fren* (London: Penguin, 2002).
Keown, Michelle, *Postcolonial Pacific Writing* (London: Routledge, 2005).
Silko, Leslie Marmon, *The Almanac of the Dead* (London: Penguin, 1991).

REWRITING
Coetzee, J. M., *Foe* (New York: Viking, 1986).
Cronin, R., '*The Hill of Devi* and *Heat and Dust*', *Essays in Criticism* 36 (1986).
Hulme, Peter, 'The Locked Heart: The Creole Family Romance of *Wide Sargasso Sea*', in Baker, Hulme and Iverson, eds, *Colonial Discourse/Postcolonial Theory* (Manchester: Manchester University Press, 1994).
Jhabvala, Ruth, *Heat and Dust* (London: Penguin, 1975).
Khair, Tabish, *Babu Fictions: Alienation in Contemporary Indian English Novels* (Delhi: Oxford University Press, 2001).
Newman, Judie, *The Ballistic Bard: Postcolonial Fictions* (London: Arnold, 1995).
Parry, Benita, 'Problems in Current Theories of Colonial Discourse', *Oxford Literary Review* 9.1 (1987).
Rushdie, Salman, *Midnight's Children* (London: Picador, 1981).
Said, Edward, *The World, the Text and the Critic* (London: Faber, 1984).
Spivak, Gayatri, 'Three Women's Texts and a Critique of Imperialism', *Critical Inquiry* 12 (1986).
Thieme, John, *Postcolonial Con-texts: Writing Back to the Canon* (London: Continuum, 2001).
Walcott, Derek, *Omeros* (New York: Farrar, Straus and Giroux, 1990).

FURTHER READING
Achebe, Chinua, *Arrow of God* (London: Heinemann, 1964).
Achebe, Chinua, *Anthills of Africa* (London: Heinemann, 1987).
Cliff, Michelle, *No Telephone to Heaven* (New York: Plume Books, 1996).
Devy, G. N., *After Amnesia: Tradition and Change in Indian Literary Criticism* (London: Sangam Books, 1992).
Driver, D. 'Transformation through Art: Writing, Representation and Subjectivity in Recent South African Fiction', in *World Literature Today* 70.1 (winter 1996).
Hutcheon, Linda, *The Canadian Postmodern* (Toronto: Oxford University Press, 1988).
McClintock, Ann, *Imperial Leather: Race, Gender and Sexuality in the Colonial Context* (London: Routledge, 1995).
Plasa, Carl, ed., *Jean Rhys:* Wide Sargasso Sea: *A Reader's Guide to Essential Criticism* (Basingstoke: Palgrave Macmillan, 2001).
Pollock, S., *Literary Cultures in History: Reconstructions from South Asia* (Berkeley, CA: University of California Press, 2003).

VIOLENCE
Césaire, Aimé, *Discourse on Colonialism*, trans. J. Pinkham (New York: Monthly Review Press, 1972).
Chakrabarty, D. *Habitations of Modernity: Essays in the Wake of Subaltern Studies* (Chicago: University of Chicago Press, 2002).
Chinodya, Shimmer, *Harvest of Thorns* (Oxford: Heinemann, 1989).
Coetzee, J. M., *The Narrative of Jacobus Coetzee*, in *Dusklands* (London: Vintage, 1974).
Dangle, A., *Poisoned Bread: Translations from Modern Marathi Dalit Literature* (Stosius Inc/ Advent Books Division, 1992).
Fanon, Frantz, *The Wretched of the Earth*, trans. C. Farrington (London: Penguin, 1986).
Grace, Patricia, *Baby No-Eyes* (London: Women's Press, 1999).
Head, Dominic, *J. M. Coetzee* (Cambridge: Cambridge University Press, 1997).

Jolly, R., *Colonization, Violence, and Narration in White South African Writing* (Athens, OH: Ohio University Press, 1996).

Keown, Michelle, *Postcolonial Pacific Writing* (London: Routledge, 2005).

Morrison, Toni, *The Bluest Eye* (London: Vintage, 1999).

Primorac, R., 'Shimmer Chinodya', *The Literary Encyclopedia*, 21 March 2002. The Literary Dictionary Company, 6 July 2006, http://www.litencyc.com/php/speople.php?rec=true& UID=863.

Spivak, Gayatri, 'Can the Subaltern Speak?', in *Marxism and the Interpretation of Culture*, ed. Nelson and Grossberg (Basingstoke: Macmillan, 1988).

Spivak, Gayatri, *A Critique of Postcolonial Reason: Toward a Critique of the Vanishing Present* (Cambridge, MA: Harvard University Press, 1999).

FURTHER READING

Coetzee, J. M., *Dusklands* (Johannesburg: Ravan Press, 1974).

Hardt, Michael and Negri, Antonio, *Multitude: War and Democracy in the Age of Empire* (New York: Penguin, 2004).

James, C. L. R., *A History of Pan-African Revolt* (Chicago: Charles H. Kerr, 1995).

Kriger, N. J., *Guerilla Veterans in Post-War Zimbabwe: Symbolic and Violent Politics, 1980–1987* (Cambridge: Cambridge University Press, 2003).

Lazarus, Neil, *Resistance in Post-Colonial African Fiction* (New Haven: Yale University Press, 1990).

Ngugi wa, Thiong'o, *Detained: A Writer's Prison Diary* (London: Heinemann, 1981).

Razack, S., *Dark Threats and White Knights: The Somalia Affair, Peacekeeping, and the New Imperialism* (Toronto: University of Toronto Press, 2004).

Said, Edward, *Peace and Its Discontents* (New York: Random House, 1995).

Salkey, A., *A Quality of Violence* (London: New Beacon Books, 1976).

TRAVEL

Buzzard, James, *Routes: Travel and Translation in the Late Twentieth Century* (Cambridge, MA: Harvard University Press, 1997).

Ghosh, Amitav, 'Foreword', *Other Routes: 1500 Years of African and Asian Travel Writing*, ed. Khair, Leer, Edwards, Ziadeh (Oxford: Signal Books, 2006).

Holland, P. and Huggan, Graham, *Tourists with Typewriters: Critical Reflections on Contemporary Travel Writing* (Ann Arbor: University of Michigan Press, 1998).

Ivison, Douglas, 'Travel Writing at the End of Empire: A Pom Named Bruce and the Mad White Giant', *English Studies in Canada* 29.3–4 (December 2003).

Khair, Tabish, 'Introduction', *Other Routes: 1500 Years of African and Asian Travel Writing*, ed. Khair, Leer, Edwards and Ziadeh (Oxford: Signal Books, 2006).

Kincaid, Jamaica, *A Small Place* (New York: Farrar, Straus and Giroux, 1988).

Kingsley, Mary, *Travels in West Africa* [1897] (New York: Dover, 2003).

Mills, Sara, *Discourses of Difference: An Analysis of Women's Travel Writing and Colonialism* (London: Routledge, 1991).

Phillips, Caryl, *The European Tribe* (London: Picador, 1987).

Phillips, Caryl, 'Necessary Journeys', *The Guardian*, Saturday, 11 December, 2004, http://books.guardian.co.uk/review/story/0,,1370289,00.html.

Pratt, Mary Louise, *Imperial Eyes: Travel Writing and Transculturation* (New York: Routledge, 1992).

Spurr, David, *The Rhetoric of Empire: Colonial Discourse in Journalism, Travel Writing and Imperial Administration* (Durham, NC: Duke University Press, 1993).

Stanley, Henry M., *In Darkest Africa* [1890] (Santa Barbara, CA: The Narrative Press, 2001).

FURTHER READING

Behdad, A., *Belated Travellers: Orientalism in the Age of Colonial Dissolution* (Durham: Duke University Press, 1994).

Hulme, Peter and Youngs, Tim, *The Cambridge Companion to Travel Writing* (Cambridge: Cambridge University Press, 2002).

Hulme, Peter, *Colonial Encounters: Europe and the Native Caribbean, 1492–1797* (London: Methuen, 1986).

Kincaid, Jamaica, *Among Flowers: A Walk in the Himalaya* (New York: National Geographic Books, 2005).

Lamming, George, *The Emigrants* (London: Allison and Busby, 1980).

Naipaul, V. S., *Among the Believers: An Islamic Journey* (London: Penguin, 1981).

Naipaul, V. S., *The Middle Passage* (London: Andre Deutsch, 1961).

Naipaul, V. S., *A Turn in the South* (London: Macmillan, 1989).

Said, Edward, *Out of Place* (New York: Vintage Books, 1999).

Said, Edward, *Reflections on Exile* (Cambridge, MA: Harvard University Press, 2000).

Suleri, Sara, *Meatless Days* (London: Flamingo, 1989).

Urry, John, *The Tourist Gaze: Leisure and Travel in Contemporary Societies* (London: Sage, 1990).

MAPS

Atwood, Margaret, *Survival* (Toronto: Oxford University Press, 1972).

Friel, Brian, *Translations* (London: Faber and Faber, 1980).

Hartley, J., 'Maps, Knowledge, Power', in Cosgrove and Daniels, eds, *The Iconography of Landscape* (Cambridge: Cambridge University Press, 1988).

Huggan, Graham, 'Decolonizing the Map: Post-Colonialism, Post-Structuralism and the Cartography Connection', *Ariel* 20.4 (1989).

Huggan, Graham, Territorial Disputes: Maps and Mapping in Contemporary Canadian and Australian Fiction (Toronto: University of Toronto Press, 1994).

Mootoo, Shani, *Cereus Blooms at Night* (Toronto: McClelland and Stewart, 1996).

Ondaatje, Michael, *Running in the Family* (New York: Norton, 1982).

Ondaatje, Michael, *Anil's Ghost* (Toronto: McClelland and Stewart, 2000).

Piper, Karen, *Cartographic Fictions: Maps, Race, and Identity* (New Brunswick, NJ: Rutgers University Press, 2002).

FURTHER READING

Brand, Dionne, *A Map to the Door of No Return* (Toronto: Doubleday, 2001).

Burstyn, V., *Water, INC.*, (London: Verso, 2004).

Devi, M., *Imaginary Maps* (London: Routledge, 1995).

Farah, N., *Maps* (New York: Penguin, 2000).

Godard, Barbara, 'Mapmaking' in *Gynocritics* (Toronto: ECW Press, 1987).

Jacobs, Jane M., *Edge of Empire: Postcolonialism and the City* (London: Routledge, 1996).

Jameson, Fredric, 'Cognitive Mapping', in *Marxism and the Interpretation of Culture* (Urbana: University of Illinois Press, 1988).

Leer, Martin, 'From Linear to Areal: Suggestions Towards a Comparative Literary Geography of Canada and Australia', *Kunapipi* 12.3 (1990), pp. 75–85.

Van Herk, Aritha, *No Fixed Address* (Toronto: McClelland & Stewart, 1986).

GENDER

Bahri, D., 'Disembodying the Corpus: Postcolonial Pathology in Tsitsi Dangarembga's *Nervous Conditions*', *Postmodern Culture* 5.1 (1994).

Conrad, Joseph, *Heart of Darkness* (London: Penguin, 1975).

Cooper, Carolyn, *Noises in the Blood: Orality, Gender and the Vulgar Body of Jamaican Popular Culture* (London: Macmillan, 1993).

Dangarembga, T., *Nervous Conditions* (London: The Women's Press, 1988).

Haggard, Rider, *King Solomon's Mines* (London: Dent, 1885).

Lewis, Reina, *Gendering Orientalism: Race, Femininity and Representation* (New York: Routledge, 1996).

McClintock, Ann, *Imperial Leather: Race, Gender and Sexuality in the Colonial Contest* (New York: Routledge, 1995).

Miller, Jane, *Seductions: Studies in Reading and Culture* (London: Virago, 1990).

Minh-ha, Trin, 'Not You/Like You: Post-Colonial Women and the Interlocking Questions of Identity and Difference', *Inscriptions* 3–4 (1988), http://humwww.ucsc.edu/cultstudies/PUBS/Inscriptions/vol_3–4/v3–4top.html.

Minh-ha, Trin, *Woman, Native, Other: Writing Postcoloniality and Feminism* (Bloomington: Indiana University Press, 1989).

Mohanty, C. T., *Feminism Without Borders: Decolonizing Theory, Practicing Solidarity* (Durham, NC: Duke University Press, 2003).

Sartre, Jean Paul, 'Preface', in Frantz Fanon, *The Wretched of the Earth* [1961], trans. R. Philcox (New York: Grove Press, 2004).

Uwakweh, P., 'Debunking Patriarchy: The Liberational Quality of Voicing in Tsitsi Dangarembga's *Nervous Conditions*', *Research in African Literatures* 26.1 (Spring 1995), 75–80.

Vizzard, M., '"Of Mimicry and Woman": Hysteria and Anti-Colonial Feminism in Tsitsi Dangarembga's *Nervous Conditions*', *SPAN: Journal of the South Pacific Association for Commonwealth Literature and Language Studies* 36 (1993).

FURTHER READING

Busby, M., *Daughters of Africa* (London: Vintage, 1992).

Emecheta, Buchi, *Destination Biafra* (London: Heinemann, 1982).

Head, Bessie, *A Question of Power* (London: Heinemann, 1974).

Jayawardena, K., *Feminism and Nationalism in the Third World* (London: Zed Books, 1986).

Ketu, K. H., *Politics of the Female Body: Postcolonial Women Writers and the Third World* (New Brunswick: Rutgers University Press, 2006).

Nasta, S., ed., *Motherlands: Black Women's Writing from Africa, the Caribbean and South Asia* (London: The Women's Press, 1991).

Stratton, F., *Contemporary African Literature and the Politics of Gender* (London: Routledge, 1994).

Tharu, S. and Lalita, K., eds, *Women Writing in India: 600 BC to the Present* (London: Pandora, 1993).

Wisker, Gina, *Postcolonial and African American Women's Writing* (Basingstoke: Macmillan, 2000).

QUEER

Brand, Dionne, *In Another Place, Not Here* (Toronto: Vintage, 1996).

Brooker, Peter, *A Concise Dictionary of Cultural Theory* (London: Arnold, 1999).

Dickinson, Peter, *Here is Queer: Nationalisms, Sexualities, and the Literatures of Canada* (Toronto: University of Toronto Press, 1999).

Djaout, T., *Les chercheurs d'os* (Paris: Seuil, 1984).

Gopinath, Gayatri, *Impossible Desires: Queer Diasporas and South Asian Public Cultures* (Durham, NC: Duke University Press, 2005).

Hawley, John C., *Postcolonial, Queer: Theoretical Intersections* (Albany: SUNY Press, 2001).

Hayes, Jarrod, *Queer Nations: Marginal Sexualities in the Maghreb* (Chicago: University of Chicago Press, 2000).

Lane, Christopher, *The Ruling Passion: British Colonial Allegory and the Paradox of Homosexual Desire* (Durham: Duke University Press, 1995).

Massad, J., 'Re-Orienting Desire: The Gay International and the Arab World', in *Public Culture* 14 (2002).

Smyth, Heather, 'Sexual Citizenship and Canadian-Caribbean Fiction: Dionne Brand's *In Another Place, Not Here* and Shani Mootoo's *Cereus Blooms at Night*', Ariel 30.2 (April 1999).

FURTHER READING

Boone, Joseph, 'Vacation Cruises; or, The Homoerotics of Orientalism', *PMLA* 110.1 (1995).

Campbell, Jane, *Arguing with the Phallus: Feminist, Queer and Postcolonial Theory* (London: Zed Books, 2000).

Das, K., *My Story* (Delhi: Sterling Press, 1976).

Hoad, N., *African Intimacies: Race, Homosexuality, and Globalization* (Minneapolis: University of Minnesota, 2007).

Soyinka, Wole. *The Interpreters* (London: André Deutsch, 1996).

Thomas, Susie, ed., *Hanif Kureishi: A Reader's Guide to Essential Criticism* (Basingstoke: Palgrave Macmillan, 2005).

Touval, Y., 'Colonial Queer Something', in *Queer Forster*, eds, Robert K. Martin and George Piggford (Chicago: Chicago University Press, 1997).

Vanita, R., ed., *Queering India: Same-Sex Love and Eroticism in Indian Culture and Society* (London: Routledge, 2007).

HAUNTING

Bhabha, Homi, *The Location of Culture* (London: Routledge, 1994).

Birney, Earl, 'Can. Lit.,', in Margaret Atwood, ed., *Oxford Book of Canadian Poetry* (Toronto: Oxford University Press).

D'Aguiar, Fred, *Feeding the Ghosts* (London: Chatto and Windus, 1997).

Derrida, Jacques, *Specters of Marx: The State of the Debt, the Work of Mourning, and the New International*, trans. P. Kamuf (New York: Routledge, 1994).

Gelder, Ken and Jacobs, Jane, *Uncanny Australia: Sacredness and Identity in a Postcolonial Nation* (Melbourne: Melbourne University Press, 1998).

Kertzer, Jonathan, *Worrying the Nation: Imagining a National Literature in English Canada* (Toronto: University of Toronto Press, 1998).

Morrison, Toni, *Beloved* (New York: Signet, 1987).

Newman, Judie, 'Postcolonial Gothic: Ruth Prawer Jhabvala and the Sobhraj', *Modern Gothic: A Reader*, V. Sage and A. Smith, eds, (Manchester: Manchester University Press, 1996).

Punter, David and Byron, G., *The Gothic* (Oxford: Blackwell, 2004).

Trevorson, Andrew, 'The Number of Magic Alternatives: Salman Rushdie's 1001 Gothic Nights', in A. Smith and W. Hughes, eds, *Empire and the Gothic: The Politics of Genre* (Basingstoke: Palgrave Macmillan, 2003).

Turner, Margaret, *Imagining Culture: New World Narrative and the Writing of Canada* (Montreal: McGill-Queen's University Press, 1995).

Walcott, Derek, 'The Muse of History', in *Is Massa Day Dead?*, Orde Coombs, ed., (New York: Anchor, 1974).

Weissberg, L., 'Gothic Spaces: The Political Aesthetics of Toni Morrison's *Beloved*', V. Sage and A. Smith, eds., *Modern Gothic: A Reader* (Manchester: Manchester University Press, 1996), pp. 115–16.

Zizek, S., *Looking Awry: An Introduction to Lacan through Popular Culture* (Cambridge, Mass.: MIT Press, 1991).

FURTHER READING

Aidoo, A., *Dilemma of a Ghost* (London: Macmillan, 1987).

Brodber, Erna, *Louisiana* (London: New Beacon, 2004).

Brodber, Erna, *Myal* (London: New Beacon, 1988).

Mudrooroo, *Master of the Ghost Dreaming* (Sydney: Collins, 1991).

Plasa, Carl, ed., *Toni Morrison: 'Beloved': A Reader's Guide to Essential Criticism* (Basingstoke: Palgrave Macmillan, 2000).

Punter, David, *A Companion to the Gothic* (Oxford: Blackwell, 2000).

Smith, Andrew and Hughes William, eds, *Empire and the Gothic: The Politics of Genre* (London: Palgrave Macmillan, 2003).

Thomas, S. R., ed., *Dark Matter: A Century of Speculative Fiction from the African Diaspora* (New York: Warner Aspect, 2000).

Yahp, Beth, *The Crocodile Fury* (Sydney: Angus and Robertson, 1992).

MEMORY

Antze, P. and Lambek, M., 'Introduction', *Past Tense: Cultural Essays in Trauma and Memory* (New York: Routledge, 1996).

Bernard, L., 'Countermemory and Return: Reclamation of the (Postmodern) Self in Jamaica Kincaid's *The Autobiography of My Mother* and *My Brother*', *Modern Fiction Studies* 48.1 (2002).

Caruth, Cathy, *Unclaimed Experience: Trauma, Narrative, and History* (Baltimore: Johns Hopkins University Press, 1996).

Coetzee, J. M., *Disgrace* (London: Vintage, 1999).

Herman, Judith, *Trauma and Recovery* (New York: Basic Books, 1992).

Heyns, M., 'The Whole Country's Truth: Confession and Narrative in Recent South African Writing', *Modern Fiction Studies* 46.1 (2000).

Kamboureli, Smaro, *Scandalous Bodies: Diasporic Literature in English Canada* (Toronto: Oxford University Press, 2000).

Kincaid, Jamaica, *My Brother* (New York: Farrar, Straus and Giroux, 1997).

Kogawa, Joy, *Obasan* (Toronto: Penguin, 1981).

Leys, R., *Trauma: A Genealogy* (Chicago: Chicago University Press, 2000).

Miki, R., *Broken Entries: Race Subjectivity Writing* (Toronto: Mercury Press, 1998).

Miki, R. and Kobayashi, C., *Justice in Our Time: The Japanese Canadian Redress Settlement* (Vancouver: Talonbooks, 1991).

Ondaatje, Michael, *Anil's Ghost* (Toronto: McClelland and Stewart, 2000).

Tal, Kali, *Worlds of Hurt: Reading the Literatures of Trauma* (Cambridge: Cambridge University Press, 1996).

Walcott, Derek, 'The Muse of History', in *Is Massa Dead? Black Moods in the Caribbean*, ed. Orde Coombes (New York: Doubleday, 1974).

Wong, C., *Reading Asian American Literature* (Princeton, NJ: Princeton University Press, 1993).

FURTHER READING

Boyarin, J., ed., *Remapping Memory: The Politics of Time and Space* (Minneapolis: University of Minnesota Press, 1994).

Brathwaite, E. K., *The Arrivants, A New World Trilogy: Rights of Passage, Islands and Masks* (Oxford: Oxford University Press, 1973).

Edwards, Justin D., *Gothic Canada: Reading the Spectre of a National Literature* (Edmonton: University of Alberta Press, 2005).

Falola, T., *A Mouth Sweeter than Salt: An African Memoir* (Ann Arbor, Michigan University Press, 2004).

Harris, Wilson, *The Guyana Quartet* (London: Faber and Faber, 1985).

Herman, Judith, *Trauma and Recovery: From Domestic Abuse to Political Terror* (London: Pandora, 1992).

King, Nicola, *Memory, Narrative, Identity: Remembering the Self* (Edinburgh: Edinburgh University Press, 2000).

Soyinka, Wole, *Ake: The Years of Childhood* (London: Vintage, 1981).

Williams, Charlotte, *Sugar and Slate* (Aberystwyth: Planet, 2002).

HYBRIDITY

Bhabha, Homi, 'Life at the Border: Hybrid Identities of the Present', *New Perspectives Quarterly* 14.1 (winter 1997).

Campbell, Maria, *Halfbreed* (Toronto: McClelland and Stewart, 1973).

Gilroy, Paul, *The Black Atlantic: Modernity and Double Consciousness* (Cambridge: Harvard University Press, 1993).

Hall, Stuart, 'New Ethnicities', in D, Morley and K. H. Chen, eds, *Stuart Hall, Critical Dialogues in Cultural Studies* (London: Routledge, 1996).

Khair, Tabish, *Babu Fictions: Alienation in Contemporary Indian English Novels* (Delhi: Oxford University Press, 2001).

Khair, Tabish, 'Unhybrid', in *When Parallel Lines Meet* (Delhi: Penguin, 2000).

King, Bruce, *Derek Walcott: A Caribbean Life* (Oxford: Oxford University Press, 2000).

Mudrooroo, *Writing from the Fringe: A Study of Modern Aboriginal Literature* (Melbourne: Hyland House, 1990).

Parry, Benita, 'Signs of Our Times: Discussion of Homi Bhabha's *The Location of Culture*', *Third Text* 28/29 (Autumn/Winter 1994).

Walcott, Derek, 'A Far Cry from Africa' [1962], in *Norton Anthology of Modern Poetry* (New York: Norton, 1988).

Walcott, Derek, 'The Schooner Flight' in *Collected Poems 1948–1984* (New York: Farrar, Straus & Giroux, 1986).

Young, Robert, *Colonial Desire: Hybridity in Theory, Culture and Race* (London: Routledge, 1995).

FURTHER READING

Brathwaite, E., *The Development of Creole Society in Jamaica, 1770–1820* (Oxford: Clarendon Press, 1971).

Dash, M., 'Marvellous Realism: The Way out of Négritude', *Caribbean Studies* 13.4 (1974). 57–70.

Hall, Stuart, 'New Ethnicities', in *Black Film, British Cinema* (London: Institute of Contemporary Arts, 1989).

Peterson, Kirsten and Rutherford, Anna, 'Fossil and Psyche', in *Enigma of Values: An Introduction to Wilson Harris* (Aarhus: Dangaroo Press, 1976).

Tiffin, C. and Alan Lawson, eds, *De-Scribing Empire: Post-colonialism and Textuality* (London: Routledge, 1994).

Young, Robert, *Postcolonialism: A Very Short Introduction* (Oxford: Oxford University Press, 2003).

Young, Robert, *White Mythologies: Writing History and the West* (London: Routledge, 1990).

DIASPORA

Appadurai, A., 'Disjuncture and Difference in the Global Cultural Economy', in Braziel and Mannur, eds, *Theorizing Diaspora* (Oxford: Blackwell, 2003).

Braziel, J. and Mannur, A., 'Nation, Migration, Globalization: Points of Contention in Diaspora Studies', in Braziel and Mannur, eds, *Theorizing Diaspora* (Oxford: Blackwell, 2003).

Cohen, Robert, *Global Diasporas* (London: UCL Press, 1997).

Gilroy, Paul, 'The Black Atlantic as a Counterculture of Modernity', in J. Braziel and A. Mannur, eds, *Theorizing Diaspora* (Oxford: Blackwell, 2003).

Gopinath, Gayatri, 'Nostalgia, Desire, Diaspora: South Asian Sexualities in Motion', in *Theorizing Diaspora*, Braziel and Mannur, eds (Oxford: Blackwell, 2003).

Gupta, Sunetra, *The Glassblower's Breath* (London: Orion, 1993).

Gupta, Sunetra, 'Interview with Bronwyn Williams', February 1996. http://social.chass.ncsu.edu/jouvert/v3i3/willia.htm.

Hall, Stuart, 'Cultural Identity and Diaspora', in *Identity: Community, Culture, Difference*, ed. J. Rutherford (London: Lawrence and Wishart, 1990).

Kureishi, Hanif, *The Black Album* (London: Faber and Faber, 1995).

Ledent, B., *Caryl Phillips* (Manchester: Manchester University Press, 2002).

Phillips, Caryl, *The Atlantic Sound* (London: Faber and Faber, 2000).

Procter, James, *Dwelling Places: Postwar Black British Writing* (Manchester: Manchester University Press, 2003).

Selvadurai, Shyam, *Funny Boy* (Toronto: McClelland and Stewart, 1995).

FURTHER READING

Ali, Monica, *Brick Lane* (London: Doubleday, 2003).

Appiah, A., *The Ethics of Identity* (Princeton, NJ: Princeton University Press, 2004).

Appiah, A., *Cosmopolitanism* (New York: Norton, 2006).

Chow, R., *Writing Diaspora: Tactics of Invention in Contemporary Cultural Studies* (Bloomington: Indiana University Press, 1993).

Desai, Anita, *Fasting Feasting* (London: Vintage, 2000).

Gates, Henry Louis, Diedrich, M. and Pederson, Carl, eds, *Black Imagination and the Middle Passage* (Oxford: Oxford University Press, 1999).

Kureishi, Hanif, *The Buddha of Suburbia* (London: Penguin, 1990).

Nasta, S., *Home Truths: Fictions of the South Asian Diaspora in Britain* (Basingstoke: Palgrave Macmillan, 2002).

Rushdie, Salman, *Imaginary Homelands: Essays and Criticism, 1981–1991* (New York: Viking, 1991).

Smith, Zadie, *White Teeth* (London: Penguin, 2000).

GLOBALIZATION

Balogun, Fidelis Ogun, *Adjusted Lives: Stories of Structural Adjustments* (Trenton, NJ: Africa World Press, 1995).

Black, S., Dir., *Life and Debt* (Tuff Gong Pictures, 2001).

Chakrabarty, D., *Provincializing Europe: Postcolonial Thought and Historical Difference* (Princeton, NJ: Princeton University Press, 2000).

Edwards, Justin D., *Understanding Jamaica Kincaid* (Columbia: University of South Carolina Press, 2007).

Hardt, Michael and Negri, Antonio, *Empire* (Cambridge, MA: Harvard University Press, 2000).

Hickley, T. and Rupprecht, A., 'Anti-Globalisation Movements', in *A Historical Companion to Postcolonial Literatures in English*, ed. Poddar and Johnson (Edinburgh: Edinburgh University Press, 2005).

McClintock, Ann, 'The Angel of Progress: Pitfalls of the Term "Post-colonial"', *Social Text* 21 (1992).

Mullaney, Julie, *Arundhati Roy's The God of Small Things: A Reader's Guide* (New York: Continuum Press, 2002).

Rofel, Lisa, 'Modernity's Masculine Fantasies', in *Critically Modern: Alternatives, Alterities, Anthropologies*, ed. B. Knauft (Bloomington: Indiana University Press, 2002).

Roy, Arundhati, *The Cost of Living* (London: Flamingo, 1999).

Roy, Arundhati, *Power Politics* (Cambridge, MA: South End Press, 2001).

FURTHER READING

Arnowitz, S. and H. Gautney, *Implicating Empire: Globalization and Resistance in the 21st-Century* (New York: Basic Books, 2003).

Chamoiseau, Patrick, *Texaco* (London: Granta, 1998).

King, A. D., ed., *Culture, Globalization and the World System: Contemporary Conditions for the Representation of Identity* (Basingstoke: Macmillan, 1991).

Klein, Naomi, *No Logo* (London: Flamingo, 2000).

Newman, Robert, *The Fountain at the Centre of the World* (London: Verso, 2003).

Nkrumah, K., *Neo-Colonialism: The Last Stage of Imperialism* (London: Heinemann, 1965).

Singh, K., *The Globalization of Finance: A Citizen's Guide* (London: Zed Books, 1999).

Stiglitz, J., *Globalisation and its Discontents* (London: Penguin, 2002).

Roy, Arundhati. *The Ordinary Person's Guide to Empire* (London: Flamingo, 2003).

Index